PIMLICO

585

UNEASY ETHICS

Simon Lee is chief executive ~~~~~~~~~~~~~~~~ ~~
College, Emeritus Professor ~~ ~~~~~~~~~ ~~een's
University Belfast and Vice-Cha~~~~~~~~~ ~~ of Leeds
Metropolitan University. He is a ~~~~~~~ ~oadcaster on
ethical dilemmas and his widely acc~~~~~ ~ books include
Law & Morals, *Judging Judges* and *The Cost of Free Speech*.

UNEASY ETHICS

SIMON LEE

PIMLICO

Published by Pimlico 2003

2 4 6 8 10 9 7 5 3

Copyright © Simon Lee 2003

Simon Lee has asserted his right
under the Copyright, Designs and Patents Act 1988
to be identified as the author of this work

First published in Great Britain by
Pimlico 2003

Pimlico
Random House, 20 Vauxhall Bridge Road,
London SW1V 2SA

Random House Australia (Pty) Limited
20 Alfred Street, Milsons Point, Sydney,
New South Wales 2061, Australia

Random House New Zealand Limited
18 Poland Road, Glenfield,
Auckland 10, New Zealand

Random House (Pty) Limited
Endulini, 5A Jubilee Road, Parktown 2193, South Africa

The Random House Group Limited Reg. No. 954009
www.randomhouse.co.uk

A CIP catalogue record for this book is available from the British Library

ISBN 0-7126-0655-6

Papers used by Random House are natural, recyclable products made from wood
grown in sustainable forests; the manufacturing processes conform
to the environmental regulations of the country of origin

Printed and bound in Great Britain by
Mackays of Chatham Plc, Chatham, Kent

This book is dedicated to my wife Patricia and
to our children, Jamie, Katie and Rebecca,
with love and thanks.

Contents

Acknowledgements

I would like to thank my family, to whom this book is dedicated, my former tutors, my past and present colleagues and all those who have worked on this book at Pimlico, Random House, especially Will Sulkin, the publisher who has supported my writing from our first book together at Oxford University Press through a time at Faber and now with Pimlico. I am most grateful to the students, staff and governors of Liverpool Hope University College, particularly my friend and colleague Dr John Elford, for the stimulation and encouragement provided by our constant discussion of ethics during the period in which these sagas have come to public attention. Most of my other intellectual debts will be clear from the text and the notes that follow.

Introduction

The five chapters of this book each tell the story of an uneasy ethical dilemma of the new millennium: should Siamese twins be separated; should the killers of James Bulger be released; should the peace process in Northern Ireland continue to embrace those who plan for terrorism; how do we account for the collapse of trust in government and business, exemplified by the fall of the government minister Stephen Byers; and how is the war on international terrorism to be conducted in the aftermath of 11 September 2001? Almost every reader will recall expressing an opinion on these matters at the time they were first in the news. Some will already have a sense of unease about their initial thoughts on these issues. This book seeks to help readers in deconstructing and then reconstructing moral thinking on each story.

Each dilemma is also an illustration of a wider area of ethics, such as medical ethics in the first chapter. Thus, while the fourth chapter, for example, discusses Stephen Byers's difficulties over the interaction of government and the economy, it is also an introduction to thinking about business ethics more generally. That is why the central story of that chapter is located in the context of other contemporary sagas about corporate and government behaviour.

A further way of looking at each chapter is as an aid to reflecting on some central concept or concepts for ethical judgement, from such virtues as justice, mercy and equal respect through to such vices as bad faith and evil.

The book as a whole is intended to challenge readers in their own opinions, in the quality of their arguments and in the robustness of their moral judgements, preparing them not only for self-analysis but also for vigorous debate with others over future cases of uneasy ethics. My aim is to cater for a wide readership, for those who think seriously about the dilemmas of the day and who sympathise with the uneasiness of those who have to make judgements on these agonising dilemmas. Moral luck strikes at random, seeming at first to require only a few citizens to face choices in the manner of the parents of Jodie and Mary. As we proceed from what appears to be an isolated case – of Siamese twins – to appreciate its relevance for us all and then to consider our responsibility as citizens for such systemic features of everyday life as the criminal justice system or a peace process or the building up of just and stable government, so we will find that we are all responsible for uneasy decisions. Most of us can learn something from reflecting on these examples when we come in our everyday lives to make our own judgements.

These moral dilemmas of the new millennium are not just hard cases, as opposed to easy ones. I prefer to think of them as *un-easy* cases. We rightly have a sense of unease in coming to a judgement on them. Anyone who finds them easy is unlikely to have explored the issues with sufficient seriousness.

At one level, we could write books on each of these cases without coming close to resolving them, but at another level we could answer the questions in one word and it may be helpful to do so as a precursor to the chapters. Should Siamese twins be separated if one will die but one might thereby live? Yes. When, if ever, should those who have abducted, tortured and murdered a child be released from custody? Depends. Is it ethical to release prisoners or to insist on the decommissioning of weapons as part of a peace process? Yes. In what circumstances are government ministers entitled to use public funds or other influence to support public or private enterprise? Depends. Is the USA justified in military action in Afghanistan as a response to terror attacks from a third party, the al-Qaeda terrorist network? Yes. Even the 'Depends' could be converted to clear answers if the question is rephrased to relate to the particular cases at the centre of the chapters. Was it right to release the child killers of James Bulger eight years after the murder when they reached eighteen? Yes. Was resignation the only ethical option for Jo Moore and Stephen Byers after her email of 11 September 2001 and his treatment of Railtrack in the following months? No.

Others, of course, will disagree with what the one word should be in each of these cases. Most observers, for instance, seemed to think that Moore and Byers should have resigned. Most young people with whom I have debated the release of the killers of James Bulger would not have allowed them their freedom so soon. Many say they would have preferred them to have been in prison for life. Some even say they think that the two young murderers deserved the death penalty.

My interest in these cases is not prompted merely by this common experience of disagreement. Even where we agree and even where we are definite about the right answer, my contention is that in these cases we still retain some ethical unease. Most of us want to say 'Yes, but . . .' or 'No, but . . .' or 'It depends because . . .'. We often wish to give more than a one-word answer to assure those who are more closely affected by the decisions, or perhaps ourselves, that we understand the countervailing arguments.

The ways in which individuals change, or hold fast to, their views on any of these cases are of particular interest. Those who speak on these sagas in the public realm tend to maintain their initial conclusions, sometimes with increasingly ingenious arguments which make me suspect that they are beginning to have doubts. Those who keep their own counsel at first may consider themselves more at liberty to change their minds as they reflect on the dilemma. The way in which we debate such cases is therefore of more than passing significance.

The first chapter, on the case of the Siamese twins, tries to set the scene by discussing some of the tactics that we use with one another in exploring such ethical dilemmas. It features, in particular, the Archbishop of Westminster's approach of setting out broad principles and the response of the judges in the Court of Appeal, whereby they used hypothetical examples to justify drawing from much the same principles the opposite conclusion to that proposed by the archbishop. Some may treat this as a crash course in how to respond at university interview to questions about the issues of the day. Others may use it as a prompt to their more leisurely reflection, perhaps in retirement, on the profound, troubling questions of our time, and in one sense of all time. In either case, readers are likely to find a tutor or a companion moving between these two modes of argument, testing putative principles by wondering how they would apply to a range of alternative facts.

This is much the same methodology as has proved so enduring in law schools on either side of the Atlantic. In US law schools, the process is known as Socratic. In one sense, then, there has not been much change since Socrates taught us how to explore these profound matters almost two and a half thousand years ago. Each generation, however, needs to address the tragic choices of its age and so this book presents some contemporary illustrations of ancient dilemmas about ethics, about what is good or bad, right or wrong, what ought to be done or ought not to be done. The beginning of wisdom is to follow Socrates who knew, in asking such probing questions, that he himself did not know all the answers.

1

Siamese Twins:
Separate but Equal?

Siamese, or conjoined twins, 'Jodie' and 'Mary', were born in the summer of 2000. Their parents, a Catholic couple from Gozo, Malta's neighbouring island, had sought expert care from a Manchester hospital. The medical team advised that Jodie and Mary would both die within months unless they were separated by an operation. One, Mary, would die as a result of the operation but the other, Jodie, would have a good chance of survival and flourishing. Their parents were reluctant to sanction the operation, citing religious reasons. The hospital authorities sought court approval for the operation to proceed, notwithstanding the refusal of parental consent. This was given by Mr Justice Johnson in the High Court who also ordered that the real identities of the children should not be revealed – hence the pseudonyms 'Jodie' and 'Mary'. International attention followed as the case was taken to the Court of Appeal. Apart from counsel for the hospital and the parents, together with the different counsel assigned by the court to represent each baby, the judges were assisted by two written submissions from interested third parties, a pro-life group and the Archbishop of Westminster.

This is what I call not just a hard case but an un-easy one because the moral dilemma is so acute that if you do not have some sense of unease, you have not understood the complexities involved. It was therefore comforting for the public, if disturbing for the judges, to hear during the course of argument in the Court of Appeal that the judges themselves were having sleepless nights. As one judge expressed it in his judgement, 'Every member of the court has been deeply troubled by this case.' Shakespeare's line about the burdens of a monarch applies to all who have responsibilities in such circumstances: 'Uneasy lies the head that wears the crown.'

Many important aspects of this case which will not be analysed here could take up a book in themselves. There is considerable *medical* interest in the operation, the pre-operation and post-operation treatment, and the wider decision-making by healthcare professionals. Several articles on the *legal* detail have already been published. In this chapter, however, the focus is on the approaches to the uneasy *ethical* dilemma taken by the Archbishop of Westminster and by the lawyers. So readers should look elsewhere for detailed exegesis of the law or analysis of the medical science. This chapter explores, instead, the way in which distinct styles of addressing the ethical dilemma emerged in the case of Jodie and Mary. The Archbishop of Westminster's intervention set out some broad principles. Although the judges engaged in arguments about legal precedent and principle, they mainly used hypothetical examples to challenge the moral force of the archbishop's conclusion on the application of those principles. These two modes of argument – principles and hypotheticals – are deployed so often in our thinking about ethics that their interaction is considered in this chapter at some length.

Why was the archbishop involved at all? The idea that this was none of his business has three main variations, two of which belong in other books. First, a legal tome might question whether there is or should be legal standing for bishops or other interveners in such cases. Elsewhere, I have long since argued for the introduction of third-party viewpoints into court hearings on human rights. Second, a book on theology might question whether the right bishop to intervene was the Archbishop of *Westminster*, rather than the bishop of the diocese in which the hospital was or in which Jodie and Mary's parents normally lived or the bishop who chairs the relevant committee of the Bishops' Conference. My view is that in a swift court process the important issue is for someone to raise the right points rather than to worry too much about exactly who should do so, but over time the Church ought to organise itself so that the Bishops' Conference or the wider Church as a whole is represented by the appropriate person, whether that is a bishop, a priest or a layperson. Third, and most significantly for an ethical discussion such as this, while some will be prepared to look at the quality of arguments whatever their provenance, others will question the moral track record of the opinion-givers. Who do they think they are? In particular, society may question whether a Catholic bishop has the standing to offer ethical principles to the wider community, given scandals such as child abuse by clerics.

The argument is often put in these or similar terms: 'Is God really to be found in an organisation that slaughtered so many innocent people in the Crusades, that used the Inquisition as a divine tool, that sanctioned racism and sexism for centuries and that has in its history so much in the way of religious wars, sinful silences and blind imperialism? Is God really to be found in an organisation that numbers some paedophiles among its ministers?' In these words, Fr Ronald Rolheiser poses the questions bluntly but then responds that, although to 'be connected with the Church is to be associated with scoundrels, warmongers, fakes, child molesters, murderers, adulterers and hypocrites of every description', it 'also, at the same time, identifies you with saints and the finest persons of heroic soul within every time, country, race and gender'. In other words, even a flawed church can offer insights. Although the courtroom may not seem to be the best place for an ethical discussion, one of the merits of the legal setting is that the arguments by an intervener such as the archbishop become a matter of record in the public domain. This enables the *quality* of the argument to be judged not only by the Court of Appeal but also by the courts of popular and expert opinion. Ultimately, then, attempts to knock the standing of the opinion-giver should be trumped by analysing the content of the opinion.

This leads us to consider how we can establish the quality of any ethical principles. Testing principles by seeing how they would be applied to examples is an established method in many disciplines, including both ethics and law. Indeed, the case of Jodie and Mary presented a real challenge of life and death to principles in a way which has for years been put to students of medical ethics as the classic hypothetical: 'What if there were Siamese twins . . . ?' The fact that yesterday's seemingly far-fetched hypothetical becomes today's actual case affirms the value of speculating on imaginary hard cases. The judgements are full of further hypotheticals although the particular examples cited by the judges will be questioned in what follows. If a six-year-old child were running amok with a gun in a playground, killing other children, and you had the opportunity to shoot the child dead, would you do so to save other children? Now that is an uneasy hypothetical case, but is it really a good analogy? The judges' examples, which included a cast of crashing planes, sinking ships, unopening parachutes and caravans surrounded by bandits, take me back to my tutorial days both as a student and as a teacher. They need to be accompanied by an ethical health warning about the dangers of citing an analogy, whether a hypothetical or drawn from an actual case, as if it were in itself a justification for a decision in a different set of facts. More work needs to be done by the judges because the presentation of a hypothetical designed to draw out an inconsistency is not in itself a conclusive argument. The supposed analogy may not be a good parallel. Even though there is much to be said in praise of using well-chosen hypotheticals to challenge students on the limits of the principles which they intuitively find attractive, the particular analogies referred to by the judges seem unconvincing as moral guides to the resolution of the uneasy case of Jodie and Mary.

This matters because, much as the judges tried to convince us that what they regarded as the extreme circumstances of Jodie and Mary should not become a precedent, this uneasy case does have a moral relevance to everyday dilemmas which pose less stark yet still important challenges. Parents, for example, are constantly taking decisions for their children and sometimes the interests of different family members can conflict, though rarely to the point of life and death. Even deciding in the best interests of a single child can be problematic, for instance in terms of choosing a school or deciding whether to accept a career move to a different area. Parents may genuinely believe that they have their child's best interests as their paramount consideration but observers may feel that it is the parents' own best interests which are more influential. When somebody else other than a parent has to act as a proxy for a child, for instance a local authority on behalf of a child in care, it can find itself being accused of deciding in the interests of the community rather than in the best interests of the child. In the late 1980s, for example, a case sped through the legal system to determine whether a seventeen-year-old with mental disabilities, referred to in court as 'B', could be sterilised without her consent. All the judges involved, culminating in the House of Lords, agreed to authorise the operation. Everybody in the case believed that they were deciding in her best interests, but it can still seem to others that the sterilisation is also relieving her carers of some concerns and that it is difficult in such circumstances to distinguish the interests of the different parties. The problems are more acute when Siamese twins are involved, but scrutiny is needed for all decisions which are promoted as being in the best interests of those who are incapable of making the choice for themselves, from female circumcision to euthanasia. In these ways, the importance of this case can be seen in relation to a whole range of dilemmas in medical ethics and in wider life.

A related element of this uneasy case which is common to so many less dramatic decisions is that a number of adults are involved with slightly different roles, perspectives and views, for example parents, doctors and judges. We tend to think of people in these three categories as each having their own moral authority but none of them is necessarily expert in ethical decision-making. The medical team's undoubted expertise, for example, is in making prognoses and carrying out the operation, not in deciding whether it is morally right to proceed with the operation. Their particular perspective is likely to produce a view which is in favour of an operation in these circumstances, just as it is likely that parents will be more circum-spect. Judges sometimes disavow any expertise in ethics but usually concede that they can offer their disinterested wisdom and their experience of making judgement in uneasy cases. Even if it is sometimes assumed that the ideal way forward is one agreed by all interested parties, it may be that some tension or disagreement between adults in these different roles is to be expected. It may even be helpful since those who are inclined to agree with one another may settle for second-best arguments whereas disagreement can sharpen the justifications offered for alternative courses of action. In what follows, the focus is not the technical legal detail, which would merit a book in itself, but on the implications for uneasy cases of these hypotheticals, on the one hand, and, on the other, the sustained line of thought in the submission by the Archbishop of Westminster, together with its reception by the Court of Appeal.

The judges said that they were grateful to Archbishop (now, Cardinal) Cormac Murphy-O'Connor for his submission. He was really what should be known as an intervener (an individual or group who makes a submission favouring a particular result), but the Latin term amicus curiae, which literally means 'a friend of the court', is used somewhat loosely to encompass such a contribution, even though that term could more strictly be reserved for arguments which assist the court without arguing for a specific outcome. The archbishop's submission, like the judgements, is also available on the World Wide Web and repays careful reading in full. He set out 'five overarching moral considerations'. These were:

(a) Human life is sacred, that is inviolable, so that one should never aim to cause an innocent person's death by act or omission.

(b) A person's bodily integrity should not be invaded when the consequences of doing so are of no benefit to that person; this is most particularly the case if the consequences are foreseeably lethal.

(c) Though the duty to preserve life is a serious duty, no such duty exists when the only available means of preserving life involves a grave injustice. In this case, if what is envisaged is the killing of, or a deliberate lethal assault on, one of the twins, 'Mary', in order to save the other, 'Jodie', there is a grave injustice involved. The good end would not justify the means. It would set a very dangerous precedent to enshrine in English case law that it was ever lawful to kill, or to commit a deliberate lethal assault on, an innocent person that good may come of it, even to preserve the life of another.

(d) There is no duty to adopt particular therapeutic measures to preserve the life when these are likely to impose excessive burdens on the patient and the patient's carers. Would the operation that is involved in the separation involve such 'extraordinary means'? If so, then quite apart from its effect on Mary, there can be no moral obligation on doctors to carry out the operation to save Jodie, or on the parents to consent to it.

(e) Respect for the natural authority of parents requires that the courts override the rights of parents only when there is clear evidence that they are acting contrary to what is strictly owing to their children. In this case, the parents have simply adopted the only position they felt was consistent with their consciences and with their love for both children.

It is unlikely that all Catholic bishops and theologians around the world, or even the country, necessarily agreed with the archbishop on the *application* of these principles to the particular case of Jodie and Mary. Many of those who disagreed would nonetheless have been encouraged that there is now in every sense a precedent for similar contributions to uneasy cases on other matters from the churches or other faith communities or others with ethical insights to share. Although its attention seems to have been concentrated hitherto on medical ethics in court cases, the teaching of the Roman Catholic Church has at least as much to say on such issues as how we as a society treat others on the margins, including prisoners and asylum seekers.

In this particular case, the archbishop's five principles of ethical decision-making pointed in the direction of respecting the parents' wishes not to proceed with an operation to separate Jodie and Mary. The judges' conclusion was the exact opposite, despite the fact that the first four of his principles seemed to be completely acceptable to each of the three judges. They cavilled somewhat at his fifth principle, there was some surprise or criticism that he had not invoked the doctrine of double effect as a sixth principle and the judges completely disagreed with the archbishop on how to apply the principles to the facts of this particularly tragic choice. Of these, it is only the differences in application, in making the judgement, which were crucial. For instance, on the fifth principle, one of the judges observed that there seemed to be little difference between the law as they had set it out and this fifth principle as formulated by the archbishop. Indeed, if the judges had put to the archbishop, or to counsel representing him, that they had their doubts about his fifth principle, he would presumably have tried to explain it or reformulate it so that the judges could understand his meaning more clearly.

Similarly, the archbishop might have been given the opportunity to explain why a judge's schoolboy recollection of Catholic teaching focused on the doctrine of double effect was not enough to persuade him that it was a relevant sixth principle. One judge, Lord Justice Robert Walker, said that the 'five salient points [are] entitled to profound respect . . . But they do not explain or even touch on what Roman Catholic moral theology teaches about the doctrine of double effect, despite its importance in the Thomist tradition . . . The term "casuistry" has come to have bad connotations but the truth is that in law as in ethics it is often necessary to consider the facts of the particular case, including relevant intentions, in order to form a sound judgement. I do not by that imply any criticism of the Archbishop's moderate and thoughtful submissions, which the court has anxiously considered.' I welcome the judge's attempt to rehabilitate the word 'casuistry', not least because this book could be considered to be an exercise in casuistry as originally understood. Whether the archbishop would have welcomed this as a fair comment is debatable. He might have responded by observing that the rich moral teaching of the Roman Catholic Church is too often reduced to the doctrine of double effect as one of the best known but least understood or helpful phrases in ethical thinking. Rather than run that risk, he tried to set out the more relevant principles. In any event, he did address the reason why the doctrine would not help in this case, although not perhaps labelling it in a way which satisfied this judge. The archbishop's submission states that

> There are those – including no doubt many Catholics – who would argue that one might embark on such an operation without having Mary's death as part of one's aim, and that her death would then be a foreseen but unintended consequence of a morally justifiable operation aimed at saving Jodie. But what is not possible is that one could embark on such an operation without foreseeing that it would do Mary no good but only lethal harm. And even if her death were merely foreseen, the invasion of her bodily integrity is nevertheless intended. The process of separation cannot be thought of with any plausibility as one of cutting into Jodie's body alone; Mary's body is necessarily cut into. And that violation of her bodily integrity is in the nature of the case lethal for her. It cannot therefore be justified.

Comments by the other two judges in the Court of Appeal, Lord Justice Ward and Lord Justice Brooke, suggested agreement with the archbishop that the doctrine of double effect could not resolve the difficulties of this case. One explained that the doctrine of double effect 'teaches us that an act which produces a bad effect is nevertheless morally permissible if the action is good in itself, the intention is solely to produce the good effect, the good effect is not produced through the bad effect and there is sufficient reason to permit the bad effect . . . I can readily see how the doctrine works when doctors are treating one patient administering pain-killing drugs for the sole good purpose of relieving pain, yet appreciating the bad side effect that it will hasten the patient's death. I simply fail to see how it can apply here where the side effect to the good cure for Jodie is another patient's, Mary's, death, and when the treatment cannot have been undertaken to effect any benefit for Mary.' The other said, 'When the Catholic nurses at the Children's Hospital in Philadelphia consulted their archdiocesan authorities . . . the comfort they received was based on the double-effect doctrine . . . I do not consider that this method of applying the doctrine of double effect would have any prospect of acceptance in an English court.' In sum, the judges and many commentators are fascinated by what one of the judges described as the 'doctrine (or dilemma) of double effect which has been debated by moral philosophers (as well as lawyers) for millennia rather than centuries', but ethical reasoning in uneasy cases has to move beyond the limited use of that doctrine and not try to extend it to inappropriate cases.

Instead of a full dialogue between the judges and the archbishop, however, the fact that his intervention was confined to a written submission means that the case leaves us without full exchanges on points of disagreement. Intriguingly, the archbishop's submission does comment on some of the judges' reported comments or questions during the course of argument, since his submission was not given until the case was underway. Had the case proceeded to appeal, then the archbishop would have had, in effect, the opportunity to reply to the Court of Appeal's doubts. The parents and the legal advisers representing the various interests chose not to appeal, however, and so we are left with the archbishop's points on the one hand and on the other a motley collection of hypothetical and real-case analogies from the judges.

Nonetheless, this is an advance on the position anticipated earlier in the chapter – the fear that the archbishop's principles could be dismissed because of hostility to his church or some other prejudice against him ('He would say that, wouldn't he, because he is a Catholic/a man/a bishop'). Religious figures and especially pressure groups are not above using similarly dubious rhetorical moves, for example retaliating by saying that doctors should not be 'playing God'. Another favourite but equally unsatisfactory tactic of church campaigners is to say that the danger of allowing doctors to proceed with such an operation is that it will lead to widespread euthanasia. Reverting to the secular opponents of church morality, those who want the operation to happen might then retort that the law and the churches should keep out of these matters because people will do what they feel they have to do, behind closed doors, regardless of what the authorities say. It is often the case that variants on these four suspect lines of attack are used as substitutes for serious ethical analysis. All that then seems to be left is precisely the process explored in this chapter whereby principles are compared to hypotheticals with, for instance, advocates of an operation in this case saying that those who oppose the operation are being inconsistent unless they also object to results in other contexts which in fact they would accept. On deeper examination, however, this can be little more than a fifth bad mode of arguing.

These five unsatisfactory tactics recur in different forms in so many discussions of uneasy cases. The first is little more than name-calling – you would say that, wouldn't you, because you are a man or a woman, fertile or infertile, a doctor or a bishop, a research scientist or a parent, a liberal or a conservative, a feminist or a chauvinist. The error behind this is its implication that people who share one facet of their identities will therefore think alike. They do not. Even if they did, incidentally, it would still be better to address the arguments on their merits rather than on their provenance. The second approach is closely related, seeking to win the argument by definition or by using morally loaded language. What exactly does 'playing God' mean? It is a linguistic smokescreen which seeks to obscure an absence of meaning. It is not the scientists or doctors who are guilty of hubris here but their accusers, in implying that humans could play God. The third approach is the so-called slippery slope argument – if we allow X, then next Y will happen and eventually we'll end up with Z (which nobody wants). This is not inevitable. It is possible to hold a position on the most slippery of slopes. The fourth approach is more commonly heard in relation to abortion (tighter laws will merely drive the activity into the backstreets) or pornography (tighter laws will merely drive the activity underground). There are many answers to this, but the basic point is that murder is not eradicated by a law and is more likely to happen in the backstreets or underground but that is no reason to allow it to flourish everywhere.

The fifth line, asserting that opponents are being inconsistent, is often presented (including in tutorials and interviews) as a knock-down or must-win argument, but there are at least two lines of rebuttal. The first is to point to subtle differences between the two sets of circumstances. The second is to admit the inconsistency but to argue that we need not necessarily be consistent across the range of uneasy choices. As Lord Millett concluded in the recent case of K: 'Injustice is too high a price to pay for consistency.' Admittedly, this was in the particular context of legislation which the Law Lords clearly thought should have been revised, the case being about whether it was a defence to the crime of unlawful sexual intercourse with a girl under the age of sixteen for the man to show that he honestly and reasonably believed that she was over sixteen. More generally, however, there are many celebrated thinkers who could help the student pinned into an apparent inconsistency. Isaiah Berlin, for example, has argued that values conflict. This notion is also behind the analysis by Guido Calabresi and Philip Bobbitt of *Tragic Choices*. Some people believe that the only way in which a society can come to terms with its conflicting values is to prefer one value in some circumstances and another in different conditions.

Of course, there are truths lurking close to some of these points, especially the fifth. The use of a debating device does not mean that there are not also legitimate ethical arguments to be prayed in aid for a similar point of view. The important point is that we should be on guard so that our consideration of uneasy cases is not deflected by the assumptions behind these manoeuvres. For example, the judges have become used to the kind of ill-informed criticism which comes their way and so in the case of Jodie and Mary anticipated some objections such as the slippery slope argument or the name-calling and prejudice caught up in the mistaken assumption that the parents were refugees from Kosovo. The judges countered these misunderstandings explicitly although they expected more – speaking to the BBC on his way into court to deliver judgement in this case, Lord Justice Ward declared that 'half the country will think we're potty'. The judges' attractive hesitancy during the hearing seemed to give way to a tone of certainty as they gave their judgements in court in summary form. The tone of off-guard comments (too jolly?) or of judgements (too adamant?) can be seen as defence mechanisms which do not undermine the seriousness with which the judges approached their agonising task. In particular, the conventions of giving judgement in court are such that we would not expect the opinions to be racked with doubt. If they were, they would be more vulnerable to reversal on appeal. Once the judges have made their decision, they have some time in which to find the best possible way of articulating their justifications and they tend to sound more confident in defending their conclusion than they may have been in reaching it. This is mirrored in our everyday conversations. Intuitions on ethical disputes are sometimes buttressed by more vigorous explanations than the initial hunches deserve.

Uneasy cases in ethics can seem like morally significant, serious versions of complex crosswords. Sometimes the answer just seems obvious but one would be hard pressed to spell out why the individual components of the clue lead to that result. On other occasions, the answer has to be worked at, it does not come for some time and it can only be completed with the help provided from the intersection of answers to other questions. The legal system, however, needs to know the reasoning (the 'ratio decidendi') and not just the answer because normally (although disavowed by the judges in this case) the reasoning will have significance for future cases as a precedent. Public articulation of reasons is also important because judges are unelected and need constantly to affirm their democratic legitimacy through being transparent. The reasons are vital for the parties to a case to decide whether to exercise any rights of appeal. Hence judges will rarely use their judgements to trace the sleepless nights and agonies of doubt during the course of argument. Rather, they will use the opportunity to do their best to defend their result against the arguments run by the losing counsel, possible arguments on appeal, the points put in some cases by amici curiae, the critical reception a case might receive from academic lawyers and those seeking to use it as a precedent or to distinguish it, together with any misunderstandings which the judges think the media and the general public might have.

Very few of the standard ploys identified above were used in any of the public discourse surrounding the case of Jodie and Mary. It seemed that the seriousness of their plight encouraged all concerned to set aside any cheap debating points. In other contemporary issues of medical ethics, however, even in other tragic cases, these five points recur, as for example in media coverage of both the Diane Pretty case, where a woman dying of motor neurone disease sought an amnesty for her husband so that he could assist her suicide, and the House of Lords Select Committee on Stem Cell Research, chaired by the Bishop of Oxford. In the former, decided by the Law Lords in November 2001, the first, most general, of the Archbishop of Westminster's five overarching moral considerations in the Siamese twins' case could also be applied to Diane Pretty: 'Human life is sacred, that is inviolable, so that one should never aim to cause an innocent person's death by act or omission.' The Roman Catholic tradition makes no distinction between one's own life or the life of another. To make this clear in the context of assisted suicide, the same principle could be expressed thus: 'Human life is sacred, that is inviolable, so that one should never aim to cause the death of an innocent person, whether another or oneself, by act or omission.'

Indeed, the Roman Catholic Church did once again intervene with its own submission. This time, however, the 'amicus' brief was not to counter a necessarily hasty first-instance judgement and it was not from the cardinal. The bishop who chaired the relevant subcommittee of the Bishops' Conference, the Archbishop Designate of Cardiff (now the Archbishop), made a submission agreeing with what he considered to be the profound judgement of the divisional court, which was itself in line with Supreme Court decisions in the USA and Canada, as well as the House of Lords Select Committee's conclusions when members of the Judicial Committee had called, in the Bland case, for the legislature to consider such matters in depth. The Bland case had arisen from the Hillsborough tragedy in which a number of football supporters died or were injured. One of the victims was a young man called Tony Bland who had survived for years in a persistent vegetative state. His parents, doctors and judges all agreed that he should be 'allowed to die'.

The Law Lords agreed that it would be wrong, albeit on a wave of sympathy for the plight of Diane Pretty and her family, for the legal system to ignore the wisdom inherent in these three interweaving strands of thought. Diane Pretty's next opportunity to press her case was before the European Court of Human Rights in Strasbourg in 2002 where she lost again. This judicialisation of ethical dilemmas is the pattern of recent times and promises to be so domestically in life after the Human Rights Act. While this has much to commend it, there is still a place for the detailed consideration of a dilemma which the legislature at its best can offer. Moreover, without challenging the right of litigants to seek, or the judges to make, ethical decisions in the courts, there is a looming issue of delimiting spheres of competence. After all, the Law Lords in the Bland case had called for the legislature to address the matter and so it did through the House of Lords Select Committee on Medical Ethics, chaired by Lord Walton. This was emphatic in its conclusions, rejecting euthanasia. The Lord Chancellor, Lord Irvine, speaking for the government in presenting to Parliament the publication of a Green Paper on mental incapacity, endorsed the Select Committee's conclusions in equally unequivocal terms:

> Euthanasia is a deliberate intervention undertaken with the express intention of ending a life, at an individual's request or for a merciful motive. The Government is absolutely opposed to euthanasia in any form. The Government fully supports the view of the House of Lords Select Committee on Medical Law in its Report of February 1994 that euthanasia is unacceptable and cannot be sanctioned in any circumstances. Euthanasia is illegal now and will remain illegal.

The Lord Chancellor soon returned to this point: 'With the exception of our absolute opposition to euthanasia, the Government has taken no fixed or final views on any of these questions.' Similarly, the Consultation Paper which he was introducing makes it absolutely clear that the matter raised in court by Diane Pretty would have had only one answer if addressed in the legislature:

> The Government has always emphasised that it does not accept that the individual's right to determine the treatment he or she is prepared to refuse or accept extends to any action deliberately taken to end the patient's life. The Government fully supports the view of the House of Lords Select Committee on Medical Ethics that euthanasia is unacceptable and should remain an offence of murder.

The Select Committee considered at great length the arguments subsequently directed to the courts in the Pretty case. It rejected them. It gave much attention to the views of Professor Dworkin, one of the two philosophers whose views were said by Lord Justice Hoffmann to have assisted him in the Bland case. It rejected them. It reflected on the experiences of the members of the Committee whose relatives or friends had died in 'less than peaceful or uplifting' circumstances and it was moved by letters from members of the public, including those in a similar position to Diane Pretty, but it then came to these conclusions:

> Our thinking must also be coloured by the wish of every individual for a peaceful and easy death, without prolonged suffering, and by a reluctance to contemplate the possibility of severe dementia or dependence. We gave much thought too to Professor Dworkin's opinion that, for those without religious belief, the individual is best able to decide what manner of death is fitting to the life which has been lived.

Ultimately, however, we do not believe that these arguments are sufficient reason to weaken society's prohibition of intentional killing. That prohibition is the cornerstone of law and of social relationships. It protects each one of us impartially, embodying the belief that all are equal. We do not wish that protection to be diminished and we therefore recommend that there should be no change in the law to permit euthanasia. We acknowledge that there are individual cases in which euthanasia may be seen by some to be appropriate. But individual cases cannot reasonably establish the foundation of a policy which would have such serious and widespread repercussions. Moreover, dying is not only a personal or individual affair. The death of a person affects the lives of others, often in ways and to an extent which cannot be foreseen. We believe that the issue of euthanasia is one in which the interest of the individual cannot be separated from the interest of society as a whole . . .

We are also concerned that vulnerable people – the elderly, lonely, sick or distressed – would feel pressure, whether real or imagined, to request early death . . . we believe that the message which society sends to vulnerable and disadvantaged people should not, however obliquely, encourage them to seek death, but should assure them of our care and support in life.

This raised the important point of palliative care. The bishops' joint submission to the Select Committee had praised the work of the hospice movement and of the development of palliative care. At first instance in the subsequent case, however, counsel instructed by Liberty for Diane Pretty had said that no such care had been made available to Mrs Pretty. In the words of the judges, 'anticipating arguments that palliative care would do much to relieve the suffering which Mrs Pretty fears, [her counsel] said simply that Mrs Pretty has not been offered any such care'. As the Select Committee observed, 'there is good evidence that, through the outstanding achievements of those who work in the field of palliative care . . . the pain and distress of terminal illness can be adequately relieved in the vast majority of cases. Such care is available not only within hospices: thanks to the increasing dissemination of best practice by means of home-care teams and training for general practitioners, palliative care is becoming more widely available in the health service, in hospitals and in the community, although much remains to be done. With the necessary political will such care should be made available to all who could benefit from it. We strongly commend the development and growth of palliative care services.' Similarly, Archbishop Peter Smith urged those with responsibilities in this case to ensure that palliative care was made available to Mrs Pretty and that changing the law on euthanasia, against all the weight of the Select Committee's examination, should not be countenanced on the basis that

17

such care was unavailable. The Law Lords agreed. The European Court of Human Rights agreed (the Archbishop of Cardiff again intervening). Mrs Pretty lost at every level and died soon after the European Court's ruling. There was much sympathy for Mrs Pretty and her husband and some considerable admiration for Mrs Pretty's courage. The judges consistently resisted the temptation to allow those emotions to affect their judgement.

The archbishop's intervention endorsed the divisional court's analysis of the Supreme Court decisions in the USA and Canada, together with their interpretation of the European Convention, now incorporated into domestic law by the Human Rights Act. There was, however, one further aspect of the US Supreme Court judgements in *Washington* v. *Glucksberg* which would have been worth drawing to the attention of the Judicial Committee, as it links to the previous point about palliative care: 'Those who attempt suicide – terminally ill or not – often suffer from depression or other mental disorders . . . Research indicates, however, that many people who request physician assisted suicide withdraw that request if their depression and pain are treated.' The references from, for instance, the New York Task Force to support these claims include the conclusion that 'more than 95% of those who commit suicide had a major psychiatric illness at the time of death' and the research finding that suicidal terminally ill patients 'usually respond well to treatment for depressive illness and pain medication and are then grateful to be alive'. Without presuming to comment on Diane Pretty's medical condition, one might have expected those who argue for overturning the whole thrust of the law, in the absence of palliative care, in pursuit of autonomy, to explain how society could be sure that genuinely autonomous, consenting decisions would be made rather than decisions affected by an underlying depression. Moreover, the judgement at first instance highlighted another dimension of this case which is in danger of being glossed over amid the debate on physician-assisted suicide: 'We are not being asked to approve physician-assisted suicide in carefully defined circumstances with carefully defined safeguards. We are being asked to allow a family member to help a loved one die, in circumstances of which we know nothing, in a way of which we know nothing, and with no continuing scrutiny by any outside person.' Not only would there be the question raised above over any person asking for assistance in suicide but there would be questions over whether society should allow family life, whether the marriage bond or parent–child or sibling relationships, to be compromised by expecting family assistance. Even without accepting the arguments for physician–assisted suicide, the switch from doctor to spouse would add two further problems, one being the strain it places on the latter to decide whether to accede to the request and the other being the lack of professional regulation. It would undermine, rather than reinforce, the right to respect for family life which is enshrined in the European Convention and the Human Rights Act.

The point of this excursus on the Diane Pretty case is that it is a strength of both courts and House of Lords select committees that they operate in the realm of public reason. That is to say, they articulate the reasons for their decisions, with humanity, passion and emotion (the judges were as moved as any media commentator by Mrs Pretty's plight), but ultimately with a concern to identify the best possible reasons for the best possible course of action. That is why courts or select committees can be a model for ethical reflection even for those who have no interest in the legal minutiae of a decision. Media commentary also has its place, not least in calling the judges and legislators to account, but it was sometimes difficult for those who respectfully disagreed with Mrs Pretty to have their voice heard in the media. This may be one reason why churches seem to have taken to both these forums with some relief. The secular media can seem, by comparison to courts and select committees, a harsh place in the modern era for those motivated by faith.

Returning to the ethical dilemma posed by the case of Jodie and Mary, therefore, we can see that if it is the most compelling, it is by no means the only example of an uneasy dilemma being resolved by constructive dialogue which, regardless of the result, has much to teach us about moral reasoning. The most intriguing way of looking at the judgements is to see how they try to cope not only with the awesome facts of the case but in particular with the profound submission by the Archbishop of Westminster. For the exchange between the archbishop and the Court of Appeal is a pioneering example in the public realm of serious, thoughtful dialogue about an uneasy case, which repays detailed consideration. Seeing what lay behind that intervention and its reception can perhaps point to ways forward for uneasy cases yet to come. In particular, the archbishop's submission was at its best when at its broadest, in setting out overarching moral principles. The judges were at their best when applying much the same principles but coming to a different conclusion. In the middle, there was something like a public tutorial on ethics, with the principles being tested by a strange assortment of hypothetical cases.

Lords Justices Ward, Brooke and Robert Walker unanimously supported Mr Justice Johnson's decision to order the separation of the twins, notwithstanding the parents' religious convictions to the contrary, with the result that the weaker twin would die during the operation, as indeed happened. Lord Justice Brooke explained the crux of the case in simple, clear terms: 'Would the proposed operation amount to the positive act of killing Mary? The answer is Yes. Would the doctors be held to have the intention of killing Mary, however little they desire that outcome? The answer is again Yes. The doctrine of double effect, which permits a doctor, acting in good faith, to administer pain-killing drugs to her dying patient, has no relevance in this case. This leaves open the single question: Would the killing be unlawful?' To that, all the judges answered No.

The judges considered that the fundamental family law principles of deciding in children's best interests or welfare prevailed. They did not believe that the criminal law of murder would apply to deliberate separation of Siamese twins even if doctors could foresee that one twin would inevitably die during the operation. The judgements are themselves book-length so any account of them needs to be seen as a necessarily selective summary. Fortunately, in the modern era, the Internet makes the full text of such judgements available relatively easily. Indeed, the legal system instantaneously published the judges' full justification on the Internet, thus allowing the whole world to examine their approach at www.courtservice.gov.uk. In a book on ethics rather than law, it is not necessary to wade through the extremely problematic issues of whether the law on murder and manslaughter allows the result which the judges wished to achieve. Nonetheless, it is important to observe that the legal process explains some of the judges' analogies and approaches to the ethical dilemma. The legal system reaches its judgements through highly intelligent and well-paid lawyers putting the best possible case for each side of any dispute, sometimes with extra lawyers hired to put independent points of view. In such a case, those lawyers will offer hypotheticals which are designed to win the case for their clients, not to provide a balanced analogy for a book on ethics. Equally, in the course of argument, the judges might put to counsel that the apparent logic of an argument could fall apart in the circumstances of such-and-such a hypothetical. When the judges come to write their opinions, they are engaged in a slightly different enter-prise, of justifying their conclusions, so again they might be expected to choose hypotheticals which work in favour of their decision. Along the way, however, they may feel duty-bound to discuss some of the examples which were put by barristers or raised by themselves in argument.

A similar process happens in philosophy or theology or law tutorials. Hypotheticals are put by tutors and adapted in the next encounter to reflect the earlier discussions. Experience (which cynics might describe as laziness) then leads to some preferred examples being refined and used year after year. Someone who studied law a few years after me at the same college has already published a book on her life and times which incidentally confirms that much the same questions were being asked at her interview as at mine. The author of one of those brilliant introductions to ethics does not explore hypotheticals or actual cases in any depth but mentions in passing the exact example which was put to me at interview a quarter of a century ago. Again, there is nothing wrong in this but it is worth reminding tutors and fellow debaters that these conventional illustrations of a dilemma need to be examined critically themselves before any lessons can be applied to the real-life uneasy case which awaits judgement. Even if we are convinced of the moral answer to a hypothetical, and even if we are in an ethics seminar rather than a legal case, there is much to be said for a quasi-legal approach to applying any precedent.

Lawyers' arguments by analogy have been much dissected and debated. Simplifying somewhat, the process involves identifying the ratio decidendi, the reason for the decision, in the precedent and then seeing whether the facts of the two cases are sufficiently similar for the precedent to apply in the case under judgement. In a hierarchical legal system, there may be another option for judges in higher courts, of overruling the precedent even if the cases are identical. In the egalitarian world of ethics, however, overruling has no place. If case A is rightly decided and the circumstances of case B are in all relevant respects the same, then B should be decided in the same way as A. If the facts are materially different, then we might describe the process in B as 'distinguishing' between A and B. This laborious spelling out of what it is to argue by analogy has a point. For if we know enough about ethics and judging the significance of facts to say that A should have been resolved in a certain way and B should follow A because it has the same relevant facts, then we do not need A at all. We could just judge B without knowing the example of A since we have been able to single out the key facts of B and make a judgement on the ethical way forward.

The law needs short cuts of precedents and reasoning by analogy to settle 'easy cases' without recourse to the expensive court system. The authority of the law and the skill of the professionals involved in the system is such that potential litigants know in case B that there is no point in pursuing a court action if A is really on the same point and works against them, unless they are prepared to take the case to a court which can overrule A. In ethics, why argue by analogy at all? It is good fun and intellectually stimulating in tutorials, but in the context of serious cases, such as that of Jodie and Mary, is there a value in the use of hypotheticals? In animated student debates, the hypothetical can have a persuasive force, out of all proportion to the substance behind it. This is what needs to be guarded against in the use of hypotheticals in ethical debates on uneasy cases. The hypothetical works best when its facts are memorable, when you agree that the result is clear-cut and when you accept that *therefore* you should judge the real case before you in the same way. The questioning student or the concerned moral agent in a case such as that of Jodie and Mary will be more sceptical when presented with an apparently compelling hypothetical. Why is this person offering this example? Is the choice to take in the hypothetical really so obvious? Are the facts really the same as in this case? Are the relationships between the characters, for example, quite the same?

To give but one reason why the examples are not perfect analogies, all the chosen hypotheticals involve a snap decision whereas the case of Jodie and

Mary took weeks. In the playground where a gun-toting child is running amok, for instance, one is unlikely to have the benefit of a written submission on the moral dilemma from the Archbishop of Westminster, a facility which was available to the Court of Appeal and which was much appreciated by them. Similarly, people faced with hypothetical or real dilemmas where there is a chance to save one life at the expense of another, have little time to ponder the nuances of the doctrine of double effect, whether facing death on a mountain (would you cut the rope which could send a fellow mountaineer to their death in order to save yourself or another?) or on a sinking ship (would you sweep aside a person frozen by fear or the cold who blocks the path of dozens to safety from a capsized ferry, as happened in the Zeebrugge disaster?). We sense that the case of the Siamese twins is more uneasy than these precisely because the parents and doctors at the bedside of Jodie and Mary had weeks in which to reflect. 'Analogies' relating to contexts where there was no time to consider or consult before exercising judgement are therefore not analogies in this important respect to the case of Jodie and Mary.

A second difficulty is that, on examination, some of the hypotheticals do not yield only one way forward to save a life or some lives at the certain expense of another life, whereas in the case of Jodie and Mary we were told that there was no way in which both could survive for long. In the playground story, for example, shooting to kill is unlikely to be the only option. There is a continuing debate as to whether shooting to kill, rather than to disarm, is ever required, even against trained terrorists, let alone against Lord Justice Ward's imaginary six-year-old.

A third difference is that most of the analogies cited by the judges do not involve the moral duties of close family, such as the parents of Jodie and Mary or the professional ethics which will have guided the doctors at the Manchester hospital, but instead involve either bystanders with no family connections and no professional obligations or others involved in the drama whose own lives are at risk. The Zeebrugge example is completely different in this way to the case of Jodie and Mary. Some of the hypotheticals may, if the details are sketched out, be adapted to become closer analogies. If the six-year-old in the playground running amok with a gun was one of your children and another was in the firing line, and you were a member of the police's armed response unit called to the scene, then it might be a more relevant analogy to know whether you would shoot the former child. It would still not be a very good one, however, because some would draw moral differences between shooting and operating or between an aggressor with a gun and a helpless baby. This hypothetical did not start from an especially plausible basis, but by the time additional facts have been read into the original formulation, it loses even more credibility and the answer becomes even more problematic, hence it is unlikely to simplify the complex task of judging what to do in relation to the Siamese twins.

These question marks against the judges' choice of hypotheticals are particular to the attempt to use these examples to make points in relation to the case of Jodie and Mary. Other difficulties which could be cited against the judges' chosen analogies are problems with the whole notion of a hypothetical but, as a regular user of hypotheticals, I have already aligned myself with those who regard the benefits as outweighing these admitted shortcomings. Nonetheless, it is worth recording that in a real case, such as that of Jodie and Mary, the facts are difficult to establish, the prognosis changes, one twin grows stronger and another weakens, the predicted life expectancy goes up and down, the timing of the operation recedes or becomes an emergency, as the issue wends its way through the legal system. In hypotheticals, in contrast, the facts are given with certainty. This is just one of the many reasons why anyone arguing about uneasy cases should be careful with their own choice of hypotheticals and sceptical about the hypotheticals introduced by others. They should be challenged, rather than accepted at face value, but they can be important in bringing home to us the implications of our approach.

It is very difficult to see, for instance, why a judge expects the following example to have helped: 'In my judgement, parents who are placed on the horns of such a terrible dilemma simply have to choose the lesser of their inevitable loss. If a family at the gates of a concentration camp were told they might free one of their children but if no choice were made both would die, compassionate parents with equal love for their twins would elect to save the stronger and see the weak one destined for death pass through the gates. This is a terribly cruel decision to force upon the parents.' Yet parents might refuse to choose between their children on the basis of strength, preferring to draw lots, or might choose the weaker thinking that the stronger might survive until freedom came through external help or they might refuse to participate at all in such an inhumane process. Hence this example does not assist us in resolving the case of Jodie and Mary, although it is at least capturing the family relationship much more closely than the other hypotheticals. Indeed, since all the judges and commentators agreed that the parents of Jodie and Mary were compassionate, did have equal love for their twins and yet did not follow what this judge regards as the inevitable choice in his concentration camp example, the judge might have pondered whether the outcome of his hypothetical was quite so obvious.

Similarly, the judicial reference to a 1977 case of Siamese twins in the USA, where rabbis advised parents that an operation in similar circumstances could be morally justified, did not assist greatly in the resolution of the dilemma concerning Jodie and Mary. A local family court apparently took only three minutes to decide that the operation in this case should proceed. The discussion of this American case led the English Court of Appeal in the case of Jodie and Mary to a very frank description of the dilemma in both: 'This was a case similar to ours, where the survival of both twins following separation was out of the question. It therefore raised the same ethical (and legal) question: could one twin be sacrificed so that the other might have a chance to live?' Lord Justice Brooke went on to explain how the rabbis and priests became involved: 'In that case the parents, who were deeply religious Jews, would not consent to the separation without rabbinical support. Many of the nurses at the hospital were Catholic, and they would not allow themselves to become involved in the proposed operation unless a priest assured them that it was morally acceptable to proceed.' Both the rabbis and the priests agreed that the operation should proceed, as did the court, although the surviving twin died only three months after the operation.

> [The rabbis] reportedly relied primarily on two analogies. In the first, two men jump from a burning aeroplane. The parachute of the second man does not open, and as he falls past the first man, he grabs his legs. If the parachute cannot support them both, is the first man morally justified in kicking the second man away to save himself? Yes, said the rabbis, since the man whose parachute didn't open was 'designated for death'. The second analogy involves a caravan surrounded by bandits. The bandits demand a particular member of the caravan be turned over for execution; the rest will go free. Assuming that the named individual has been 'designated for death', the rabbis concluded it was acceptable to surrender him to save everyone else. Accordingly, they concluded that if twin A was 'designated for death' and could not survive in any event, but twin B could, surgery that would kill twin A to help improve the chance of twin B was acceptable.

As the judge conceded immediately after citing this passage, 'There is, however, no indication in the submission we received from the Archbishop of Westminster that such a solution was acceptable as part of the philosophy he espoused.'

The classic student response to the rabbis' first hypothetical would be to observe that parachutes can support two people. I am indebted to a rabbi and friend, Julia Neuberger, for observing that students might also spend some time doubting whether the second man would succeed in grabbing the legs of the first. Attempting to deny the plausibility of the imagined facts enlivens tutorials but distracts from the fundamental ethical challenge. Let us suppose that the parachute is damaged to the point where one man can land safely but two could not. Again, the parachuting classes in the student body will argue as to whether, nonetheless, the second could be allowed to hold on to the legs of the first until sufficiently late in their falls for the second to have a chance of survival when kicked away. Just when the tutor believes that the student has no option other than to address the question 'Is the first morally justified in kicking the second away?', the inventive student will counter with a hypothetical variation on the hypothetical: 'What if the first has a heart attack when his legs are grabbed; is the second entitled to hold on and use the dead or dying first to cushion the fall; or could the second now claim that the first is designated for death and somehow take over the parachute, forcing the first to plummet unaided?'

A whole tutorial can pass speculating on the moral impact of a family relationship between the two, or of roles as instructor and learner, or of the assumption that the first packed the parachutes and is somehow responsible for the failure of the second parachute, or of the extreme case where the designating was by the first who maliciously interfered with the second parachute. In my experience, such attempts to avoid the simple question often spring from a reluctance to being corralled into being presumed to agree with a course of conduct (in these cases, relating to Siamese twins) on the basis of an example constructed for this purpose. Sometimes, a student who has a special commitment to another issue may suspect that the hypothetical will be used in evidence against them on the consistency line of attack mentioned above and so spars rather than answers the question. For example, two men sharing a parachute is not far away from a famous hypothetical example used in abortion debates of one person being plugged into another's body as a life-support system. A student who is avowedly pro-life or pro-choice in campaigning about abortion may be wary of expressing a view on the hypothetical, even if they are relatively unperturbed by the rare case of Siamese twins.

What may seem a major digression is necessary here to disentangle the tentacles of abortion debates from the case of the Siamese twins. Lord Justice Brooke chose an interesting reference point in the case of Jodie and Mary when he commented on recent changes to the law on abortion:

> It is true that there are those who believe most sincerely – and the Archbishop of Westminster is among them – that it would be an immoral act to save Jodie, if by saving Jodie one must end Mary's life before its brief allotted span is complete. For those who share this philosophy, the law, recently approved by Parliament, which permits abortion at any time up to the time of birth if the conditions set out in Section 1(1)(d) of the Abortion Act 1967 (as substituted) are satisfied, is equally repugnant. But there are also those who believe with equal sincerity that it would be immoral not to assist Jodie if there is a good prospect that she might live a happy and fulfilled life if this operation is performed. The court is not equipped to choose between these competing philosophies.

The substitution referred to was in fact a spectacular farce. Amendments to what became the Human Fertilisation & Embryology Act 1990 were used by pro-life campaigners to try to restrict the law on abortion. The Act was in any event going to involve votes of conscience (all votes in Parliament, one would like to think, should be votes of conscience, but in the United Kingdom's politics, the term signifies that Members of Parliament are free to vote without any party line) and pressure to address abortion law had been building up through the courts. The Oxford student abortion case in the late 1980s had seen the then Master of the Rolls, Lord Donaldson, express some exasperation with the legislature for not addressing the issue. The government agreed to give some time to consideration of abortion law and a complex series of amendments aimed to give legislators a choice of time limits.

The pre-existing law was complicated and this process made matters worse. The Abortion Act 1967 was itself a private member's bill, introduced by David (now Lord) Steel, and sought to minimise the opportunities for filibustering or wrecking manoeuvres by building on bits and pieces of pre-existing common law and statute. In essence, that law made it an offence to procure a miscarriage unlawfully and the uncertainty came in what was meant by unlawfully. Judges seemed to think that it would be lawful to save the life of the mother in extreme cases. An uneasy case led a judge to direct a jury to acquit where the mother, a teenager victim of a multiple rape, would have been a 'mental wreck'. This is a phrase, used in evidence in the case, which might make sense to the jury in a particular case but it is not the language which is customary in legislation. The Abortion Act 1967 gave more precision in the defences to the charge of procuring a miscarriage, spelling out 'unlawfully' and no doubt extending it:

Subject to the provisions of this section, a person shall not be guilty of an offence under the law relating to abortion when a pregnancy is terminated by a registered medical practitioner if two registered medical practitioners are of the opinion, formed in good faith –

(a) that the continuance of the pregnancy would involve risk to the life of the pregnant woman, or of injury to the physical or mental health of the pregnant woman or any existing children of her family, greater than if the pregnancy were terminated; or

(b) that there is a substantial risk that if the child were born it would suffer from such physical or mental abnormalities as to be seriously handicapped.

Instead of giving a time limit, the 1967 Act referred to the time limit established by the Infant Life (Preservation) Act 1929. This created a presumption of twenty-eight weeks but the presumption was rebuttable and the definitive time limit was when the baby was 'capable of being born alive'. This meant that the time limit would vary as technology improved the chances of survival and flourishing. Over the decades, the effective time limit therefore came down to some twenty-four weeks. Twenty-eight weeks, however, was lodged in the minds of the media and campaigners. Reformers therefore came to the ludicrous position of trying to reduce the time limit from what they thought it was to what it actually was yet they did so with such incompetence that the time limit was actually removed from the category of cases where it was most needed (since late abortions were most likely when there was a late diagnosis of disability). This is such a confusing story that many find it difficult to believe but this is what happened.

The focus of reforming the law was in relation to time limits but the opportunity was also to be taken to unpack the separate grounds lumped together in (a) and also to tighten the law somewhat by spelling out, for example, that not just any injury to the mother would suffice, only a grave and permanent injury. Hence the 1990 Act substituted for those original (a) and (b), a revised formulation of (a), (b), (c) and (d). Unfortunately, a drafting error meant that the campaigners included the time limit in (a) rather than in an initial clause which would have then governed all four of the grounds. Since the old (b) ground of handicap was now the new (d), it did not have any time limit applying to it. Thus the 1990 Act takes away the reference to the 1929 Act time limit and substitutes for the original defences in the 1967 Act:

(a) that the pregnancy has not exceeded its twenty-fourth week and that the continuance of the pregnancy would involve risk, greater than if the pregnancy were terminated, of injury to the physical or mental health of the pregnant woman or any existing children of her family; or

(b) that the termination is necessary to prevent grave permanent injury to the physical or mental health of the pregnant woman; or

(c) that the continuance of the pregnancy would involve risk to the life of the pregnant woman, greater than if the pregnancy were terminated; or

(d) that there is a substantial risk that if the child were born it would suffer from such physical or mental abnormalities as to be seriously handicapped.

Whereas what the reformers should have put is that section 37 substitutes

that the pregnancy has not exceeded its twenty-fourth week and

(a) that the continuance of the pregnancy would involve risk, greater than if the pregnancy were terminated, of injury to the physical or mental health of the pregnant woman or any existing children of her family; or

(b) that the termination is necessary to prevent grave permanent injury to the physical or mental health of the pregnant woman; or

(c) that the continuance of the pregnancy would involve risk to the life of the pregnant woman, greater than if the pregnancy were terminated; or

(d) that there is a substantial risk that if the child were born it would suffer from such physical or mental abnormalities as to be seriously handicapped.

The late Cardinal Winning of Glasgow criticised Tony Blair and other politicians for their voting on abortion law. In so far as pro-life groups or bishops or the media regard voting on the 1990 Act as the touchstone, there is a surreal character to such condemnation or praise. For those who thought they were improving the law from a pro-life perspective actually made matters worse, again as seen from that same own perspective, and vice versa. The question of whether an abortion is ever morally defensible has too often been confused with the question whether it is legal. Within the many legal questions surrounding abortion, false targets have too often been attacked. Too often, incompetence and undue complexity in legal drafting have obscured the moral questions. Abortion law is especially complicated by its tortuous legislative history. Observers can be forgiven for thinking that prominent Catholics who spoke out against an operation on Jodie and Mary were influenced by the impact they thought the case might have on abortion and, for that matter, for thinking that Catholics who kept their own counsel were equally affected by the abortion question.

Returning after that long detour to the rabbis' second hypothetical about caravans and bandits, this example is likely to encounter the same avoidance tactics regularly deployed to dodge the fundamental questions posed by applying principles to sets of real or imaginary facts. Thus students will tend to question the naivety of the hostages in imagining that the bandits will keep to their word. Alternatively, they may question why the individual has been singled out from the crowd and imply that discrimination, rather than say a record of war crimes, could make a difference. Students would be more willing to offer up Hitler than to offer up one of their number who has been designated because of ethnic background by a racist group of bandits. The most common student instinct is to counter politely by avoidance rather than confront directly the idea of sacrificing one person in this way on the flimsy assumption that they are 'designated for death'. The weighing up of one life against several is by no means as clear as the rabbis seemed to imply, but even if it were, it is not a precise analogy to a Siamese twins' case where it is not one-life-for-many-lives but one-for-one or one-for-two.

If we turn from judicial citation of hypothetical cases to their references to actual choices, again it is not proven that the real example of strangers facing an uneasy decision helps parents or doctors in the Siamese twins' context:

> At the coroner's inquest conducted in October 1987 into the Zeebrugge disaster, an army corporal gave evidence that he and dozens of other people were near the foot of a rope ladder. They were all in the water and in danger of drowning. Their route to safety, however, was blocked for at least ten minutes by a young man who was petrified by cold or fear (or both) and was unable to move up or down. Eventually the corporal gave instructions that the man should be pushed off the ladder and he was never seen again. The corporal and many others were then able to climb up the ladder to safety.

The corporal was not, however, the parent of the fearful young man, it was not a one-for-one or one-for-two case and the corporal's life was one of those at risk. This is not the same as the position of the parents of Jodie and Mary, who were not at risk themselves, who were not having to decide in a matter of minutes and who were in a close family relationship of love and responsibility to both those who might die.

The judicial fascination with analogies meant that they could not resist other examples without any analysis to show whether they have a message for the case of Jodie and Mary:

> There is another class of case in which a person may be faced with the dilemma of whether to save himself or others at the cost of harm or even death to a third person. The dilemma generally arises as the result of an emergency and the examples (real or imagined) are typically concerned with disasters at sea, or emergencies during mountaineering or other hazardous activities . . . Of the many real and imagined examples put before the court it is worth mentioning two incidents which really did happen, although neither was the subject of a court decision. One is the awful dilemma which faced the commander of an Australian warship, in peacetime, when a very serious fire occurred in the engine room. He ordered the engine room to be sealed off and flooded with inert gas, in order to save the ship and the rest of the crew, although the order meant certain death for anyone who was still alive in the engine room. The other is the equally awful dilemma of a mountaineer, Simon Yates, who held his fellow climber, Joe Simpson, after he had slipped and was dangling

over a precipice at 19,000 feet in the Andes. Yates held Simpson for an hour, unable to recover him and becoming increasingly exhausted. Yates then cut the rope. Almost miraculously Simpson landed on a snowy ice bridge 100 feet below and survived. When they met again Simpson said to Yates, 'You did right.'

More might have been expected from the judges by way of explanation as to how their chosen examples illuminate the matter for decision before them. In the first of these hazardous cases, for example, we might have expected to have had clarified the issue whether not giving the order meant certain death for the others on board, even though for me that, or other arguments-by-numbers, would not have been decisive. From an ethical point of view, some work also needs to be done on explaining whether the expectations and duties of members of the Australian Navy are a good analogy to the role of parents and children in the case of Jodie and Mary. In the second example, there is an intriguing hint that reluctance to take the action, as demonstrated by heroic efforts to save the other, is morally significant. Adults who have freely chosen to undertake a risky enterprise, such as mountain climbing, may have an understanding of what someone in Yates's position may have to do, as illustrated by Simpson's generous comment. Suppose, however, that a less forgiving Simpson had been paralysed in the fall and that a rescue helicopter had reached Yates only minutes later, leading to the comment, 'You did wrong.' Is the ethical choice determined by the outcome or by the reaction of those affected?

No doubt lawyers in this case were drawn to the Simpson/Yates example because of the voluminous literature arising from mountaineering, including many books by Joe Simpson and at least one by Simon Yates. Simpson imagined what Yates might have been thinking in his book about the incident, *Touching the Void*. Yates then confirmed the accuracy of that account in a book about a different climb, *Against the Wall*, and also gave his own version:

I knew I had done all that could reasonably be expected of me to save Joe, and now both our lives were being threatened, I had reached a point where I had to look after myself. Although I knew that my action might result in his death, I took the decision intuitively in a split second. It simply felt the right thing to do, like so many critical decisions I had taken during the climb . . . My decision had been right; we had both survived. In subsequent years, I have overheard numerous heated debates about the ethics of my decision and many 'what if' scenarios. I have met people who are understanding of my actions and others who are openly hostile.

Simpson went on to say, 'You saved my life, you know. It must have been terrible for you that night. I don't blame you. You had no choice. I understand that and I understand why you thought I was dead. You did all that you could have done. Thanks for getting me down.' Indeed, the book is dedicated 'To Simon Yates for a debt I can never repay . . .'

The image conjured up by the truncated version of the story is that the two were climbing up the mountain and at the first experience of trouble, Yates cut the rope sending Simpson to a likely death. The reality is that Yates had saved Simpson higher up the mountain after the latter had fallen and broken his leg badly early in their descent. Yates was bringing Simpson down heroically when a further fall meant that Simpson's survival depended on Yates holding him by the rope which joined them. After an hour, Yates's grip began to give way and he thought that they would both die unless he cut the rope.

This intriguing story has absolutely no relevance to the Siamese twins' case but is of interest in itself. It may surprise some that, however misplaced they were, the judges' striking analogies, hypothetical and real, did not capture the public imagination. This may simply be because of the awesome facts of the case itself or because the analogies are just not very apposite, but another possibility is that the media have yet to learn how to unpack the richness of the human drama and ethical argument from the detail of legal cases. There is an assumption that the public will not be interested in the legal minutiae and that therefore all they need to know are the facts, the result and the odd gaffe by a judge. If so, then we need to work harder at listening to, or observing, or decoding, what goes on in our name in our courts. A distinguished professor of ethnomusicology, the anthropology of music, at Queen's University, Belfast, the late John Blacking, drew attention to the way in which our culture prizes musical performance but other cultures value listening more than we seem to do. Without the ability in others to appreciate their music, performers would not be able to perform in quite the same way. Similarly, we seem to regard philosophy in general, and ethics in particular, as about elite performance, almost behind closed doors rather than as an activity in which wide participation should be cultivated. Hypotheticals have a role to play in this, not least because, at their best, they can help us test our intuitions. In the third chapter, a more complex method of testing our hunches is applied to the endless dilemmas posed by Northern Ireland. Whichever way we use to reflect on our instincts, this process of arriving at what has been called a reflective equilibrium is not just to be reserved for uneasy cases. It is a way of testing and then improving our judgement in everyday dilemmas.

Ultimately, however, even the judges conceded that hypotheticals would not solve the problem which they faced in this uneasy case of Jodie and Mary: 'In truth there is no helpful analogy or parallel to the situation which the court has to consider in this case. It is unprecedented and paradoxical in that in law each twin has the right to life, but Mary's dependence on Jodie is severely detrimental to Jodie, and is expected to lead to the death of both twins within a few months.' Even without the benefit of well-chosen, apposite hypotheticals, speculation on the fate of Jodie and Mary was tantamount to a national, indeed international, seminar on ethical choices. Although commentators and judges sometimes seemed to be desperately clinging to the position they first adopted, using ever more dubious arguments to justify an initial hunch, so-called ordinary citizens, in contrast, were disarmingly prone to say that their first thought was such-and-such but now that they had learned more, thought about it, heard other people talk about it, prayed about it, they had come to think the exact opposite. A turning point for some was the widely publicised artist's illustration, drawn from a photograph, of Jodie and Mary. This picture demonstrates the power of an image over words in today's society. I have heard people say that it changed their minds from supporting the operation to opposing it and vice versa, so I am not claiming that the impact was unproblematic. Rather, the point is that we can be so touched one way or another by having the reality of uniqueness yet interdependence brought home to us visually. This is especially salutary for authors, lawyers and tutors or students of philosophy, all of whom are traditionally wordsmiths.

The Court of Appeal's judgements illustrate another health warning in debates on uneasy cases. Although I have some sympathy with both the judges' reasoning and their conclusion, I do not see how they made the leap from the former to the latter. Their often enriching, sometimes uneasy reasoning did not, it seems to me, lead ineluctably to their stark conclusion. This is a feature of many arguments about uneasy cases. Someone makes a good point and seems to advocate a sensible result but it is not clear how they are connected. Bad points seem to get in the way and the crucial link between best points and ultimate conclusions is never explained. Indeed, it is my contention that the best single argument for ordering the operation and the best single argument for respecting the wishes of the parents were not articulated in the courts. This again is a general lesson against the beguiling narrative force of a justification unless it is comprehensive.

Those who disagree with the archbishop seem to me, though apparently not to the Court of Appeal judges, to have almost lost the ethical argument before they have begun if they adopt the rhetoric of the rights or best interests of the more vulnerable twin. For it is difficult to see how this way of thinking can allow for a decision which deliberately takes her life. The better line for the judges to have run would have been what American lawyers have called a 'substituted judgement' test. Rather than talk of her rights or interests, ask instead what she would decide if she were capable of analysing her predicament but was otherwise the person she was at the time of the court hearings. Would she not have chosen heroic self-sacrifice:

greater love hath no sister than this, that she lay down her life for her twin? There are answers to this approach, including the fact that the rights rhetoric is embedded in the law and that there are obvious dangers in medical ethics and elsewhere if there is too ready a willingness to allow X and Y to convince themselves that Z would make a judgement of self-sacrifice. Nonetheless, it is arguable that this is in fact the way in which future generations will try to make sense of the death of the more vulnerable twin now that the Court of Appeal's conclusion has been carried into effect.

The best counter-argument about parental interests, also omitted from the deliberations of the Court of Appeal, is that the new Human Rights Act requires judges to have particular regard to the importance of freedom of thought, conscience and religion. This is especially significant as the Human Rights Act 1998 came into force less than a month after the Siamese twins' case, on 2 October 2000, with its emphasis in section 13 on the courts being under a duty to pay particular regard to freedom of religion. This special clause, and the Home Secretary's explanation thereof in Parliament, was a matter of great importance for the late Cardinal Hume, who could see how crucial these matters are to our understanding of the human condition and, to use the phrase invoked by the parents in this case, to our under-standing of God's will. The court's determination could be said to have affected not only the right to life of Jodie and Mary but also the right to respect for family life, the right to freedom of conscience and the right against inhuman treatment of those directly involved, together, possibly, with the exercise by a religious organisation – the Roman Catholic Church – of the European Convention right to freedom of thought, conscience and religion. It was therefore a missed opportunity that this case, with its profound moral challenges, was not taken to the House of Lords and there illuminated by judicial reflection on the importance of paying particular regard to religious freedom. Trumping parental wishes is not to be undertaken lightly, as explained in the archbishop's fifth principle, and it is difficult to see how parental wishes arising from religious convictions could now, with the Human Rights Act fully in force, be trumped at all in these circumstances.

Not only do I think that we were denied the best arguments for either ordering the operation or respecting the wishes, I also believe that we have seen some of the worst arguments feature or lurk beneath the surface of attitudes struck in and out of court. For example, arguments about parental interests always need to be handled carefully in cases affecting children. In this case we were treated at the High Court stage to an equation of disability and sin akin to that which brought about Glenn Hoddle's demise as England manager. Mr Justice Johnson reported that 'Due to the customs of the community in which they live the mother feels that she must have done something wrong for her to have conceived in this way. She is concerned about how the twins would be received in their community where there is a belief that this disability must be punishment for some earlier sin.' This is part of a bigger issue, whether the Church or interest groups or doctors or courts genuinely value any parental wishes and/or whether they invoke parental wishes only when those wishes correspond to their own stance.

We must beware of taking at face value accounts of what the parents think or what the customs or facilities are in another country. On the other hand, we should be extremely wary of hidden dismissals of what the parents say they think. Underlying some reactions to this case, it is possible to detect a paternalism which could be articulated thus: the parents genuinely think that they cannot bring themselves to choose death for one of their children, they therefore genuinely want to argue vigorously for the non-intervention but actually they will have a sense of relief if the authorities trump those arguments because honour will be satisfied, the best case has been put for the weaker twin and they may emerge from the case with one child to cherish. Again, as with the 'substituted judgement' test, we are only a short distance away from professional and state reinterpretation of wishes, rights and interests. The first safeguard against a move too far is to spell out the possible influences which are underlying the public arguments.

This is one of the benefits of the appellate process, that we participate in a continuing conversation rather than make a once-and-for-all snap decision in a school playground or on a mountain. For example, in a chilling passage at first instance, Mr Justice Johnson had said of the weaker twin that her life 'would not simply be worth nothing to her, it would be hurtful'. One of the successes of the archbishop's intervention was that this error of judgement by Mr Justice Johnson was explicitly rejected by the Court of Appeal. Lord Justice Ward said, 'I am satisfied that Mary's life, desperate as it is, still has its own ineliminable value and dignity. In my judgement, the learned judge was wrong to find it was worth nothing.'

Another successful aspect of the archbishop's argument was that it brought to the attention of the judiciary three powerful critiques of the Law Lords' ruling in the Bland case, on withdrawing a feeding tube from a patient in a persistent vegetative state with the result that the patient would die. One of the judges, Lord Mustill, confessed to 'acute unease' about adopting a way 'through the legal and ethical maze', fearing that the decision 'may only emphasise the distortions of a legal structure which is already both morally and intellectually misshapen'. On the same page, the Law Lord again uses the word 'acute' to describe the moral dilemma in Bland: '[t]his appeal obviously raises acute problems of ethics, but this should not obscure the fact that it is also exceptionally difficult in point of law.' The reason is, to give a fuller quotation, that 'the acute unease which I feel by adopting this way (drawing a distinction between acts and omissions) through the legal and ethical maze is I believe due in an important part to the sensation that however much the terminologies may differ the ethical status of the two courses of action is for all relevant purposes indistinguishable'.

The most philosophically sophisticated judgement was given in the Court of Appeal by Lord Justice (now Lord) Hoffmann who described the case as presenting a 'terrible decision' and chose to answer the legal point very briefly so that he could instead focus on the ethical issues because 'this case has caused a great deal of public concern'. He explained:

> This is not an area in which any difference can be allowed to exist between what is legal and what is morally right. The decision of the case should be able to carry conviction with the ordinary person as being based not merely on legal precedent but also upon acceptable ethical values . . . To argue from moral rather than purely legal principles is a somewhat unusual enterprise for a judge to undertake. It is not the function of judges to lay down systems of morals and nothing which I say is intended to do so. But it seemed to me, in such an unusual case as this, it would clarify my own thought, and perhaps help others, if I tried to examine the underlying moral principles which have led me to the conclusion at which I have arrived. In doing so, I must acknowledge the assistance I have received from reading the manuscript of Professor Ronald Dworkin's forthcoming book, *Life's Dominion*, and from conversations with him and Professor Bernard Williams.

His conclusion was that Tony Bland's 'body is alive, but he has no life'. In a critique which the Archbishop of Westminster commended to the Court of Appeal in the case of Jodie and Mary, Professor John Finnis lambasts Lord Justice Hoffmann's approach: 'This sort of dualism, which thinks of the body as if it were some kind of habitation for and instrument of the real person, is defended by few philosophers indeed (religious or otherwise). It renders inexplicable the unity in complexity which one experiences in everything one consciously does.'

On appeal to the House of Lords, there was more attention given to the legal arguments, but the judges still perceived the need to address, or distance themselves from, the moral dimensions of the case. Lord Browne-Wilkinson noted that the Court of Appeal's approach, 'reaching the conclusion that the withdrawal of food and Anthony Bland's subsequent death would be for his benefit, attaches importance to palpable factors such as personal dignity and the way Anthony Bland would wish to be remembered but does not take into account spiritual values which, for example, a member of the Roman Catholic Church would regard as relevant in assessing such benefit'. Whether this distinction makes sense is debatable. We are told at first instance that 'Anthony Bland was not religious but that he had attended Sunday school in the Church of England'. Contrary to the impression that the Church of England is wishy-washy and that the Roman Catholic Church is absolutist on these and other matters, the two churches agreed on the principles which ought to apply in such a case in a subsequent joint analysis, explicitly rejecting the 'false contrast' between religious and secular values and which insisted that neither 'of our Churches insists that a dying or seriously ill person should be kept alive by all possible means for as long as possible'.

Lord Browne-Wilkinson's judgement continues by stating that 'Where a case raises wholly new moral and social issues, in my judgement it is not for the judges to seek to develop new, all-embracing, principles of law in a way which reflects the individual judges' moral stance when society as a whole is divided on the relevant moral issues.' In practice, however, judges do make key decisions in ethically uneasy cases and they have tended to do so in cases such as this by unconscious manoeuvres which reduce the moral dilemma to two extreme views, crudely utilitarian on the one hand and crudely religious on the other, leaving judges to glide through the middle as if an enlightened, not-too-utilitarian and not-too-religious, but rather a right-on or at least rights-on, way.

This has been exposed by the three critiques of the Bland decision which the Archbishop of Westminster drew to the attention of the Court of Appeal in the case of Jodie and Mary. In addition to the article by John Finnis mentioned above, he referred also to another masterful analysis of Bland by another academic lawyer, John Keown and, most importantly, he introduced to the Court of Appeal the joint submission from the Anglican and Roman Catholic bishops in this country to the House of Lords Select Committee established in the aftermath of the Bland decision to review the law. The churches' analysis is more simply expressed, and yet could be said to be more profound, than are the Law Lords' opinions. Drawing judicial attention to the underlying richness of the churches' contributions could prove to be crucial in the development of human rights jurisprudence in the United Kingdom and should give all-comers pause for thought in considering uneasy cases. Hitherto, there has been a tendency for judges and others to create space for themselves in the middle ground of what they take to be public opinion by caricaturing a crude utilitarianism as one extreme and the views of, as Lord Browne-Wilkinson put it in the Bland case, Roman Catholics and Orthodox Jews on the other extreme. This enables the judges to think of themselves as pretty much in the centre ground. The fact is, however, that a broad spectrum of Judaeo-Christian opinion agrees on these issues and is itself firmly in the mainstream of great humanitarian thinking, as illustrated by the bishops' joint reaction to Bland:

The arguments presented in this submission grow out of our belief that God Himself has given to humankind the gift of life. As such, it is to be revered and cherished. Christian beliefs about the special nature and value of human life lie at the root of the Western Christian humanist tradition, which remains greatly influential in shaping the values held by many in our society. They are also shared in whole or in part by other faith communities. All human beings are to be valued, irrespective of . . . their potential for achievement.

The central argument of the churches' reflection on the issues raised by the Bland case was that

Those who become vulnerable through illness or disability deserve special care and protection. Adherence to this principle provides a fundamental test as to what constitutes a civilised society . . . Because human life is a gift from God to be preserved and cherished, the deliberate taking of human life is prohibited except in self-defence or the legitimate defence of others . . . *a pattern of care should never be adopted with the intention, purpose or aim of terminating life or bringing about the death of a patient* [my italics].

This was quoted with approval by the Court of Appeal in the case of Jodie and Mary. Its route to the legal system is worth consideration. The Law Lords called in the Bland case for the legislature to review the law. The bishops put these points to that review. Then one of the bishops, now the Archbishop of Westminster, referred to this argument in his submission to the Court of Appeal in the case of Jodie and Mary and the point commended itself to the judiciary. This illustrates a more general point that we should not judge a contribution to our understanding of uneasy ethics solely by its immediate impact on the particular uneasy case. Lodging in the public realm a penetrating analysis is always of worth, even if it sometimes requires more than one reference for the judiciary to accept its insights. Similarly, we are reflecting on the Siamese twins' case, not because we expect a similar set of circumstances to arise but because we appreciate the humanity of all involved in an agonising decision and we believe that we can learn lessons for our own lives and our own decision-making. When the case began, these Siamese twins may have been seen as posing an unusual dilemma. As the case proceeded, however, all-comers began to see that our unease at any quick or simple conclusion arises from the profound way in which this dilemma speaks to us of the human condition and of the eternal struggle to discern a divine will.

An extraordinary feature of the case in what we are told is a secular age is that the moral teaching of the new Archbishop of Westminster was so swiftly accepted as a significant factor, even by those such as the judges who disagreed with his conclusions. The fact that his submission to the Court of Appeal features so prominently in the judgements is itself a lesson for uneasy cases. Any lawyers' monopoly on arguing about these uneasy cases before a court has been broken. Any scepticism about the standing of the churches in these matters should also give way to the need for detailed rebuttal of arguments or acceptance of them.

This is not to say that the churches or other faith communities have all the answers for the rest of society, and it is worth pausing to ask why not, if a religious tradition does claim some insight into fundamental truths. One line of explanation which can be confused with uneasiness is uncertainty. The Anglican theologian, Dr John Elford, for example, has argued for the churches to be more liberal in what he calls an age of uncertainty. He thinks that the technological and other uncertainties in the modern world are so great that we cannot be certain in our ethics. Uncertainty is, for him, caused partly by 'the simple fact that we live in an age of widespread moral disagreement' and partly by 'the increasingly evident limitations of our knowledge'.

As is apparent from the titles of books on this matter, I prefer to think of unease, rather than uncertainty, as the key feature in these ethical debates. We can be very certain that one twin will die and almost certain that the other will live. The unease does not come from the uncertainty. Rather it comes from the certain conviction that one will die from the operation and both will die without it. Of course, John Elford is talking about uncertainties which go beyond a medical prognosis, taking us towards an interpretation of pluralism which implies moral relativism. I would argue, however, that it is possible to be uneasy about this case, to respect those who in conscience disagree but still to believe in objective goods or values and still to be certain that the best ethical way forward is for the operation to proceed or not to proceed. The unease does not have to come from, or result in, indecisiveness, uncertainty or lack of conviction about the preferred way forward. It can come from appreciating that the countervailing arguments, while less persuasive, are still of value and that the people involved are touched by a tragedy. From my perspective, the strength of John Elford's analysis does not lie in his emphasis on uncertainty. In his book on pastoral theology, compassion, understanding, practical wisdom and grace all feature prominently. The book on the uncertainty of ethics also has great value in identifying why what I call uneasy cases are such a profound link between the human and the Divine: 'Human beings are unique in their ability to make ethical choices because they can reason about the options available to them and because they also have the freedom and the will which enables them to implement those choices.'

From John Elford to the judges, however, there is a tendency to paint the ethical dilemma as difficult because of uncertainty engendered by two conflicting rights or principles. This seems to me to obscure the possibility that there is also uneasiness when a single, simple principle has to be applied to a particular case. For all manner of reasons, which will have to await a further book on law, ethics' cousin, lawyers have become conditioned to think in terms which I have described as owing unacknowledged debts to Isaiah Berlin and Guido Calabresi, as if the difficulty always comes from a conflict of values. In outline, the assumption of uncertainty being rooted in clashing principles arises thus. Lawyers talk of hard cases where the rules seem to run out and where judges therefore have a discretion to do the best they can or, according to some, an obligation to discern the underlying principles and apply them. The former approach held sway on this side of the Atlantic for some time, seeming as it did to fit the reality of judicial creativity and demonstrating a refreshing candour. On the other side of the Atlantic, however, it did not seem sufficient to justify an activist, liberal Supreme Court challenging the elected branches of government in the 1950s and 1960s. The idea that the judges were not simply making it up as they went along but rather discerning the underlying principles which were already there had an attraction to liberal America. It seemed to carve out a distinct but still democratic niche for the court. Sceptics observe, however, that judges and commentators always seem to find that the underlying principles allegedly inherent in the law are the very ones which the judges or commentators would wish to prevail in a political setting. In other words, liberal judges think they find underlying liberal principles while conservative judges think they find underlying conservative principles. The Supreme Court splits along ideological lines. The principles are to be found in the judges' hearts and minds rather than somehow hidden in constitutional texts, subtexts or contexts.

The distinction between hard and easy cases in law seems simple at first. Hard cases are the ones which come before appellate courts because lawyers can reasonably disagree about them. Easy cases are those which can be resolved without elaborate argument about what the law is or how it should be applied to the facts of a dispute. Much of the procedural reform sweeping through the English legal system in the wake of a thoroughgoing analysis by Lord Woolf is designed to prevent unmeritorious appeals clogging up the courts when determined litigants, supported by their own wealth or by the public purse, try to convert their easy case into a hard one by seeking a replay. The hierarchical system of the law is designed instead to filter out these cases and leave the more senior and expensive levels to focus on the hardest cases, where their judgements can then ripple out through the system to be applied in the easier cases by relatively junior judges.

One problem with this approach is that the dividing line between hard and easy can itself be problematic. The conditioning that leads us to assume that the uncertainty of hard cases arises from two conflicting principles is also complex and subtle. It is a feature of the fact that legal systems tend to reduce multidimensional problems to two-way disputes. Lawyers are well advised to put their best arguments only, preferably their single best argument. If there are only two parties, this leaves us with the impression that even hard cases can be reduced to two conflicting positions. The incentives are also there for each set of lawyers to argue as if the principle which would help their client win is already somehow inherent in the law, latent but lurking just for this judge in this case to articulate it.

This partly explains why the Archbishop of Westminster's submission has changed the dynamic of litigation in hard cases. Third-party interventions undermine this assumption that there are only two ways of looking at any dispute and that they arise from a conflict of values. This is one reason why it may be considered that the ideal amicus curiae brief would not have gone quite so far as the archbishop's. He could have left his contribution at the level of his five overarching moral considerations, together with more of the ethical thinking which underpinned them. By clearly favouring the arguments of those who opposed the operation, his submission can be seen as 'taking sides' and thus reinforcing these assumptions about there being only two perspectives. Nonetheless, the archbishop came close to establishing that even in the hardest of cases we can agree on the relevant rights, principles and values. Where we disagree is in the application of those norms to the facts of a particularly troubling case.

John Elford is right in that sometimes there is uncertainty surrounding the law, the facts or the ethical framework of a case. 'The result' of a case is by no means always 'the result' in real life. Abortions, for example, which were deemed lawful by courts in famous cases on either side of the Irish Sea have not always been carried out, either because of a change of mind by those involved or because of a miscarriage. To give another way in which uncertainty has prevailed, I have described abortion law in Northern Ireland as a twilight zone. The English legal system has had several legislative attempts to establish the law on abortion. The Irish and American legal systems have had major cases before their respective Supreme Courts. Society in Northern Ireland, in contrast, seems to shy away from facing the issue squarely. The result is that campaigners pretend that the law is more conservative than it is, but the law has for some time seemed not to measure up to the international standards of certainty expected, for instance, by the European Court of Human Rights. The Human Rights Act will see domestic arguments about uncertainty or certainty in the law, just as the European Court ruled against the UK in the mid 1980s on the issue of telephone tapping, because the rule of law or legal certainty or the doctrine of legality demands an answer, but the UK had left a vacuum, trying to dodge the issue. In an earlier case on freedom of expression, the European Court had explained:

> Firstly, the law must be adequately accessible: the citizen must be able to have an indication that is adequate in the circumstances of the legal rules applicable to a given case. Secondly, a norm cannot be regarded as a 'law' unless it is formulated with sufficient precision to enable the citizen to regulate his conduct: he must be able – if need be with appropriate advice – to foresee, to a degree that is reasonable in the circumstances, the consequences which a given action may entail.

There can still be unease, however, even when the law or, to return to ethics, when the guiding morality is perfectly clear and certain. There can still be unease when the determining factor is a single, simple principle. The reason why the archbishop's faith or some other fundamental ethical position does not necessarily yield a clear answer to every case is to be found elsewhere, in levels of generality. Law is necessary as a coordinating authority if people are going to live in society. It is necessary to agree on which side of the road to drive, for the common good to flourish. It is not necessary to drive on the left. Societies flourish just as much when they drive on the right. Trying to deduce which side of the road we should drive on from the general principle is trying to make the higher level of abstraction do too much work. To take a more profound example, life itself should be respected but what that means in detailed application to a particular set of facts can be more problematic. Those who believe that God created us with moral reasoning and free will can regard it as part of the human condition and the divine plan that we should work away at what to do in these most uneasy of dilemmas, where the general injunctions seem to run out of detailed advice. Although the parents invoked the expression 'God's will' in an endearing way, for a theologian or bishop to decree that proceeding with the operation or refraining from it is God's will might seem hubristic in these circumstances. The strength of the tradition is therefore not necessarily that there will always be a single conclusion at the most detailed level but rather that there will always be wisdom available at some level of generality. It is primarily for the individuals most closely involved to exercise their judgement, having fully informed their consciences by trying their best to absorb the relevant teaching. Ultimately, it requires judgement to resolve an uneasy case.

One of the central texts of the Second Vatican Council, *Gaudium et Spes*, explains this in terms which give the lie to the hostile assumption that the Roman Catholic Church has one answer which it thinks is right in every single moral decision:

The laity should also know that it is generally the function of their well-formed Christian consciences to see that the divine law is inscribed in the life of the earthly city. From priests they may look for spiritual light and nourishment. Let the laity not imagine that their pastors are always such experts, that to every problem which arises, however complicated, they can readily give him a concrete solution or even that such is their mission. Rather, enlightened by Christian wisdom and giving close attention to the teaching authority of the Church, let the laity take on its own distinctive role.

Often enough the Christian view of things will itself suggest some specific solution in certain circumstances. Yet it happens rather frequently, and legitimately, so that with equal sincerity some of the faithful will disagree with others on a given matter. Even against the intentions of their proponents, however, solutions proposed on one side or another may be easily confused by many people with the gospel message. Hence it is necessary for people to remember that no one is allowed in the aforementioned situations to appropriate the Church's authority for their opinion. They should always try to enlighten one another through honest discussion, preserving mutual charity and caring above all for the common good.

If it is primarily a matter for lay people, for all citizens, to take responsibility for making ethical judgements, the archbishop's submission of five overarching moral principles has the merit of guiding (but not, to my mind, determining or dictating) such judgements through being rooted in a living tradition of thought which has been exploring these questions continuously, not just in recent cases but for century after century. A common question to ask in a tutorial or in a discussion between friends about any uneasy case is whether there is any underlying philosophy behind your surface conclusions in the particular dilemma. How can the archbishop justify his five salient principles? He could point to a number of sources. To give but one: in 1998, on the occasion of the fiftieth anniversary of the Universal Declaration of Human Rights, the Catholic Bishops' Conference of England and Wales issued a thoughtful statement on Human Rights and the Catholic Church. The bishops based their approach on the 'Catholic belief that two vital truths about human persons must always be held together'.

Firstly, all persons are unique, irreplaceable, destined for transcendent life, and so are not just units of some larger mass or entity, who could properly be treated as interchangeable, or merely as the instruments of another's purpose. (For example, each person is embodied: all our thoughts and perceptions are inseparable from our senses, from their openness to the world and their active response to it. It follows that everyone's experience is unrepeatable.)

Secondly and equally important, everyone is a person-in-relationship whose well-being cannot be attained alone, and whose life can never be considered apart from the many relationships (more or less intimate or enduring) that make up its fabric.

In practice, the individual person and the community will always have claims against each other: and their true fulfilment goes together. Neither an individualism that denies the claims of community, nor a corporate prosperity that excludes the well-being or dignity of individual persons, is ultimately tolerable.

These two truths, articulated in this passage well before the Siamese twins' case, are relevant not only to the uneasy case of Jodie and Mary but to all the litigation which the Human Rights Act will witness. Even before the Human Rights Act, openings were there for these kinds of arguments through the principles of the European Convention which has now in effect been incorporated into our domestic law through the 1998 Act. While this chapter is concerned primarily with the first right in the European Convention – the right to life – the next substantive right listed in the European Convention has played a significant part in the issues addressed in the second and third chapters: 'No one shall be subjected to torture or to inhuman or degrading treatment or punishment.' There is European case law on what that means, some of it involving decisions against the UK government, such as that relating to interrogation techniques in Northern Ireland in the 1970s. What the case law needs is a jurisprudential or philosophical or theological underpinning. Just as the Roman Catholic Church has given the European Union, and now domestic politics, the concept of subsidiarity, so it can now offer the domestic and European courts these two truths and the way in which they are united in the concept of the common good to provide that foundation for human rights.

Although the bishops welcomed the Human Rights Act, they were cautious about its impact on their own freedoms. The Act and the Convention are wide-ranging but not comprehensive. The right to marry and the right to respect for private and family life are protected by the Human Rights Act. So are the rights to freedom of thought, conscience, religion, expression, assembly and association. There is a prohibition on slavery, a right to liberty, to a fair trial and to freedom from retrospective criminalisation of behaviour. There is a prohibition of discrimination in the exercise of all these rights. Some Church reactions to the Human Rights Bill concentrated on perceived threats in some of these rights. In particular, would a public authority, such as a church, be forced to conduct marriages of which it did not approve or be unable to dismiss headteachers of whose lifestyle it did not approve? On the former, the European Convention has been most respectful of churches – too respectful in the judgement of some other human rights lawyers. On the latter, there is no right to employment enshrined in the Convention or the Act, so direct attacks on 'discrimination' in employment are not clearly covered. Nonetheless, it is possible to imagine creative legal arguments which buttressed the cases already being taken to industrial tribunals where a head is dismissed from a church school (or indeed by other schools).

Partly to allay these fears, the Home Secretary added section 13 to the Human Rights Act. It states that 'If a court's determination of any question arising under this Act might affect the exercise by a religious organisation (itself or its members collectively) of the Convention right to freedom of thought, conscience and religion, it must have particular regard to the importance of that right.' Various stances can be taken on the importance of a right. Some hold that all rights are equal. Some think that some rights are more equal than others. Section 13 could be taken as suggesting that freedom of religion is the most important. Others argue that 'absolute rights', such as that against degrading treatment, are more important than 'qualified rights' such as freedom of expression where there is a balancing act inherent in the European Convention. The structure of such rights is that the first part of the article sets out the right in absolute terms: 'Everyone has the right to freedom of . . . religion.' The second part, however, explains that the right 'may be subject only to such limitations as are prescribed by law and are necessary in a democratic society in the interests of public safety, for the protection of public order, health or morals, or for the protection of the rights and freedoms of others'. It is the essence of European Convention jurisprudence that the first part of the article is to weigh heavily in the balance and that the word 'only' sets the scene for the second part. The right is only qualified where it is necessary. Rephrasing the article, it could be put as 'where it is necessary in the public interest'. This seems to me to be too loose a formulation, however, and the vital contribution of Christian theology here might be to introduce the notion of 'the common good' as the term to capture the circumstances in which the right has to give way or be restricted.

A third-party intervention in court ought to be judged on its merits, on the quality of its argument. Indeed, this may well be part of the reason why the Catholic Church has warmed to the role of providing amicus briefs, not just in this country but around the world, because in court its teaching is not filtered through media indifference or hostility but available to be judged for the quality of its reasoning. In practice, of course, a court is more likely to pay attention to a submission which comes with the moral and spiritual authority of church leaders where they have established a system to promote human rights and where their own record on human rights is regarded as exemplary. On the former point about a systemic rather than solo intervention, the Siamese twins' case moved through the courts and to the hospital so swiftly that there might not have been time for more than the individual leadership of the archbishop, but this is likely to be exceptional. It is a moot point whether a cardinal has, as cardinal, any greater authority than other bishops in his national conference. Indeed, it could be argued that cardinals have no authority on cases which concern another diocese. In practice, the bishops band together and create a system for addressing matters of mutual concern – the Bishops' Conference – which has committees usually chaired by a bishop who is then the effective spokesman for the Church in the particular country. When the cardinal is the president of the Bishops' Conference, he will have more justification than otherwise for providing an overview. On the latter point, about human rights' records of interveners, a submission from bishops known for their prison visiting or their acts of solidarity with refugees is more likely to impress the judiciary than a submission on a case involving child abuse where the bishops sadly are perceived to have shown poor judgement in not acting with sufficient speed and vigour. There are few short cuts, therefore, to the task of building up a culture of promoting human rights and the common good. Nor should there be.

Most importantly, the two truths identified by the Catholic bishops show that the uneasy case of Jodie and Mary is not to be regarded as on the margins, only one remove from implausible hypotheticals and thus so unusual that fundamental principles can be disregarded. On the contrary, the Catholic bishops' twin principles show why the case of the Siamese twins has touched the consciences of the world: the interdependence yet uniqueness of the two vulnerable children involved posed in stark form questions of the ultimate truths about human dignity and the human condition. This is why the case engages us so much and why virtues and emotions such as love, generosity, dignity, compassion, respect, awe, wonder and hope mingled with reactions to the plight of the family. It is not enough to say that the right landscape in such an uneasy case is to be found by clambering to the moral high ground. It is our duty to craft a space, a public realm, which is shaped by arguments of the highest calibre and yet simultaneously of the deepest humility in the face of the Siamese twins' profound experiences of uniqueness and interdependence.

In this shared endeavour, the archbishop's submission has shown that Christian views are not the result of an extreme position which can be easily disregarded by those who do not share that particular religious faith. There is a role for theology in public and private life, contrary to the influential but flawed view of Professor Glanville Williams who in the 1950s sought to banish this discipline from the ambit of the law: 'For the legislator (a fortiori the judge), it seems sufficient to say that theological speculations and controversies should have no place in the formulation of rules of law, least of all the rules of the criminal law which are imposed on believers and non-believers alike.' This proposal was memorably described by Professor Basil Mitchell as being that 'we should be permitted to listen to Lady Wootton but not to the Archbishop of Canterbury (unless, perhaps, he forgets his theology)'. Lady Wootton was a social scientist and the spirit of the contrast could perhaps be translated in the modern era by updating the example to, say, Professor Anthony Giddens, director of the LSE and exponent of the Third Way, or substituting for the social sciences a media-friendly scientist, such as a leading medical researcher. Professor Mitchell rejected Professor Williams' proposition, suspecting that 'the critic likes theology to be doctrinaire enough to be discounted with impunity. We are more comfortable with stereotypes. We are happy to know that our theologians are doctrinaire and irrelevant, just as we are happy to know that our dons are remote and ineffectual.'

The churches' insights are not irrelevant and they are not only of value to those who share their beliefs. On the contrary, they are part of the mainstream of ethical thinking through the centuries, across the boundaries of time, faith and nationality. Professor John Finnis has explained lucidly in *Natural Law and Natural Rights* the ways in which natural law and Roman Catholic teaching dovetail but the one is not dependent on, nor restricted to, the other. As Finnis observes, the principles are 'well recognized in other formulations: most loosely as "the end does not justify the means"; more precisely, though still ambiguously, as "evil may not be done that good might follow therefrom"; and with a special Enlightenment flavour, as Kant's "categorical imperative": "Act so that you treat humanity, whether in your own person or in that of another, always as an end and never as a means only".' It does not follow, of course, that John Finnis would agree with the archbishop on what these general principles mean for the particular case of Jodie and Mary. More generally, other bishops and Catholic thinkers will disagree with one another on the application of principles to facts, as they probably did in this case.

They will agree, however, that Catholic social teaching has another vital concept to offer to all who are troubled by uneasy cases. Secular commentators have tended to suppress what had been their preferred utilitarian rhetoric in recent years, relying instead on human rights to explain their judgements in such uneasy cases as that of Jodie and Mary. This seems to be all the more plausible given the incorporation of the European Convention on Human Rights, drafted in 1950, into our domestic law through the Human Rights Act 1998. For some time now, rights rhetoric appears to have held sway in the public realm, which could well be regarded as an improvement on utility. Where rights conflict or otherwise fail to resolve the dispute, a deeper approach to ethics is needed, grounding rights talk in a broader understanding of the human condition. In Catholic social teaching, the relevant term is the 'common good'. In the run-up to the 1997 general election, the Roman Catholic bishops in England and Wales published a substantial document entitled *The Common Good*, and just before the 2001 general election, the bishops updated it with *Vote for the Common Good*. As we have seen, in fact, the votes of judges will be just as important as the votes of politicians in the new constitutional order, but the point holds good that the bishops' selection of 'a few of the vital issues facing our society' rightly identifies the issues of the marginalised as 'families, human life, global poverty and injustice, asylum seekers and refugees, family members needing care and crime and prison'. These are the topics on which we can expect future amici curiae briefs to assist our understanding of uneasy cases. According to the bishops, we all (not just politicians and judges) have a duty to show concern: 'All governments, political parties, politicians, communities and individual voters have a moral responsibility to be concerned about the most vulnerable human beings in our society.'

The bishops explain that the common good is not the same as the utilitarians' 'greatest happiness of the greatest number'. Rather, it is 'the sum of all those social conditions which allow the human dignity of all to be respected, and their basic needs to be met, while giving men and women the freedom to assume responsibility for their own lives'. Human rights are not the whole story in ethics because they may conflict or may have to be forgone in the interests of the common good. As the bishops observe, 'Key elements of the common good such as peace, justice, compassion and mutual respect can only be protected and promoted through the collaboration and engagement of all.' Inclusivity is a close ally to clear thinking about uneasy cases. Thinking about the issue from the full range of perspectives can change our understanding of the moral imperatives and, just as importantly, of moral considerations which involve going the extra mile, of showing more generosity or more restraint than is necessary given one's own rights. For those who think that human rights discourse is the ultimate trump card in ethical argument, however, there seems to be no way of explaining, or perhaps even understanding, the concept that it can be right not to exercise a right. I tried to capture this point a decade ago in relation to freedom of expression, with particular reference to the saga surrounding Salman Rushdie's novel, *The Satanic Verses*. A similar limitation will arise in discussions of punishment if justice is regarded as the last word, leaving no space for going beyond what justice requires through showing mercy. The common good, however nebulous a concept it might seem to those unfamiliar with Catholic thought, has the merit of encompassing all these aspects of ethical judgement.

No concept, however compelling, can absolve the individuals concerned from exercising judgement, especially one at such a high level of generality. In an uneasy conclusion to this introductory uneasy case, then, it is worth pointing to another confusion on the part of the judges:

> I am satisfied that there has been the closest consultation between the medical team, the parents, their friends, their priest and their advisers. Just as the parents hold firm views worthy of respect, so every instinct of the medical team has been to save life where it can be saved. Despite such a professional judgement it would, nevertheless, have been a perfectly acceptable response for the hospital to bow to the weight of the parental wish however fundamentally the medical team disagreed with it. Other medical teams may well have accepted the parents' decision. Had St Mary's done so, there could not have been the slightest criticism of them for letting nature take its course in accordance with the parents' wishes. Nor should there be any criticism of the hospital for not bowing to the parents' choice. The hospital have care of the children and whilst I would not go so far as to endorse a faint suggestion made in the course of the hearing that in fulfilment of that duty of care, the hospital were under a further duty to refer this impasse to the court, there can be no doubt whatever that the hospital is entitled in its discretion to seek the court's ruling. In this case I entertain no doubt whatever that they were justified in doing so.

In other words, the Court of Appeal said that the doctors were not under a duty to challenge the parents before the court, yet this is difficult to reconcile with the judges' decision, which was that, in these circumstances, the stronger twin's interests had to prevail. The logic of that conclusion, right or wrong, is that those with responsibility should have come to court to secure authority for the operation. This is but one example of a running theme in the judgements, that they did not wish this case to be regarded as a precedent, preferring to think of their decision as confined to its particular facts. This is muddle-headed, as we have seen that the very opposite is true, that the case ought to be regarded as a core illustration of the human condition.

This is why leaving the Court of Appeal judgements unchallenged was such an unsatisfactory conclusion to the legal system's handling of the case of Jodie and Mary. An appeal to the House of Lords would have given a further opportunity for reflection, still within the time frame for an operation if one were to be ordered. What would have happened then? It seems to me as if the parents would have been under some considerable pressure to reconsider their initial position. One might have begun to change his or her mind. Since the parents were reported as agreeing with one another, the judgements did not address the implications for uneasy ethics if parents were to disagree on whether to consent to a course of action. This can complicate cases in law, for example where an estranged boyfriend seeks an injunction to prevent his girlfriend proceeding with an abortion. Even where the couple are a harmonious family unit, however, there can be disagreements in good faith on what is in the best interests of their children. Politicians sometimes hint, for instance, that their children's attendance at a kind of school not favoured by their party is due to their spouse's conscience and judgement trumping their preference.

If one parent or both parents had begun to doubt their initial judgement, this in turn would have caused the archbishop to clarify whether he was really in favour of parental wishes being respected by the law or only if the parents agreed with him. The Human Rights Act would have come into force and it is more likely that the better arguments would have been presented. As discussion of Tony Bland's case has demonstrated, however, a case is never completely closed. Subsequent cases will give opportunities to re-examine the arguments in the case of Jodie and Mary. In the court of public opinion, that debate is already taking place. The debate, indeed the unease, persists because the choice is tragic – to sanction the operation and breach the moral prohibition on consigning one twin to a premature death or to prevent the operation and thus consign the other twin to a premature death. What the judges missed is that hypotheticals about instant judgements in emergencies are *easier* than a case where there is time to ponder such a choice, at least in that they prompt less uneasiness. In the case of Jodie and Mary, the barrister for the hospital reported that 'The surgeons are . . . not in any great hurry, as from the cardiac point of view things remain steady'. Although Mary seemed to be drawing nutrition from Jodie, 'this could have implications for the timing of the operation but there is no immediate rush', leaving the expected 'point of separation at three plus months . . .'. It may be easier to live with having made a snap decision which you now believe to be wrong than to have agonised for weeks.

This discussion has been intended to convey a fascination with working through the implications of hypotheticals, a wariness of dubious debating moves, an awareness of the richness of the Catholic tradition, a reluctance to condemn those who take a different view and an enthusiasm for thinking about how to apply some of these thoughts to dilemmas in one's own life. More specifically, what I take from the case of Jodie and Mary is that it is possible to argue, with integrity but also with unease,

- that it was right for the parents to stake out their position
- that the doctors were entitled to challenge their decision
- that it was right, given some public criticism of the parents' standpoint, the challenge from the doctors and the decision by the first instance

judge (who was deciding without the benefit of all the arguments which the Court of Appeal heard), for the archbishop to articulate the overarching moral considerations

- that it was permissible nonetheless for the judges to apply this framework, or their own variation on its themes, to reach a different conclusion
- that the best reasoning to defend such a decision has yet to be formulated
- that we are all therefore still learning from this uneasy case

Some will dismiss this as descending to relativism, but my argument – adapting the imagery of Monet painting different studies of the cathedral at Rouen, in his case from the same place but capturing the differences in light – is that our impression of a cathedral varies with our vantage point and we can never fully understand the cathedral (here the divine will) but can only glimpse and describe how it seems to us, from where we stand. We are uneasy partly because we know that we cannot grasp the whole in a single impression or see everything from one human perspective. It is possible to believe that it would not have been right for the parents to have had to decide that one child should die that the other might live but nonetheless right for the state to intervene, with judges coming to a decision in good faith which we could not expect of the parents. The judges' task has been compared, mistakenly, to Solomon's, whereas the better biblical reference is to Abraham's willingness to follow what he took to be the divine will even to the point of sacrificing the life of his child. Morality is not just about instant decisions in catastrophic cases. Neither is it solely concerned with refraining from doing bad things. It also entails positively doing good things to build up the common good. Hence, even exercising a right judgement in uneasy cases does not exhaust morality and we need to turn to more complex cases, involving more families and professionals than does this initial, uneasy case of Jodie and Mary.

2

Child Killers: Uneasy Mercy

The complex ethical dilemmas surrounding punishment were reduced in the summer of 2001 to a deceptively simple question about the timing of the release of the killers of James Bulger. Was eight years too short a period for Robert Thompson and Jon Venables to have served in custody? In the autumn of 2002, an even more notorious child killer, Myra Hindley, died after thirty-six years in prison. Should she have been released? Answering these questions, consistently or otherwise, is not easy. The quest is often assumed to be for a theory of just punishment whereas in my view the issue is one of *mercy* rather than of *justice*. A *theory* needs to do more than simply state that mercy can be either given or withheld. How does mercy differ from justice? Is it meaningful to talk of showing a mercy too far? When should mercy be shown – after eight or thirty-six years?

On 12 February 1993, these two ten-year-old boys – Thompson and Venables – had played truant from school, abducted the two-year-old James Bulger from a shopping precinct in Bootle, Merseyside, took him to a railway embankment, subjected him to various indignities, battered him with bricks and an iron bar before leaving him on the railway line so that his body was sliced in two. They were arrested later that month and detained. In November that year, after a trial held in public with some concessions to their youth and with protection from hostile crowds who attacked the van which brought them to court, they were convicted of abduction and murder. As they were under eighteen, the sentence was an order to detain them during Her Majesty's pleasure, in other words at the discretion of the authorities.

The writer Blake Morrison followed the case, attended the trial and subsequently wrote a powerful book, *As If*. He understood why the case attracted from the very beginning such horrified interest: 'Some deaths are emblematic, tipping the scales, and little James's death . . . seemed like the murder of hope . . .' Yet he feared the demonisation of the child child killer: 'A child has died and become an icon. A nation's conscience must be appeased. The intricacies of responsibility are not at issue. The public mood is bleakly vengeful. The boys must be put away, and quick.' He expected the father of James Bulger, Ralph, to make the kinds of comments which he did to the media, for instance, after the conviction of the two boys: 'One day they'll be out of jail and I'll be waiting for them.' He was more disappointed when the judge said, 'The killing of James Bulger was an act of unparalleled evil and barbarity,' because Morrison had read confidential reports on the boys' backgrounds from social services, not used in the trial, and because he spent some time candidly exploring our moral confusions in childhood more generally. He realised, however, that the judge may have been talking tough before offering a relatively soft sentence. Blake Morrison's writing has had some considerable influence on attitudes in this case, so it is worth setting out his thoughts at the conclusion of the trial, which turned out to be prophetic:

> Only a culture without hope cannot forgive – a culture that doesn't believe in progress or redemption. Have we so little faith in ourselves we can't accept the possibility of maturation, change, cure? Have we so little faith in children? . . . Children can be restored socially and psycho-logically as well as medically. Robert and Jon could be rehabilitated, remorseful as they are. Prison shouldn't just be incarceration, but incarceration with therapeutic aspirations. It's inhuman not to forgive damaged children, and despairing not to try to save them. As if kids who kill come from another planet, and don't deserve the chance to be human, to atone, to repair.

The trial judge recommended that they serve a minimum of eight years. The Lord Chief Justice of the day recommended ten years. The trial judge was clear that the minimum figure would have been eighteen years had they not been so young. It is also worth recording his thinking, which again has some claim to have been prophetic in that his proposed eight years proved to be exactly the period of their detention. The trial judge regarded eight years as a very long period from the perspective of a ten-year-old boy:

> Very great care will have to be taken before either defendant is allowed out into the general community. Much psychotherapeutic, psychological and educational investigation and assistance will be required.
> Not only must they be fully rehabilitated and no longer a danger to others but there is a very real risk of revenge attacks upon them by others . . .
> If the defendants had been adults I would have said that the actual length of deterrence necessary to meet the requirements of retribution and general deterrence should have been eighteen years.
> However, these two boys came from homes and families with great

social and emotional deprivation. They grew up in an atmosphere of matrimonial breakdown where they were exposed to, saw, heard, or suffered abuse, drunkenness and violence. I have no doubt that both boys saw video films frequently showing violent and aberrant activities.

In my judgement the appropriate length of detention necessary to meet the requirement of retribution and general deterrence for the murder, taking into account all its appalling circumstances and the age of the defendants when it was committed is eight years . . . eight years is 'very very many years' for a ten- or eleven-year-old. They are now children. In eight years' time they will be young men.

The parents of James Bulger gathered more than a quarter of a million signatures supporting a petition to the government to make sure that Thompson and Venables would serve a longer period than the judiciary seemed to be envisaging ('seemed to be' signifies that in fact the judges were recommending a minimum and the actual time would depend thereafter on the progress of each in custody; if they turned eighteen and were not to be released, and then again if they were not released by the age of twenty-one, each landmark would require a different kind of custody, ultimately moving them to adult prisons). The huge numbers who supported the petition are explicable in the light of the gruesome details of the abduction, abuse and murder of James Bulger, followed by the callous discarding of his body, left on a railway line. Of the many descriptions of the features of this case which explain the extraordinary public antipathy to Thompson and Venables and their families, perhaps the most succinct is by Lord Reed, concurring with the decision of the European Court some six years later:

The murder of James Bulger by [the defendants] was an appalling act. James was two years old. The grief of his parents, who took part in the proceedings before the Court, is inexpressible. The fact that [the defendants] were themselves only ten years old at the time of the murder makes it particularly disturbing. Other aspects of the murder, such as the abduction of James from his mother, the brutal nature of the killing, and the severing of James's body, provoke shock and revulsion. The video pictures which showed [the defendants] abducting James, and leading this defenceless little boy to his death, brought the events before his parents, and before the public, with a haunting clarity. In the circumstances it is unsurprising that the case has given rise to great public concern and has received a high level of publicity.

When Michael Howard was Home Secretary, it was the practice for the holder of that office to set the tariff, or minimum term, in such cases. Influenced in part by this almost unprecedented level of public outrage, he decided that the figure should be fifteen years for these two child killers. Although they had not appealed against their convictions, they challenged this setting of the tariff by the Home Secretary and their cases were considered by judges in both the English legal system and the European Court of Human Rights, who also addressed some other aspects of the trial. The House of Lords, in a 3–2 split decision, and the European Court both ruled against the government on this issue of determining their release, while the government succeeded, for example, in defending before the European Court the process of prosecuting such young children for murder, not least because some other European jurisdictions, including Ireland, have even lower ages for responsibility.

Of particular significance to this discussion is that in 1999, after Howard had been succeeded by Jack Straw as Home Secretary and while the Home Office was absorbing the implications of the House of Lords' ruling against the government on the tariff, the European Court also ruled against the United Kingdom on such a determination of the liberty of young offenders by a government minister. Either the trial judge or the Lord Chief Justice, not the Home Secretary, should set the minimum term. A central reason for this was the judicial view that the time served in custody was a judicial matter and should be treated judiciously, free from the pressure of public opinion, such as petitions which might be expected to hold some sway with an elected politician.

The relevant passage of the letter from the Home Office to each of the killers explained how Michael Howard as Home Secretary had been influenced in setting fifteen years:

> In making his decision, the Secretary of State had regard to the circumstances of the offence, the recommendations received from the judiciary, the representations made on your behalf and the extent to which this case could be compared with other cases. He also has regard to the public concern about this case, which was evidenced by the petitions and other correspondence . . . and to the need to maintain public confidence in the system of criminal justice . . .
>
> He takes the view that this was an exceptionally cruel and sadistic offence against a very young and defenceless victim committed over a period of several hours.

The reaction of Thompson and Venables was reported to be that they became preoccupied, in the light of this, by the feeling that they were being treated like Myra Hindley who was convicted of the Moors murders in 1966 and who was still in prison when they were found guilty of their crimes three decades later. The Lord Chief Justice in 1982 had decided that she should serve a minimum of twenty-five years, in which case she might have been released in 1991, before the murder of James Bulger. In 1990, however, the Home Secretary of the day, David Waddington, determined that life should mean 'whole life' in the case of the Moors murderers. Successive Home Secretaries seemed adamant that she would never be released.

Rather than suffer the same fate, Thompson and Venables challenged the Home Secretary's decision. They succeeded, ultimately by the 3–2 split decision in the House of Lords. According to the Law Lords, the Home Secretary should not have ignored the progress and development of the children in custody. He should have been 'detached from the pressure of public opinion', showing a judge's 'dispassionate fairness'. At the core of standard liberal unease about punishment is the knowledge that the wider public does have draconian views in favour of lengthy prison sentences. In a liberal democracy, how do we reconcile democracy, rule by the people, with liberalism? The answer is that democracy is not simply the same as majoritarianism. The whole human rights movement is a counter to the notion that the majority should be allowed to rule unfettered by concerns for rights, justice and the common good. Elected politicians are good at reflecting the views of majorities or sizeable minorities, otherwise they would struggle to be elected, but unelected judges have a countervailing role to play in standing apart from, and up to, popular opinion. This is why there seemed to be a problem in the English system of entrusting an elected politician with the effective determination of a minimum sentence. Even so, how exactly do we incorporate the public's attitudes to crime and criminals within our legal system and how do we acknowledge the anguish of victims' families and friends if we have to discount those views when it comes to sentencing?

One of the Law Lords, Lord Goff, offered a cogent answer when he explained that he wished to 'draw a distinction in the present context between public concern of a general nature with regard to, for example, the prevalence of certain types of offence, and the need that those who commit such offences should be duly punished; and public clamour that a particular offender whose case is under consideration should be singled out for severe punishment'. The former general concern is relevant, the latter clamour is to be set aside by anyone who has to make a judgement about the continued detention of particular offenders. The Home Secretary was not the right public office-holder to resolve the tariff in individual cases. The responsibility passed to the Lord Chief Justice.

In 2001, it emerged that there were some seventy cases where child killers had been invited by the Prison Service to make representations on their tariffs. Lord Woolf, the new Lord Chief Justice, now has the responsibility in all these cases to set the tariff which is, more precisely, the minimum time a detainee must serve before the parole board may consider the case. Lord

Woolf decided that the time had come in the cases of Robert Thompson and Jon Venables. The matter then became one for the parole board and the Home Secretary, David Blunkett, who had in 2001 succeeded Jack Straw. There had been some indication of the likelihood of this happening a year or two earlier when the then Inspector of Prisons, Sir David Ramsbotham, annoyed the government and courted controversy in opining that Thompson and Venables should be released around the time they became eighteen, rather than proceed to adult prisons.

Much the same arguments were replayed when this actually happened in July 2001 after those with responsibility for the development of Thompson and Venables advised that they should be released. One difference from the earlier dry run was the tabloid horror at the care and cost of giving the young men new identities. An irony of this, however, was that it was judged necessary because of the hostile reactions of those who then bemoaned the cost. Draconian injunctions were issued by the courts to prevent any British media from revealing anything which would help identify the two young men formerly known as Robert Thompson and Jon Venables.

Some commentators seemed to think that eternity would be too soon to release the perpetrators of such a crime as the murder of James Bulger. The question could be asked whether the timing of such judgements on these matters was itself right. Was the moment of release not in one sense too soon to be so definite that the release was timely or untimely? In another sense, was it not too late, given that the issues had been argued exhaustively before the courts more than two years earlier? Certainly, timing affects attitudes as even a few days seemed to make a difference to the way the public thought about the matter. Thompson and Venables were released on a Friday, with the result that there was intensive media coverage over the weekend. On the Monday, BBC Radio 4's *Moral Maze* asked me to participate in their programme on the subject, partly because of my jurisprudential interest in crime and punishment but partly also because of my involvement in the community in Merseyside. To a BBC researcher in London, it seemed as if people on Merseyside had spent the weekend being appalled at the early releases and were baying for revenge. The prospect loomed of a debate about whether communities in Liverpool were any different to communities elsewhere. On the Tuesday, therefore, I bought Liverpool's local evening paper, the *Echo*. There was no mention of the issue what-soever, not even in its outspoken letters to the editor. The front page lead story was about a grandmother in her eighties who beat off an intruder with a stick. By the time I came to comment on the Wednesday, then, the weekend 'outrage' of local communities had begun to subside as a media story.

Beginning to come to terms with the release of Thompson and Venables does not imply any callousness in relation to James Bulger or his parents. On the contrary, the memory of James Bulger is enduring on Merseyside and beyond. If there was more hostility on Merseyside than elsewhere at the time of the releases (which is not proven), it could be regarded as natural for the community surrounding the scene of such a crime. If this were the case and we were looking for another reason, it could be seen as a positive comment on Merseyside's instinct to sympathise with the most vulnerable. Hence most people would align themselves with James Bulger and with his family on the release of his murderers. If those killers were to be threatened with exposure by the tabloids, however, opinion might well rally to protect them because they would then have become the hunted rather than the hunter. If they were to sell their stories to the tabloids, somehow circumventing the prohibitions on identifying them, then opinion would certainly return to being unremittingly hostile to them.

One lesson of the first week of the release of Thompson and Venables is that whether or not public opinion is significant to any ethical question surrounding an uneasy case (and in my view it is not), it can be so volatile that a few days can make all the difference in measuring that opinion. Pressure groups or commentators who pronounce instantly on what is or is not acceptable to the community can find themselves out of date. Rushing to judgement is a dangerous enterprise. This is not because the public is fickle. It is an illustration of this process of changing opinions at its most vibrant.

Compared to our first uneasy case, that of the Siamese twins, it is not so clear in the case of the child killers what exactly is the reference point when members of the public or expert commentators question the judgement of the authorities. In what sense can we say that eight years, or any number of years, is too soon or too late to release murderers? Those who seemed so convinced that the period was wrong talked as if we should mark the heinousness of crimes by demanding that those convicted should serve longer than the authorities have determined. The circular reasoning involved in this is a warning of unease, however, since a system of justice should have matters the other way round: the term to be served is determined on the basis of how serious the crime was, the deterrent effect of the sentence and whether there has been rehabilitation. If the minimum tariff has been served and there has been genuine remorse and rehabilitation so that there is no risk to the public, then it would be incoherent to deny release.

Another way in which reactions seem to be more complex than in our first uneasy case is that deciding on an operation was a stark 'yes/no' choice whereas people have a huge range of alternatives when a release date is being considered. Indeed, this is so much a feature of discontent that I sometimes wonder whether the authorities need an artificial deadline or a contrived deadline to reduce the options from infinity to two. In the case of sterilising a mentally handicapped seventeen-year-old in the 1980s, mentioned in the previous chapter, the legal drama came at a rush as her eighteenth birthday neared. In similar fashion to the cases of Thompson and Venables, we were told that she would have to change to a different regime on reaching eighteen, hence the 'urgency'. Had such a deadline been missed, it would have been more difficult at any time in her twenties to argue that there was a pressing need for a virtually irreversible step. The easiest response to this uneasy case is to say that they should have served a few more years. Making eighteen a focal point, with a harsher regime in which their progress could be halted or reversed, ruled out such fence-sitting and had the effect of concentrating minds on a now-or-never variation of the yes/no verdict on an operation.

In the horrendous circumstances of such a gruesome child murder, it is easy for tensions to be raised on the release of the killers by any journalist seeking comments from the parents of the murdered child and those closest to them. Then again it is easy to blame journalists, but a free press has a duty to present a broad range of reactions. The media can argue that asking the family of James Bulger or their neighbours for their immediate reactions is a neutral act or even the positive provision of a voice for the often voiceless relatives or acquaintances of victims. The media can certainly point to the salutary fact that their awkward questions at seemingly impossible times have sometimes been answered with a grace that is awe-inspiring. In the immediate aftermath of the Enniskillen tragedy, for instance, Gordon Wilson's forgiveness of the killers of his daughter Marie would have been unknown to us if what others might have regarded as intrusive media reporting had not been pursued. Even in this moving case, however, there are difficulties of timing and focus. Not all of those who were injured or bereaved at Enniskillen had the same reaction and certainly not at the same time. Christians and others who found his example inspirational need not imagine that there is no space in God's embrace for those whose timescale of compassion is slower than Gordon Wilson's.

The media need not, however, restrain themselves unduly in the interests of minimising controversy. Suppressing the natural anguish of James Bulger's family would have served no helpful purpose. The media should, however, be self-critical in their reporting of the aftermath of tragedies. For example, when they focus relentlessly on the relatives of those who have died in multiple tragedies such as Enniskillen or Omagh or Oklahoma or Dunblane or Hillsborough or Heysel, they are relegating those who have been injured but who have survived to also-rans every time they describe the families of those who died as 'the' victims. Of course, those who are bereaved deserve our sympathy, and their day in court if necessary, but they are not the primary victims of an outrage such as Omagh. Nor is it clear that remaining in the public eye or being encouraged to comment on anniversary after anniversary is good for those who grieve, let alone conducive to merciful or even just decision-making.

On the other hand, there can be a nobility in the way in which grieving families keep alive the memory of those who were murdered. They remind us that the murderers are responsible for their actions, which is an especially valuable lesson if there are signs of a murderer manipulating campaigners and the media in an attempt to be released from prison. The longest running vigil in this respect was for the victims of the notorious child killers Ian Brady and Myra Hindley, known as the Moors murderers. Brady and Hindley abused and murdered five young people – the oldest was seventeen, the youngest ten – between 1963 and 1965. Hindley lured the first victim, a girl she knew, to Saddleworth moor where Brady raped her and killed her by slitting her throat. The pair taped the last quarter of an hour of the ten-year-old's life, with Hindley telling her to shut up as Brady raped and killed her. They were caught when Hindley's brother-in-law witnessed the fifth murder and told the police. They were convicted in 1966 for two of the murders, Brady also for a third murder and Hindley for shielding Brady after that murder. It was only two decades later that they confessed to the other two murders, the delay meaning that one body has not been recovered. The Murder (Abolition of the Death Penalty) Act 1965 came into force just before they were arrested. Hence they received life sentences for the murders and Hindley received a 'further' seven years for the other offence of shielding Brady. Reporters in court described them as unmoved even by the tape recording being played to the jury. Hindley was said to be 'sullen, defiant and silent'.

Yet during her record term of imprisonment, Myra Hindley seemed to come to regard herself as a victim. Ann West, the mother of Lesley Ann Downey, the ten-year-old girl who begged Hindley to stop Brady, vowed to oppose the release of Hindley. When Hindley seemed to be gathering public support for her release, Ann West used the media to oppose the notion. Before she died three years ahead of Hindley, she vowed to haunt the murderer from beyond the grave. As Professor Terence Morris observed, 'For almost forty years the mothers of her victims were gathered like some latterday Greek chorus minding the grief that would never leave them, by day or by night or by season, until the hour when death should come for them too.'

Successive governments seemed heavily influenced by public and media opposition to the release of Myra Hindley. In line with Robert Thompson and Jon Venables being reported to have been frightened by the prospect of becoming Hindleyesque figures who would die in prison, the authorities were influenced, I suspect, by the Hindley precedent in their decision to release Thompson and Venables at the age of eighteen. For if they were transferred to the adult prison system at eighteen, it might then have become as difficult to release them as it proved to be for Hindley. In fact, they were released ahead of her in 2001. Then, just when the Law Lords looked set to issue a further ruling in the case of another murderer which would have made it difficult for Hindley to be kept in prison indefinitely, she died while still in custody in November 2002.

An insidious, potentially corrosive, development in cases of uneasy ethics is that the media can sometimes create the expectation, even in the minds of leading public figures, that everyone must have something to say publicly on everything at the instant there is a development, such as the release of Robert Thompson and Jon Venables or the death of Myra Hindley. Again, this is not to say that the media are at fault but it is to question whether public figures need to have more resolve to maintain their own counsel on such occasions. It is possible to have nothing to say publicly, not because we are soft or tough on crime or the causes of crime, not because we have no time for the victims of crime but because the moment of release, or death, of the perpetrators is no time to be using the media to say anything about the merits of particular decisions. Instead, we could all have benefited from recovering the spirit which came so naturally across the country in the wake of James Bulger's death and the tragic murders at Dunblane, together with the other disasters mentioned above. In each case, people took to their churches and other places of prayer, lighting candles and marking appropriate sites with flowers. Similarly, when the release of the killers was pending, we needed sound bites less than we needed the candles and the still small voice of calm, the space to reflect on James Bulger's innocence, on the awful brutality of his murder, on the awesome task which faced those then charged with responsibility for the futures of his killers, on the possibility which almost dared not surface in the media that those public servants could have succeeded against the odds in discharging that duty and then again on the qualms we have that, even so, this may not yet have been the right time for release.

The rhythm of American death-row sagas lends itself to vigils as well as to almost continuous litigation. Even the Oklahoma bomber, the mass murderer Timothy McVeigh, who had seemed determined to accept the death penalty, allowed his legal team to mount appeals at the end. Relatives of those who were murdered argued strongly for the right to witness the execution. A compromise was reached in which a limited number of relatives watched on closed-circuit television. Even in the USA, which stands apart from most of the Western world in its insistence on the death penalty, ten-year-olds would not be executed. In an uneasy case, it is worth asking why, and then relating this to our sense of what should happen to ten-year-old killers in a system which would not stoop to taking their lives in response even to their heinous crime.

All these cases, from Oklahoma to Bootle to the Moors, raise the question of how images can affect our views of uneasy cases. As they were themselves children, Thompson and Venables were spared the publicity and notoriety which would have come with their photographs being used by the media every time their releases were discussed. Their anonymity was protected by court order while they were in custody. On their release, a further injunction prevents the media from revealing their new identities and their whereabouts. In contrast, a haunting photo of Myra Hindley played a large part in shaping views against her release. The same photo was pervasive in media coverage of her death. Her death while still a prisoner prompted debate about the power of the image of her from the 1960s. Vanora Bennett wrote: 'Freeze-framing her in the Sixties, before her long odyssey through prisons, religious conversion, protestations of repentance and energetic battle to secure her freedom (which, ironically, may finally have been about to succeed), has made it easier for the British public to deny the possibility that the woman within, like her external image, was capable of change.' Hindley herself had come to the same conclusion that 'most people don't want to accept that people like myself can change. They prefer to keep me frozen in time together with that awful mugshot so that their attitudes, beliefs and perceptions can remain intact.'

She seemed oblivious to the way in which the grief of her victims' families was frozen by her actions. Although much of the debate about the photo regards it as unfair to freeze-frame how she was, another way of considering the matter is to regard the photo as an appropriate reminder of the unvarnished murderer rather than the seasoned campaigner. Perhaps the photo achieved a macabre, iconic status precisely because it did capture the attitude of Hindley as illustrated by her demeanour in court. Of course, she would have presented a different image over the years, whether through age, genuine change or a desire to be released. There is some controversy about whether any change in Myra Hindley was genuine or contrived for effect, attention, power and the prospect of release. Terence Morris distinguishes remorse and contrition, the 'former a longing that she had never done what she did and brought all this trouble upon herself, the second a heart-felt cry of sorrow at the enormity of her sin. While there was much evidence of the former, the latter was never publicly vouchsafed.' In a similar analysis, Theodore Dalrymple identifies the essence of the unease which many experienced at the way in which Myra Hindley seemed to revel in publicity: 'The very fact that she campaigned for her own release demonstrated her lack of true remorse: for if she had fully understood the enormity of what she had done, she would have realised that she had lost all moral standing to decide for herself in her own case. She might have wished for release and accepted it if granted: but not campaigned for it. Her stridency in her own cause was a sign of continuing moral deficiency.' He concludes that Myra Hindley 'never received justice: she was far too well treated for that', she benefited instead from 'immense mercy' but that 'releasing her from prison, however, would have been a mercy too far'.

The political, judicial and media establishments firmly resisted all campaigns and court actions in Myra Hindley's name. A judgement in the House of Lords, for example, labelled her crimes as 'uniquely evil', placed 'in terms of comparative wickedness in an exceptional category'. We will return to the challenge of evil in other contexts but, whether this case is categorised as evil or unique or not, even if we accept that the murderer has atoned and changed, that does not necessarily mean that she should be released. We can go beyond what is deserved, the sphere of justice, and enter the realm of mercy without abandoning all discernment or judgement. Almost everyone knows the Shakespearean lines about the quality of mercy without necessarily understanding them or therefore knowing whether or not the sentiments are helpful. Seamus Heaney's famous line about peace will surface in the next chapter. Shakespeare gives Portia the image that mercy 'droppeth' and Heaney notes how peace comes 'droppin' slow'. It can be an insight in certain contexts, and this is one, to think of both mercy and peace as being offered drop by drop rather than in a gushing, all or nothing manner. The willingness of society to show a murderer some mercy does not require society to offer more. Even if the drop is received with dignity and remorse, the next drop cannot be demanded as of right. Indeed, mercy is less likely to be proffered when the recipient acts as if mercy is their right, for that suggests a misunderstanding of their own actions and position as well as of the nature of mercy. By definition, mercy can only be relevant in the moral world beyond what is required by rights or by justice.

The interconnectedness of moral decisions is apparent when the contrasting fate of Ian Brady, the principal Moors murderer, is considered. Whereas Myra Hindley was frustrated by death in custody when she sought release from her life sentence, Ian Brady is frustrated by life as he has sought death through a hunger strike which was in its fourth year by the time Myra Hindley died. He is detained in a special hospital and is force-fed through a tube. This has echoes of the previous chapter's account of whether society should allow euthanasia, suicide or assisted suicide, although the circumstances are significantly different. Brady has emphasised that he will not seek parole. He wants to die. A feature of the approach of both Brady and Hindley during their long prison terms has been their attempt to control their destinies. This itself may seem to some as an echo, this time of their crimes during which they controlled, abused, tortured and murdered children. Others will take a more indulgent view of the struggle for power in a prison. Prisoners have time to focus on how to assert themselves. The prison system is premised on depriving prisoners of not only liberty but also many aspects of the power of self-determination. Some of Hindley's supporters interpret the refusal to release her as a manifestation of a discriminatory attitude in society which penalises the female accomplice more than the male murderer. What some see as Hindley being manipulative, they see as others fearing that they might be manipulated. What some see as an image which captures evil, they see as a stark, overlit police photo of a frightened suspect who may have been unused to having her photograph taken. In this way, the Moors murderers have been a subject of uneasy public debate for almost four decades.

Myra Hindley's death will not bring that to an end. On the contrary: her death while still in custody after thirty-six years in prison highlights a deeper unease or malaise as well as challenging some of us in our instincts on these matters. In the public sphere, the significance was partly that she died just days after the government had announced yet another 'tough on crime' legislative programme and only weeks before the Law Lords were expected to issue a judgement pointing in the opposite direction. The Labour government's major constitutional reform, incorporating the European Convention on Human Rights into a domestic bill of rights through the Human Rights Act, was coming back to haunt the government, since it gave power to the judges who are relatively liberal on punishment whereas the government itself wanted to promote a more draconian approach to punishment. In the private arena of our own thoughts on punishment, the puzzle (for me at least) is why it seems right to support a position in which the authorities have resisted calls for Hindley's release from prison and yet have set Thompson and Venables free.

All the possible variations on answering these dilemmas can be heard in almost any discussion. Some would have kept all three in prison for ever, some would have released all three after eight years or twelve years or some such number well short of Hindley's thirty-six years, some would have released Hindley but not Thompson and Venables. Yet I think it right to have detained Hindley way beyond the shorter period served by Thompson and Venables. Is this being unfair on the woman in the trio or the one who had her photo taken, or are the crimes different, or were the different ages of the murderers relevant, or is it their subsequent conduct which affects my judgement? The determining influence is not, in my thinking, public opinion. If anything, there may be a contrary element of challenging the consensus which seemed to have been edging towards sympathy for Hindley while expecting time in adult prison for Thompson and Venables.

As explained in the first chapter, it is possible also to challenge the presumption that we have to be consistent in our judgements on such matters. Nonetheless, I would like to think that I can defend my conclusions on society's response to Hindley, Thompson and Venables, albeit with some unease. Anyone who is confident that they know exactly when, if at all, to release life prisoners has not grasped the complexities of punishment. So I am not pretending that eight years or more than thirty-six years are somehow the precise answers in the particular circumstances of the different crimes. Rather, our personal judgements depend to a considerable extent on what we can glean from those closer to the prisoners and from our own observations, through the media, about their stories in the round, including the stories of their victims and their victims' families. Moreover, none of this is meant to pre-empt divine judgement, including divine mercy, and is therefore nothing to do with tabloid headlines or quotes about rotting in hell.

It seems to me a bold but proper step for society to exercise mercy in releasing Thompson and Venables on their reaching adulthood, after being assured that they are fully conscious of, and remorseful for, their barbaric abduction, torture and murder of James Bulger on 12 February 1993, without it being wrong to have kept Hindley in prison for the rest of her life. Her crimes came in her twenties, not while she should have been at primary school. Hers was a series, not a single case, of abduction, torture and murder. She did not take a single person spontaneously but planned the luring of five victims. Her cruelty was not on a single day but spanned the five abductions of 12 July 1963, 23 November 1963, 16 June 1964, 26 December 1964 and 6 October 1965. If it is somewhat crude to put these differences in the facts so starkly, nothing is meant to diminish the awful torture and murder of James Bulger. Nonetheless, Myra Hindley was involved in five even more brutal murders and died before she had served five times the length of custody for Thompson and Venables. Even if she had changed, even if she was genuinely sorry, even if we ignore the plotting to escape and her twenty-year delay in confessing to two of the murders, the argument from consistency based purely on the murders themselves did not require her release by way of analogy to the release of Thompson and Venables.

To argue in this way, of course, is to repeat the process of the first chapter, of testing principle against examples, albeit in this case real tragedies rather than hypotheticals. In this chapter, we know much, perhaps too much, of the detail of the examples. The principles in this context seem more elusive, however, since we have quickly passed the notion of justice in punishment and have gone straight to extreme circumstances in which only an exercise of mercy can release murderers. So what is mercy? Lord Bingham, on behalf of the Judicial Committee of the Privy Council, in quashing a death penalty in Belize on 11 March 2002, put the conventional wisdom in simple, compelling terms:

Mercy, in its first meaning given by the *Oxford English Dictionary*, means forbearance and compassion shown by one person to another who is in his power and who has no claim to receive kindness. Both in language and literature mercy and justice are contrasted. The administration of justice involves the determination of what punishment a transgressor deserves, the fixing of the appropriate sentence for the crime. The grant of mercy involves the determination that a transgressor need not suffer the punishment he deserves, that the appropriate sentence may for some reason be remitted. The former is a judicial, the latter an executive, responsibility.

On what basis, then, did the executive come to the conclusion that it was safe and right to show mercy to Venables and Thompson?

The argument *against* mercy would have some of the same elements as in the debate about Myra Hindley. In particular, public perceptions are shaped by images. Part of the reason why James Bulger's name is known and will continue to be known is that, unlike most child victims, the beginning of his ordeal was captured on video. That image is one of innocence, of childlike trust, walking hand in hand with nemesis. This is haunting not just for those who witnessed this abduction but for anyone who has ever failed to intervene as a child is led screaming away, anyone who has stood by, or walked by on the other side, trusting in those who have proceeded to abuse the trust of children. Although public impressions of the Moors murders and murderers include the horrendous audiotape of one murder and the chilling photo of one murderer, the visual imagery of the initial abduction of James Bulger is much closer to a familiar sight. Its poignancy works at several levels. Primarily, the imagery works against those abducting James Bulger as it highlights the betrayal of trust. On the other hand, the youth of the boy leading James Bulger away is also evident, whereas the Hindley photo and audiotape create more sinister impressions.

The case *for* an eventual release had to be made by those public servants whom society charged with the daunting task of working alongside these child killers. It is their responsibility to cling to the fellow humanity of those guilty of the most appalling crimes. This can be a chilling and unrewarding role. So if indeed their work has helped Thompson and Venables demonstrate remorse, atonement and rehabilitation, then they deserve society's admiration for coming as close as human beings can come to facilitating redemption in the most unpromising of circumstances. The exercise of mercy in relation to Thompson and Venables is in some senses an act of faith in, and affirmation of, all those who worked with them between the ages of ten and eighteen.

As the panel observed on that *Moral Maze* programme, I tend to use religious language in discussing this case or other questions of punishment. Atonement and redemption, for example, are associated with the witness of faith traditions. The other guests questioned by the regular panel were Michael Howard and Blake Morrison. The latter's book ends with him thinking 'of hands being taken, and of a journey beginning in hope, and ending not in tragedy but miracles. I think of sunlight falling through the stained-glass Resurrection of a parish church, and of sins I've committed and people I've hurt, and of words from the Bible I'd forgotten: penance, shrift, expiation, propitiation, atonement.' Looking at Pope John Paul II's message to prisoners on the occasion of the millennium, the key concepts for him do, of course, include the notions which Blake Morrison, you and I will use in reflecting on this uneasy case, such as redemption. He also places great emphasis on the dignity of the human person and on the common good. The Pope marked the millennium as a great jubilee. His statement in July 2000 on prisoners explained his approach in these terms:

> To celebrate the jubilee means to strive to find new paths of redemption in every personal and social situation, even if the situation seems desperate. This is even more obvious with regard to prison life; not to promote the interests of prisoners would be to make imprisonment a mere act of vengeance on the part of society, provoking only hatred in the prisoners themselves . . .
>
> We are still a long way from the time when our conscience can be certain of having done everything possible to prevent crime and to control it effectively so that it no longer does harm and, at the same time, to offer to those who commit crimes a way of redeeming themselves and making a positive return to society . . .
>
> For all to play their part in building the common good they must work, in the measure of their competence, to ensure that prisoners have the means to redeem themselves, both as individuals and in their relations with society. Such a process is based on growth in the sense of responsibility. None of this should be considered Utopian. Those who are in a position to do so must strive to incorporate these aims in the legal system . . .
>
> Jubilees have been an incentive for the community to reconsider human justice against the measure of God's justice. Only a calm appraisal of the functioning of penal institutions, a candid recognition of the goals society has in mind in confronting crime, and a serious assessment of the means adopted to attain these goals have led in the past and can still lead to identifying the corrections which need to be made. It is not a question of an automatic or purely cosmetic application of acts of clemency.
>
> Prison should not be a corrupting experience, a place of idleness and even vice, but instead a place of redemption.

This is more challenging than is the standard liberal unease. Secular liberals might wrestle with their desire to affirm the value of citizens' views and their realisation that the wider populace's views can be illiberal. The Pope goes further, with a call to *action*. We must *do* something to improve our system of punishment. This is a more demanding ethic, an uneasy one. Its scriptural basis is well-known – 'I was in prison and you visited me'. That biblical injunction was lived out by the late Cardinal Hume. It was his visiting of the Maguire and Conlon families in prison that led him to challenge infamous miscarriages of justice. One of those freed as a result, Gerry Conlon, described the cardinal's contribution to the release of the Guildford Four as 'quiet, serious and enormously influential'.

This is part of a more general approach to ethics which the Christian tradition, other faith communities and great secular reformers such as Jeremy Bentham have all lived out at their best. As well as being the father of utilitarianism, Bentham was a noted prison reformer. Reflecting on the ethics of alternative courses of action is not a spectator sport but invites participation and positive action, whether from a religious or a secular perspective. In the religious corner, Pope Paul VI sent an apostolic letter to the cardinal with responsibility for laity, justice and peace in 1971. Dispatched on the eightieth anniversary of Pope Leo XIII's encyclical on the condition of the workers, *Rerum Novarum*, this was entitled 'A Call to Action':

> Let each one examine himself, to see what he has done up to now, and what he ought to do. It is not enough to recall principles, state intentions, point to crying injustices and utter prophetic denunciations; these words will lack real weight unless they are accompanied for each individual by a livelier awareness of personal responsibility and by effective action. It is too easy to throw back on others responsibility for injustices, if at the same time one does not realise how each one shares in it personally, and how personal conversion is needed first . . .
>
> In concrete situations, and taking account of solidarity in each person's life, one must recognise a legitimate variety of possible options.

Again, this could be applied to the issue of imprisonment and other forms of punishment. Reflecting on the James Bulger case should lead to action to make it less likely that ten-year-olds could repeat such an appalling series of crimes and less likely that custody for longer and longer is seen as the only response, regardless of the effect it has on the lives of offenders.

Popes' calls to action are echoed in the stirring secular addresses which inspire American law students to imagine they will become ethical crusaders for justice as they graduate, of which genre my favourite is the speech by Justice Higginbotham, a distinguished American judge from an ethnic minority background:

> In my opinion, lawyers must be the visionaries in our society. We must be the nation's legal architects who renovate the palace of justice and redesign the landscape of opportunity in our nation . . . When it comes to

moral values and ethical commitments, lawyers have been found on all sides of every major issue. Some lawyers have ruthlessly exploited the helpless while others have tirelessly aided the weak, the poor and the dispossessed . . . Each lawyer – whether judge, or political, professor or entrepreneur – must make personal judgements. Those critical moral and human values cannot be acquired by even the most meticulous reading of opinions or statutes. Each lawyer must consciously and constantly assess his or her values and goals in forging rules of law for the future . . . in moving towards the goal of social and legal justice for all . . . where will each of you stand? Will you be aligned with those forces that expand the horizons of opportunity for the weak, the poor, the powerless, and the many who have not had our options? Or will you become members of the indulgent new majority in our society who seem to feel that the quality of morality in our nation's public life is unimportant as long as they have good salaries and comfortable suburban homes or luxurious condominiums in the city? Will you as a lawyer merely become a technical expert, detached and indifferent? Will you be concerned solely with obtaining the highest fees for the least amount of effort, untroubled by the quality of life in our nation or world? Or will you care enough to make a difference?

On rereading those words, I realise that they have influenced my regular pleas to all graduands, whether lawyers or not, that they should not be indifferent but should dare to be different, to respect differences and to make a difference. So how can we move from a sense of unease about the murder of James Bulger and the punishment of his murderers to an active involvement in building up a better society? The immediate inhibition is the feeling that any step we take will be too small to make a significant difference. This is to misunderstand how change works and how it is up to us to make the difference, however small, of which we are capable. As the famous lawyer-politician Robert Kennedy observed in 1966, speaking to university students in South Africa when Nelson Mandela was in prison and had decades further to serve in jail, 'Each time you stand up for an ideal, or act to improve the lot of others, or strike out against injustice, you send forth a tiny ripple of hope, and crossing each other from a million different centres of energy and daring, those ripples build a current that can sweep down the mightiest walls of oppression and resistance.' In other words, a small step can play a part in the long journey to a more just society. The law is not an aimless endeavour.

With Robert Kennedy, I see hope as the substantive answer to a pressing question, a variation on the theme of 'what is a legal system a system for?', namely 'what are the socially excluded actually excluded from?' We need a rounded understanding of hope. Dr Jonathan Sacks, the Chief Rabbi, has written repeatedly and movingly on this: 'There is such a thing as an ecology of hope. There are environments in which it flourishes and others in which it dies.' Criminal justice, as Blake Morrison observed, can play a part in creating the conditions in which hope can emerge. Even in the wake of heinous crimes, the criminal justice system and those who make it work should not give in to a sense of despair or hopelessness. If we are to trust the judgement of those charged with responsibility for Thompson and Venables, their cases exemplify the progress which can be made, the belief that there is always hope.

Here, we are close to the reason why the question of timing was highlighted at the beginning of this discussion. Punishment is a process, involving legislature, judiciary and executive. It happens over time. At different stages of the process, the primary aim may vary and therefore the branch of the state with primary responsibility will change accordingly. Some arms of the state are elected, some unelected, reflecting democracy's need to balance majoritarian factors and the protection of hated figures and other vulnerable individuals from the dangers of unchecked majoritarianism through fearless advocacy of rights. In the latter case, judges are well placed precisely because they are unelected and have tenure. They can resist the lynch mob, the popular mood, and they can play a part in educating the public towards a more sophisticated understanding of how progress can be made.

The standard debate on these matters is for tutors or media interviewers to ask what is the purpose or justification of punishment, without specifying the timing of this generic enquiry. The purpose and the justification of punishment are not exactly the same, and my argument is that the answer is not the same at different times in the cycle of punishing any individual offender. Nonetheless, generations of interviewees and tutees have been expected to pick one from the favoured three theories in answer to either variant of the question: deterrence, reform, retribution. My preferred approach would be to say that since punishment is a system or process which involves all three branches of government and all three elements of deterrence, reform and retribution, the mark of a just or good or merciful system is that it matches the right branch and purpose to the appropriate stage or phase or time of the process. It is understandable for those closest to James Bulger or other victims of appalling crimes to think and feel as if time has stood still. They are condemned to relive the agony each time the case returns to a high profile, at the trial, when the tariff is set, at the judicial review hearing in the High Court, the Court of Appeal, the House of Lords, at Strasbourg for the European Court hearing, when that decision is announced, when the tariff is revised, when the Chief Inspector of Prisons comments, when the killers are released, and so on. What society has to do, however, is to respect the memory of James Bulger but also appreciate that the characters of the killers have moved on from their ten-year-old selves, that the punishment system has changed them. This is what we are being told by the authorities in the decision to release them. We are assured that they have changed, otherwise the conditions for release would not have been met. If there has been an error, they can be recalled to custody at any time throughout their lives. Of course, it would be too late, but there is as high a degree of certainty as anyone can expect from the authorities that the killers are not going to kill again. They have also served the term required for deterrence and retribution, otherwise the tariff would not have expired. It therefore misses the point of the punishment process to argue as if we were all back in 1993 and as if there is still an argument for a longer period to satisfy the conditions established by any of the three main theories of punishment. Each has been addressed.

To explain this requires some analysis of each of the terms in turn. Deterrence is a subset of a wider utilitarian approach to punishment. One obvious aim is to stop these ten-year-olds from repeating their crime, or any other crime, almost certainly by a period of incarceration and possibly by isolation. More generally, a substantial sentence sends out a message which is designed to deter others from committing similar crimes. One could quibble at whether this is necessary or whether it works. The latter complaint, of course, implies that deterrence is necessary but not always achieved. A negative answer to the former makes the latter redundant. If we find ourselves using both criticisms, and are subjected to the charge of inconsistency, one answer may be that we regard different crimes as needing deterrence in different ways. For example, it is often supposed that burglary is more responsive to deterrence than so-called crimes of passion. Even to express the alternatives in this way is to engage with some dubious reasoning (crime of passion, for example, seeks to convey the answer in the terminology) and to dabble with only part of a more complex whole. If burglars, for instance, are calculating, they will not only be following the length of sentences but will be assessing the risk of being detected, being caught, being prosecuted, being convicted before it comes to sentencing. All of these negatives will be balanced by the lure of what they expect to make from the burglary.

This point can be illustrated by an offence more often committed by those who think of themselves as the law-abiding classes, namely driving faster than the speed limit. Here many citizens routinely display some of the characteristics of the calculating burglar: what are my chances of getting caught and how stiff will the punishment be, as balanced against how much I would like to get somewhere more quickly than the speed limit allows? Tougher penalties and blanket surveillance work in tandem.

Retribution is often regarded as a bad thing and often identified with the God of the Old Testament as if that were bad company to be keeping. Yet an eye for an eye or a tooth for a tooth can be regarded as a limiting principle, that is to say *only* an eye for an eye, *only* a tooth for a tooth. Or, to pay homage to Shakespeare, when justice demands a pound of flesh, it requires *only* a pound of flesh. The popular expressions which express the principle of retribution, 'the punishment must fit the crime', 'just deserts' and the like, can all be regarded as demonstrating balance and proportionality, ruling out sentences which are too tough as well as those which are too soft. For instance, hanging, drawing and quartering speeding motorists would probably have an even greater deterrent impact than three penalty points on a licence but we would not regard this as a just punishment since it would be disproportionate, the punishment would exceed the enormity of the crime, it would leave little room to express our horror at crimes yet to come, it would exhaust our sense of awfulness, as well as being barbaric and possibly leading to perverse acquittals because the common sense of the jury would baulk at such a draconian punishment. So retribution is not necessarily an arcane, nasty element in our thinking about punishment and it is not deterrence by another name. It is, however, an even more difficult concept to relate to a precise number of years. The word 'relate' and its relations need to be explored here. For while we may not be able to produce an absolute scale of years for crimes which makes sense, we can produce a relative table and rule out some punishments if they are, by comparison, too lenient or too drastic.

During my years of teaching law, using hypotheticals and actual cases, the example on punishment which most riled students was the true story of the sentences in what became known as the Ealing vicarage rape case. What outraged the public at the time, and continues to outrage students and other readers, is that one defendant received the same sentence of five years for both burglary and rape when the two crimes were carried out in the same incident while another defendant in the same case received only three years for the rape. This was taken by many to signal that the legal system rated attacks on property as highly as attacks on the person, especially when the judge seemed to place great store by the fact that the victim had made a 'remarkable recovery'. The leading civil liberties lawyer, Helena Kennedy QC, has observed of this, 'Lucky defendants . . . Any recovery was no thanks to them.'

The victim and the public had a clear sense that the relative scales had been crossed – either the sentence for rape should have been longer or the sentence for burglary should have been shorter. The judge's best explanation would have been to acknowledge the risk of being seen to be underrating the horror of the rape but to spell out that he had to discount the sentence in line with precedent and the public interest in protecting victims because the defendants pleaded guilty. If there is no discount in the sentence, defendants are more likely to plead not guilty which would subject the defendant to the further ordeal of a trial. Moreover, the scale of sentencing for burglary is higher than might be expected because it is a crime which does seem to be affected by sentences being increased. Repeat offenders in burglary can expect high sentences. Rapists can escape a long sentence by pleading guilty. The two crimes rarely come together in the same trial but comparing the two does make the system seem to undervalue the person, as compared to property. No doubt the judge was uneasy about the logic of the two lines of sentencing policy when brought together and could foresee the furore which would follow (he would say that, wouldn't he, because he's a man; the law is being inconsistent). What would society have judges do and why? Helena Kennedy accepts that the answers are not easy:

> Sentencing is a minefield for judges. The pressure is on to reduce the prison population, to give due credit to those who plead guilty and save victims the degradation of giving evidence about some appalling event. The youth of a defendant should reduce the length of a prison term, because of their inexperience of life and a greater optimism about their rehabilitation. Many factors count, and a cold appraisal or comparison of sentences can be a fruitless exercise.

It is worth noting that Helena Kennedy dedicated this influential book, *Eve Was Framed*, to 'women in prison'. She was writing in 1992, before the murder of James Bulger, and took the line on the Moors murderers which has been questioned in this chapter. Although I do not think that Myra Hindley was treated harshly because of sexist attitudes, respect for Helena Kennedy merits recording her contrary view:

> Myra Hindley's name is one that comes to everyone's lips as soon as criminals come into the conversation, regardless of sex. Crimes involving children always engage our deepest emotions and we all feel a particular empathy with the families of the victims. But although the Moors Murderers must come near the top of any catalogue of atrocities, public horror has concentrated more and more on the female of the two offenders, and I think that, while this is partly because she has not sought to avoid visibility, it is largely because of her gender. Even if women do not themselves have children, society expects them to embody the nurturance and protectiveness associated with mothering, and there is a heightened outrage when they run in the face of those ideas.

It will nowadays rightly be part of almost everyone's instinctive approach to uneasy cases to consider whether there is some prejudice, on grounds such as gender or race or sexual orientation or religion, lurking beneath conclusions. Indeed, this has become so dominant an approach that it can sometimes exclude consideration of other factors. The first two extended examples in this book, the separation of female twins and the incarceration of two boys for the murder of another boy, do not seem to raise questions of discrimination although the third, Northern Ireland, is preoccupied with it. It is a good check on the purposes of punishment to consider whether any theory could sustain differences in the treatment of men and women. If the point is to deter, is there any sense in which punishments are more likely to deter one or other gender? Or if the point is to express society's denunciation of the crime and to ensure that offenders receive their just deserts, is there any sense in which retribution could lead to different sentences for men and women convicted of the same crime?

Turning to the third major theory of punishment – rehabilitation – one of the most frightening aspects of the debate about the release of Thompson and Venables is that reform features not only at its very best but also at its very worst. The progress apparently made by both these child killers is a testimony to the success of those responsible for their educational, social and psychological care while in custody. That is the system at its best. The system at its worst, however, seems to accept almost without demur that to put them in an adult prison would be to invite regression. This is a damning indictment of our society's approach to those who are in adult prisons. Going into prisons is enough for many people to feel deeply uneasy about the whole issue of conditions and expectations in our system of punishment.

British judges have had the opportunity to rule on death-row cases in recent years through their role in the Judicial Committee of the Privy Council. This functions as the supreme court for a limited number of Commonwealth legal systems and is usually composed of Law Lords, sometimes supplemented by a judge from another Commonwealth jurisdiction. There have been several appeals from Caribbean death sentences. The common constitutional provision is a version of the European Convention rights. These allowed, when drafted in 1950, capital punishment as an exception to the right to life, so lawyers have relied instead on the right against torture and inhuman and degrading treatment and punishment. Death sentences have been quashed when the process of appealing has dragged on for five years or more with a series of expected dates for execution deferred in the last few hours.

The uncertainty which this has generated for the prisoner has been deemed to be inhuman punishment. This seems to some observers to be a contrived argument which would only appeal to judges who probably oppose the death penalty or are otherwise sceptical of the merits of the legal system's verdict on the particular prisoners. Indeed, it must be an uneasy ethical and professional dilemma for judges who conscientiously object to the death penalty as to whether

- to declare that their minds are made up and recuse themselves, playing no part in such a case, or
- to maintain a front of neutrality but find an ingenious way of ruling against execution, or
- to rule in favour of the death penalty if the merits of the law require it even though the judges believe it to be immoral.

Such a choice is not confined to death-penalty cases but is a variation on the classic uneasy question for judges in unjust regimes: should they resign or work to mitigate the worst effects of an unfair legal system, not least for fear of judges who support the regime replacing them? Not only in the Nazi legal system or South Africa's apartheid years but throughout history and across the globe, the guardians of justice have had to examine their own consciences.

Few, if any, public comments on what should have happened to Thompson and Venables went beyond 'life should mean life', the refrain of the petition to the Home Secretary, to demand that 'life should mean death'. No state in the world has a policy of executing ten-year-old murderers. Even those countries which still have capital punishment, such as the USA, tend to have qualms and legal prohibitions on executing such young children. The USA has attracted international opprobrium, amid the attentions of Amnesty International, for being prepared to countenance executions of those who are in their late teenage years. Unease in ethics nowadays can come from a sense of being out of line with thinking in other cultures which we respect. It was the fact that European countries had such differing ages for criminal responsibility in cases of murder which prevented the European Court ruling against the British government for the public trial of Thompson and Venables. In the same spirit of internationalism, the Privy Council was impressed, in the course of one of its decisions on the Jamaican constitution, where the bill of rights was effectively based on the European Convention on Human Rights, by the arguments put to the US Supreme Court which were taken from a Zimbabwean Supreme Court case which in turn was influenced by an amicus brief from that country's Roman Catholic bishops. This is an example of the impact of that church and theology generally on the development of the law, as well as being a striking illustration of the way in which ethical ideas can reverberate around the world now that legal jurisdictions seem so willing to learn from one another.

Although the uncertainty argument was restricted to the extreme case of death row, there is an analogy to Myra Hindley and to the cases of Robert Thompson and Jon Venables. It is inhumane, however inhumane their crimes, to leave prisoners with no hope of release or to dash their hopes at the last, repeatedly. More generally, conditions in prisons can be inhuman or degrading not only in their physical awfulness but also if the full range of provision is not there to make a coherent theory of punishment work in practice. To be punishment in this full sense, there must be opportunity for reform, not merely incarceration. Not least to release resources in support of this, it may well be that lesser offences should not lead to prison in so many cases.

What is certain is that prisoners will be regular litigants under the Human Rights Act for the obvious reasons that they have little to lose, they have time in which to ponder litigation and the public purse may provide the funding to pursue it. It would be churlish, however, not to accept that another reason is the unsatisfactory state of our overcrowded and under-resourced prisons. This is not to claim that there are easy solutions to serious crime, still less that prisons are the be-all and end-all of deterring or preventing violence. On the contrary, I was criticised by the former minister with responsibility for prisons, Ann Widdecombe, at a Catholic bishops' conference on Catholics and public life for being long on analysis and short on solutions when it came to prison policy. My response was that this is how I like religion to be in public life, long on analysis and short on solutions. As someone who has spent my whole life in education, including eight years heading the university college which is the leading trainer of teachers on Merseyside, my unsurprising conclusion is that our education systems and social services have to be considered alongside our system of punishment in the light of the abduction and murder of James Bulger.

The two child killers were *not* inseparable friends for years. What seemed to bring them together was their school's decision, no doubt understandable on educational grounds, to keep them down a year the previous September. By the beginning of the following term, a month before the February murder of James Bulger, one is recorded as having played truant on forty of the 140 half-days and the other forty-nine. This is extraordinarily high for a primary school. The social services reports astonished Blake Morrison and clearly played an influential part in shaping his conclusions on the case. He is sympathetic, however, to those who passed by on the other side of the road as they saw James Bulger being led away by Venables and Thompson. Although we might all like to think that we would have acted as good Samaritans, Morrison understands the reality that many conclude it is safer not to intervene nowadays.

All the social and educational factors need to be brought together before we focus on the prison system. Undoubtedly, the education and rehabilitation of Venables and Thompson cost millions of pounds, but it is a price worth paying if we have not first built up the common good in other ways to prevent them from carrying out the crime, perhaps by the state insisting on attendance at school or by the intervention of social services in their lives generally or of a bystander on that particular day.

Like Blake Morrison, I would not wish to blame anyone for their good-faith judgements as professionals or as citizens, in school or the social services or on the streets of Bootle. It is important, however, to ask what we can learn from the case, from decisions which might have been handled differently given what we now know.

The Duc de la Rochefoucauld is credited with the insightful comment, 'Everyone complains of their memory, but no one complains of their judgement.' We make wrong judgements from time to time in all aspects of our lives but we very seldom set about systematically learning how to judge or how to improve our judgement. It is just possible that the legal system's judges have something to teach us here because they are exposed, in a hierarchical system of publicly delivered reasons, to systematic critiques of their decisions. Again, it is not my suggestion that there are some simple, instant solutions to the complex problems revealed by the uneasy case of Thompson and Venables.

As explained elsewhere in this book, while the immediate comment has its place in a tutorial or sometimes in the public realm, I have valued the time which I have had to reflect on this uneasy case and the stimulus provided by others. For example, it is not easy to establish exactly what we mean by that litany of religiously inspired words which feature in the debates on punishment. A book could be written on almost any passage in Dostoevsky's *Crime and Punishment*, as when Sonia says to Raskolnikov, 'You must make atonement, so that you may be redeemed thereby . . . You shall have it [her cross] at the moment of your expiation.' To use simpler rhetoric, what exactly is the difference between justice and mercy? Is it our judgement that Thompson and Venables have been dealt with justly or mercifully? It may be that, in eternity, justice and mercy will rhyme but in the here and now of the seventy child killer cases being examined by the Lord Chief Justice, do we expect him to live up to that precise title or to become the Lord Chief Mercy? Lord Bingham, himself previously a Lord Chief Justice, is clear in the Belize judgement already quoted that judges should focus on justice and leave mercy to the executive. In practice, the division of responsibilities is not so clear.

In reflecting on all this while rereading Blake Morrison's extraordinary book, it dawned on me that part of the attraction of his searingly self-revealing approach to punishment was that he had recovered a tradition which is particularly associated with Calvinism. The approach is described by Professor Duncan Forrester in *Christian Justice and Public Policy* by reference to this Scots Calvinist order for receiving a forgiven offender back into the congregation, dating from 1564:

If we consider his fall and sin in him only, without having consideration of ourselves and of our own corruption, we shall profit nothing, for so shall we but despise our brother and flatter ourselves; but if we shall earnestly consider what nature we bear, what corruption lurketh in it, how prone and ready every one of us is to such and greater impiety, then shall we in the sin of this our brother accuse and condemn our own sins, in his fall we shall consider and lament our sinful nature, also we shall join our repentance, tears and prayers with him and his, knowing that no flesh can be justified before God's presence, if judgement proceed without mercy.

Forrester quotes David Garland's comment on such an approach:

The sinner-offender was not conceived as 'other' but rather as a kind of Protestant Everyman, a living example of the potential evil which lies in every heart and against which every soul must be vigilant. In keeping with this conception, the denouement of each public ceremony was aimed not at the vanquishing of the enemy but instead at the reinclusion of the atoned and repentant sinner.

It is this sense of involvement and inclusiveness that is needed in answering the questions posed by criminal justice and in the even more complex saga of working for peace and justice in Northern Ireland, to which we will soon turn. In both cases, the religious language and ethics which underpin our debates are calling for us to *live out* our philosophies of justice and mercy. In other words, it is not enough to be an armchair liberal mocking those who might take to the streets in protest at the release of Thompson and Venables. To earn the right to be soft on crime or soft on the causes of crime, we should be matching our rhetoric with our action, visiting the prisons, supporting the charities which reintegrate them into the community, employing offenders and simultaneously doing what we can to ensure that the victims and their families are helped to cope with their own predicament and with the knowledge that those who caused them harm have garnered such attention.

This in turn poses uneasy challenges. For example, although the Open University has performed wonders in offering educational opportunities in prisons, including to Myra Hindley, and deserves much credit for this, especially in Northern Ireland, university application (UCAS) forms require those who have been released from prison to disclose convictions. Although liberals believe that education, reintegration into the community and employment prospects are more constructive than long sentences, do we make it easy for those who were in prison to pursue their education on release? The requirement to disclose does not, of course, mean that those with a criminal record will be discriminated against, but university administrators and tutors seem, in my experience, rather uneasy at the prospect of matching liberal ideals by welcoming former murderers, drug dealers and thieves into their campus communities. Thank goodness for that, will be the reaction of many liberal, middle-class parents of liberal, middle-class students. Yet these parents and students are the very ones who are most likely to support the release of Thompson and Venables at the age of eighteen. Alongside the possibility of a career in the armed forces, one of the most plausible developments for them would be to go to university. Given the judicial order which bans them from returning to Merseyside, they will not be students in Liverpool, but the arguments for their release could bring them to a campus near you. On the arguments used in this chapter, this is right and proper, for they would not have been released if the experts had not judged that they have satisfied the conditions for release which include not being a danger to anyone. Universities are also major employers. Should a member of staff who is imprisoned for dealing in drugs be welcomed back, on release, into working in a student setting? Throwing the question back to tutors or the university authorities is one, uneasy, tactic for a student whose philosophy of punishment is being tested on a range of hypothetical or actual cases in a tutorial. Would you insist on high minimum sentences for burglars, for those convicted of violent assaults, for drug dealers? Indeed, whatever the sentence was, what would you do if they had served the maximum and then came looking for the opportunity to study or work?

What emerges from the qualms shown by universities when we are asked to follow the logic of our calls for leniency, clemency and mercy by taking risks ourselves is that, deep down, we are not too sure that 'deterrence' or 'rehabilitation' have worked. We fear recidivism. If that is the case, however, then should we not be doing something about the system of criminal justice, including if necessary arguing for more resources to be committed to it? Or perhaps we fear prison, either because we do not know much about it, fearing the unknown, or because we have visited prisons and found the experience distinctly unpleasant, fearing the fearful and frightful. Again, though, should we not be taking action in either case? Earlier, I agreed with Blake Morrison that we should be wary of judging the thirty-eight adults who recalled seeing James Bulger being led away by Thompson and Venables but who did not intervene. After all, we ourselves may be in the position of standing idly by while those convicted of crime, and those who work with them, labour in appalling conditions.

As someone who cannot claim to have a good record in prison visiting, it is with some unease that I take this chapter any further to pursue this point. The four groups, beyond those with family connections, who do seem to visit prisons regularly are ministers of religion, prison charities, lawyers and politicians. As a rare visitor myself, I think that these four groups deserve praise for their presence in prisons. Nowadays, the first three tend to argue with the fourth on the lessons which the rest of us should learn from their experiences. Politicians were prison reformers in the liberal sense in the 1960s, but in the 1980s, 1990s and now in the new century they seem to be trying to show that they can be tough on crime by telling judges and the prison service what to do. A turning point came in the 1990s when Leon Brittan was Home Secretary and told a Conservative Party conference that life imprisonment should mean life. One of many rows between Michael Howard, when he was Home Secretary, and the judges revolved around sentencing. As with Leon Brittan, it was a party conference that provided the occasion for pandering to supporters who wanted to hear of tough action: 'No more automatic early release. No more release regardless of behaviour. No more half-time sentences for full-time crimes . . . If prison, and the threat of prison, are to work effectively, there's a strong case for greater certainty in sentencing – for stiff minimum sentences for burglars and dealers in hard drugs who offend again and again and again.'

The Lord Chief Justice of the day, Lord Taylor, was appalled:

> Minimum sentences must involve a denial of justice. It cannot be right for sentences to be passed without regard to the gravity, frequency, consequences or other circumstances of the offending . . . To impose a minimum sentence of seven years on those convicted for the third time of trafficking in proscribed drugs will simply fill our prisons with addicts who sell small quantities to support their own addiction.

His successor, Lord Bingham, continued the disagreement:

> A skilful professional burglar who avoids detection until he is brought to book on the same occasion for fifty domestic burglaries or a professional drug dealer eventually tracked down for the first time are not subject to the mandatory penalties. A feckless small-time burglar who is caught each time, or an addict dealing in small quantities at street level, is so subject. Anomalies of this kind are not the stuff of sound lawmaking. . .
>
> If, as the century and the millennium slide to a close, our penal thinking is to be judged by the thinking which animates this Bill, then I, for one, will shrink from the judgment of history.

Now, we have another Lord Chief Justice, Lord Woolf, with whom this chapter began because it was his responsibility to decide the length of the tariff in the cases of Thompson and Venables. He had earlier conducted the inquiry into the Strangeways and other prison riots which took him into prisons and which caused him to reflect deeply on the purposes of punishment and the practical conditions in prisons. In the aftermath of that report, I took part with Lord Woolf and others in a 'Question Time' event arranged by the Butler Trust in the cathedral-like chapel of Wormwood

Scrubs prison. This was an extraordinary occasion. The chair of proceedings was Jon Snow of Channel 4 and the other members of the panel, in addition to Lord Woolf and myself, were a life prisoner, a prison governor and the Home Secretary of the day, Kenneth Clarke. The specially invited audience were mostly prisoners plus some prison officers, civil servants, Sir Stephen Tumim (then Her Majesty's Inspector of Prisons) and Lord Longford. Questions from prisoners centred on the long periods spent on remand. Lord Woolf thought that the legal system needed more resources from government. Kenneth Clarke, a QC himself, replied robustly to the effect that when courts sat for a full day, then the government might consider more resources but time spent on remand could otherwise be reduced by judges working for longer hours. Douglas Hurd and Kenneth Clarke were the last of the liberal Home Secretaries but even they had their disagreements with the judges. Jack Straw and David Blunkett seem to be from the Michael Howard wing of the Home Office, so that confrontations with other elements of the criminal justice system have become more likely.

The Michael Howard dispute with the judges seems at first not to be related to conditions. The Home Secretary was arguing for certainty. The Lord Chief Justices were saying that his method would lead to unfairness between prisoners and would lose the sense of relative seriousness between crimes. Underlying the dispute, however, is an issue to do with what it is then like to be in prison, because the judges clearly think that longer minimum terms increase prison overcrowding and decrease the effectiveness of educational or reform programmes. Politicians want to appear to be doing something about crime but do not want to fund the extra prison places which would be needed to support more time in prison for more prisoners with conditions at the same level.

The phrase 'appear to be doing something' is important because part of our uneasiness at prison policy is to do with the suspicion that politicians, and perhaps wider society, are settling for a false target instead of really aiming to prevent or diminish crime. Lord Chief Justice Taylor, for example, was adamant that if the Home Secretary's objective was to reduce crime, increasing the chances of being caught would have far more effect than lengthening sentences. Since politicians cannot seem to respond to voters' demands for something to be done about crime rates, they resort to talking tough about a different measure – the length of time spent in prison. Through their legislative majority, this is something which they can affect, even if, as we have seen in the case of Thompson and Venables, there is some doubt, especially in the new human rights-led constitutional order, as to the propriety of trespassing on judicial territory. This is aiming at a false target, just as golfers who cannot correct their hooks or slices just aim for a false target to the right or left of the flag respectively. In the USA, Bill

Clinton and several other state governors used the death penalty as a false target for being seen to be tackling crime. Here, it tends to be the number of years in a prison sentence.

Which takes us back to that figure of eight years in custody for Thompson and Venables. During those eight years from their trial to their release, from 1993 to 2001, politicians had been competing with one another to push up the number of years for relatively minor crimes, so it is perhaps understandable that, for some, eight years now seems too short a period (by comparison with what politicians are now demanding as the minimum sentence for lesser crimes) to mark the horror with which society responded to this most appalling of crimes.

There is another element beyond the sheer number of years in custody which may be the rationale behind the intuition that Thompson and Venables have been lucky. Just after they were released, Lord Archer was imprisoned for perjury. He expected to spend most of his custody in a category D prison, an open prison, but he was initially allocated to a category C prison, apparently because there were other investigations continuing. It was clear to the public from this episode, if it had not been clear before, that there is a huge difference between categories of prison which may matter more than the number of years. Moreover, Thompson and Venables had never suffered the regime of any adult prison. In other words, those who would have liked them to stay in custody for longer were not just arguing about an arbitrary number. A figure higher than eight would have entailed time in an adult prison. This would have been more difficult for them, so the argument goes, amounting to real 'punishment' rather than education. As identified earlier, two factors worked against a transfer to an adult prison. The first is that it would seem to invite regression rather than progress in their rehabilitation. The second is that once that Rubicon had been crossed, the Myra Hindley factor could have begun to operate so that there would never have been a politically acceptable time for their release. Each of these reasons is premised on a flaw in our system of punishment which therefore worked in favour of the child killers. The first flaw is that adult prisons are not sufficiently well resourced or well run to aid prisoners. The second is that the system is itself a prisoner to the public's prejudices. The link between these two problems is that the public, or at least the media, focus on length of sentences as a false target has led to more than 90,000 prisoners already being in custody, of whom almost 5,000 are serving life sentences. The economics of punishment should not be ignored in the debate on the ethics of criminal justice. Indeed, we have already touched on the concern at the cost of first educating Thompson and Venables before then providing them with new identities.

The imprisonment of Lord Archer also highlights another element in punishment, namely stigma. The ritual of the criminal justice system is not only a good safeguard to ensure that only the guilty are punished, it also adds to the sense that the community is making a statement about what is respectable and what is disreputable behaviour, as with Lord Archer's offence of perjury. The denunciation of the offence is emphasised by the publicity which is associated with the court system. It would be a mistake for a society to assume that the appropriate stigma only comes with the denunciation being followed by a long, custodial sentence in conditions which reflect badly on the society. Far from being required by justice, such a sequel would undermine the society's reputation for fairness.

Indeed, Lord Woolf's 1991 report into the prison disturbances of April 1990 concluded that one of main reasons for the riots was society's failure to address the question of justice in prison. In July 1994, just before the first IRA ceasefire of the modern Troubles, there were disturbances in the Crumlin Road prison opposite the courts. Given the security restraints during the conflict, this prison held both people convicted of serious crime and those on remand, especially because the latter could be taken into court through an underground tunnel which connected the prison to the courthouse. Overcrowding resulted and the conditions, for example in terms of sanitation and exercise facilities, in the Victorian prison could not cope with the numbers. In September 1994, the Standing Advisory Commission on Human Rights, of which I was a member, visited the prison and in October recommended to the Secretary of State its closure. The chair of the commission, Charles Hill QC, was particularly concerned that those who had not been convicted of any crime were being held in intolerable conditions. Some improvements were made and the commission was invited to revisit in February 1995, but while acknowledging the amelioration in conditions, we still concluded that the prison was not fit for purpose and should be closed as soon as the availability of alternatives and the practicalities of security allowed.

Visiting an overcrowded prison as a member of a statutory body with responsibility for advising the Secretary of State on human rights took me back to my first visit to a prison, when I was a student at Yale Law School. Prisoners who were mounting litigation against the authorities for overcrowding and the denial of rights were being helped by Yale students who needed a large number of fellow students to interview prisoners about their conditions. Yale is in the state of Connecticut. Although Yale's home town, New Haven, is a tale of two halves, in that the delightful university environment contrasts sharply with run-down areas a short distance away, the state as a whole seems privileged and beautiful. To go to the state capital and enter the prison was a shock, primarily because the overwhelming majority of inmates seemed to be Hispanic, with a few who were black, whereas the rest of Connecticut seemed almost exclusively white. The secondary shock was that many of the prisoners seemed unable to communicate fluently in English. Another jolt was appreciating the seriousness of their crimes. Then we came to the overcrowding, which was unworthy of any system of punishment but all too typical of many.

Seeing these conditions for myself, before I began teaching law, was a personal education, as was, some fifteen years later, the opportunity to participate in the recommendation to close a prison with similarly inhuman conditions. On both those occasions, and on my rare prison visits in between, I had considerable sympathy for those who worked within the prison service. To give one other example, I was invited once to address a conference of prison medical officers. I talked about the rapidly developing area of medical ethics and law, especially the emerging doctrine of informed consent. The first question from the floor came close to flooring me quite literally as my squeamishness was confronted with some lurid facts. The thrust of the question was, 'That's all well and good in theory but what should I do faced, as I was yesterday, with a patient who is HIV-positive and has hepatitis B, who is in isolation, who self-mutilates and who finds a way to cut his arm and squirt infected blood at anyone, including the doctor, who comes into the cell?'

Prison doctors, prison chaplains and prison officers are taking on an unpleasant task at society's behest. The appalling conditions of many prisoners are the appalling conditions of these workers. The 'life must mean life' lobby would take away what little incentive remains for some of the most difficult prisoners to improve their behaviour. Those of a more liberal disposition, however, should not dismiss the criticism which will come in turn, that worrying about prison conditions and arguing against tough sentences is being 'soft on crime'. On the principle of questioning the rhetoric, I would prefer 'just deserts' as a (retributive) phrase to trump talk of being soft or tough. Incidentally, even key government papers seem unable to spell 'deserts' correctly in this debate. The concept of 'just desserts' relates more to the issue of having cake and eating it than to a fair system of punishment where the focus is on what is deserved – just deserts. To achieve just deserts, to keep the scales of justice in balance, is an uneasy task. After all, what is being put into one side of the scales is a crime whereas something incommensurate, a number of years in custody, is being used as a counterweight. We will never succeed, however, if we are confused about the task. Nothing can ever compensate for such a vile crime as the murder of James Bulger, but that is not the issue. The confusion here is between the moral duties owed to the victim of a crime and to those close to them by the perpetrator, and the debt incurred to society by the criminal's attempt to superimpose his or her will as against the common good.

The trend to involve the victim, or victim's relatives, in the determination of punishment, is itself a blurring of these two concerns. There is an element of legitimate overlap, as recognised by the European

Court being willing to involve the parents of James Bulger in the Strasbourg hearing. Ultimately, however, the two are distinct. Nor is the 'common good' to be confused with 'public clamour', as the Law Lords and the European Court observed. It is because society is punishing the transgression against the common good, not acting as a wronged individual, that we can make some sense of the symbolic nature of punishment. The criminal's will is in turn subjugated to the determination of the common good. Although two wrongs do not make a right, the two actions are not morally equivalent. The criminal's actions are an assertion of power, the state's are a reassertion of authority. Part of the difference is to do with the systemic nature of the legitimate authority's approach to punishment. This is also partly why it is so important that the punishment does not descend to violations of human rights. It is also why the misnamed 'punishment beatings' in Northern Ireland are such an affront not only to human rights and dignity of the victims but also to the state, as they are an attempt by those who support violence to intimidate and usurp the state.

The kneecapping of a teenager by paramilitaries, perhaps because the youngster had been stealing cars and driving them recklessly (which, in another misnomer, is often called 'joyriding') or dealing in drugs, has been a feature of the Troubles. This kind of assertion of power has continued beyond the ceasefires. Distinguishing it from a legal system's punishment is possible in a variety of ways. A legal system should have clearly defined primary rules of conduct and secondary rules about interpreting and applying those primary rules. Typically, those accused of breaching the primary rules have rights to challenge their accusers, for example to plead mistaken identity, and to explain themselves, to make pleas in mitigation. Punishments must not only deter but must not be disproportionate. They must only 'fit the crime'. They should not exceed 'just deserts'. They should not themselves be administered in a way which violates human rights. For self-appointed 'judges' to act as juries and executioners is a world away from a legal system's ideal image of itself.

We see in this example several reasons why the state should not allow its role of protecting the common good to be challenged in this way. One of the reasons why the paramilitaries carry out such beatings is because they can depict themselves as protecting 'their' communities while the state stands idly by, incapable of deterring even young teenagers from causing disruption to the community. The word 'punishment' is therefore one worth contesting, from all points of view. If the state acquires a reputation for not acting justly in its own treatment of suspected criminals, then it becomes difficult for it to distinguish itself from those who administer such beatings. In Northern Ireland, the legal system has for decades had judges acting as juries, albeit because the jurors' own security and freedom from prejudice were in question. At times, the legal system did suspend the normal panoply of primary and secondary rules, as with internment. The European Court of Human Rights ruled that there had been inhuman or degrading treatment of prisoners.

For some, the overcrowding and unsatisfactory conditions in prisons were only one step away from the violence of the paramilitaries. For others, any such analogy is misplaced. On either view, the struggle to re-establish a decent, humane system of punishment is not simply necessary in terms of the human rights of those subjected to it but is also part of distinguishing the rule of law from the rule of the gun and of the baseball bat. These are some of the reasons why 'liberals' are so insistent that the law must be so conscious of prisoners' rights. Since we all have a natural identification with the rights of victims and their relatives, punishment becomes a central uneasy case for working out our ethical framework.

In extreme cases, such as the killing of James Bulger or the peace process in Northern Ireland, the right thing to do may make at least two impossible demands. First, any act of mercy by society carries with it the cost of superhuman tolerance on the part of those closest to the victim. Second, it may only be justifiable in superhuman, that is to say divine, terms and not by rational, secular morality. Religious texts in general, and the Bible in particular, place great emphasis on liberating those who are captive, whereas the secular logic of deterrence seems to leave little room for mercy, clemency and grace. These factors were, however, central to the remarkable chain of events in Northern Ireland, to which the next chapter turns, and it is when those virtues are forgotten that progress seems imperilled. In much the same way that the answers to these uneasy cases of punishment are to do with mercy rather than the common assumption of justice, so the answers to Northern Ireland are to do with justice (and again sometimes going beyond justice) rather than the common assumption of peace.

3

Northern Ireland: Uneasy Peace

Moral unease has featured throughout the Northern Irish peace process. In particular, on all sides there has been some considerable distaste for treating generously those opponents whom they regard as having behaved badly. Yet many could see that generous actions, if reciprocated, could present a way forward, perhaps the only way forward. Here, then, is an ethical dilemma which has not only been a major public issue but which has much to teach us about relatively minor private choices. The linked questions for consideration at every stage of the 'peace' process are more about justice than they are about peace: what does justice demand and should those who have behaved badly be included in the determination of just progress? In the autumn of 2002, the Northern Irish Executive was suspended. This, like most other hiatuses in the peace process, is normally explained as happening because 'trust broke down' between Unionists and Republicans in government. There will be more to say on trust in the next chapter, but this seems an inaccurate way of capturing the difficulties in Northern Irish institutions since they are characterised by distrust in the first place. Moreover, even if the police raid on Sinn Fein offices in Stormont, the centre of government, was the occasion of the 'breakdown', there were probably deeper causes. Whether or not Republicans were spying on Unionists and other establishment figures from within that very establishment, there were almost unbearable tensions and electoral problems for the Unionists within the executive.

In many quarters, however, there has been a grudging appreciation that the early release of prisoners was vital for progress and that including people who have behaved badly is a necessary feature of building a just society. Temporary release for some in the run-up to the referendums on the Good Friday Agreement helped secure overwhelming support in Ireland, north and south, for that framework. Republican prisoners, for instance, spoke in favour of the settlement in pre-referendum rallies. In turn, the positive support for the agreement led to the almost-permanent release of almost all prisoners who had been convicted of crimes associated with terrorism.

'Almost-permanent' refers to the fact that, like Robert Thompson and Jon Venables, these prisoners can be recalled if they violate the terms of their release. One prominent loyalist prisoner, Johnny Adair, was soon returned to prison under this clause.

Well before the Good Friday Agreement, however, the churches and human rights groups in Northern Ireland were expressing in this particular context much the same views on prisoners as set out by popes, Scot Calvinists, Cardinal Hume and Blake Morrison in the previous chapter. In 1979, Pope John Paul II's historic visit to Ireland, famous for its insistence on an end to violence, included a call to the Irish hierarchy to

> have special care for those who live on the margin of society. Among those most needing pastoral care from bishops are prisoners. My dear brothers, do not neglect to provide for their spiritual needs and to concern yourselves also about their material conditions and their families.
>
> Try to bring prisoners such spiritual care and guidance as may help to turn them from the ways of violence and crime, and make their detention instead be an occasion of true conversion to Christ and personal experience of love. Have a special care for young offenders. So often their wayward lives are due to society's neglect more than to their own sinfulness. Detention should be especially for them a school of rehabilitation.

This is not an easy story, however, of simple moral teaching being uncontroversially applied with the result that meek prisoners were freed to widespread satisfaction. On the contrary, turmoil surrounded every phase of the next twenty years. Indeed, what happened next, in the wake of the Pope's visit, was that the Republican hunger strikers and Margaret Thatcher's government became locked in one of the uneasiest of cases to resolve. When the Labour government was in power in the mid to late 1970s, some prisoners had staged first a 'blanket protest', in which they wore only blankets rather than prison uniforms, and then a 'dirty protest', in which they also smeared their excrement over their cells. Originally focused on five demands for status as 'political prisoners', this turned into a battle with the new Prime Minister who took office in 1979 and hunger strikes began in 1980. There appeared to be a solution around Christmas but it proved illusory and the fasts were resumed. Bobby Sands began his fast on 1 March 1981 and died sixty-six days later, having been elected as an MP in a by-election while on hunger strike. In their day, the hunger strikes were seen as profoundly uneasy cases to address with the world watching and adopting different rhetoric: suicide, choice, martyrs, manipulation, propaganda, sacrifice, blackmail, injustice. The five demands for political status turned into a battle of wills. Communities in Northern Ireland were polarised in their reaction to the hunger strikers. Many Protestants in

Northern Ireland seemed to think that the Roman Catholic Church could somehow persuade the hunger strikers to stop their campaign and often assumed therefore that the continuation of the strike was a sign of a sinister support for Republicans from the Catholic hierarchy. Republicans seemed to think that the Catholic Church was trying to break the hunger strikes by negotiating a compromise and putting pressure on the prisoners' families to put pressure in turn on the individual hunger strikers. The Catholic Church seemed to think of itself as powerless while being regarded by its critics as powerful.

In the unpromising aftermath of the conclusion to the hunger strikes, after the deaths of Bobby Sands and others, it fell to Cardinal Tomas O'Fiaich and then Cardinal Cahal Daly to lead the Irish Catholic bishops' responses to the Pope's clarion call. The latter, for example, emphasised the Old Testament roots of engagement with prisoners, Christ's call to forgive others unconditionally and the practice of the Church in placing such a high priority among 'works of mercy' in visiting prisoners: 'A society will be truly Christian in proportion to its readiness to forgive. It surely follows that forgiveness, compassion, re-education and rehabilitation will be distinguishing characteristics of the prison system in a Christian community, rather than merely punishment, retribution and deterrence.' All this could be applied to the previous example of child killers. Indeed, the youth of prisoners in Ireland, north and south, was a feature to which Cardinal Daly drew repeated attention: 'It is characteristic of subversive or politically motivated prisoners, both in Northern Ireland and in the Republic, that they are young, mostly in their twenties'; 'In the Republic of Ireland, nearly 80 per cent of all prisoners are between fifteen and thirty years of age . . . It also seems to be taken for granted in our society that imprisonment is the most effective and perhaps the only way of eliminating crime. That assumption needs to be vigorously challenged.'

The bishops understood, of course, that the conflict in Northern Ireland complicated the uneasiness of developing an ethical approach to punishment and prisons in the Irish context, compared to the problem of dealing with child killers in England. Cardinal Daly appreciated that those who regard themselves as prisoners of war pose challenges which tend to tilt 'the balance of prison policy towards security rather than towards the other objectives of a human prison system'. Nonetheless, the bishops were emphatic, from before the ceasefires, that there is an ethical imperative to work with prisoners and constantly to question the way in which the criminal justice system classifies and treats people:

Christians, with motivation derived from their faith, should be prominent among those who work professionally or voluntarily for the welfare of prisoners and ex-prisoners and for the welfare of their families

. . . Even a casual visitor to a typical prison will notice that the immense majority of the prison population come from the lower income groups, the more deprived parishes, the unskilled and semi-skilled sectors, the educationally deprived, the subliterate and subnumerate groups . . . It is not either cynical or subversive to ask whether it is the real criminals who are in prison; or is it simply, in the words of Hemingway's *The Old Man and the Sea*, that 'the poor ain't never got no chance'.

Again, it is worth recalling that this was written before the talks which led to the Downing Street Declaration and then the Good Friday Agreement. The ethic of mercy and clemency was being advocated by cardinals, and by others in the churches and by secular human rights groups, throughout the Troubles and indeed throughout history. This in turn raises the possibility that the peace process was made possible in part by this consistent ethic of generosity. Cardinal Daly praised government ministers for courageous decisions, such as closing the Long Kesh compounds, the scene of the hunger strikes, and granting compassionate Christmas parole. He went on to say:

If it be argued that such decisions amount to going soft on crime or on terrorism, it must not be forgotten, least of all by Christians, that clemency has an important part to play in facilitating a change of heart, both in the offending individual and in the wider community. Authority has to make itself admired and not just feared . . . Prudent acts of clemency, conducted in a responsible and systematic manner, could be a recognition of society's collective responsibility for what the whole community did and failed to do in allowing a political and social situation to develop in which young people were left at the mercy of . . . forces stronger than themselves . . .

There are many young men, both loyalists and republicans, who . . . became victims of the tragic circumstances surrounding them in their early and middle teens and who made ruinous errors of judgement, with disastrous consequences for their young lives and often for their victims . . . Society and in particular those responsible for political decisions in society cannot absolve themselves from their share of responsibility for the conditions that allowed or even encouraged these young people to be so calamitously misguided.

Our society is desperately in need of a change of heart. A change of heart cannot be forced, but it can be evoked. Only mercy can evoke mercy. Compassion cannot be compelled by force or fear; it can only be shown. By being shown, it justifies itself and indeed justifies justice. Clemency and mercy are not simply Christian virtues. They can also be forces for political change and social transformation.

As with the release of Robert Thompson and Jon Venables, however, one can sympathise with the bereaved when those who killed their loved ones are allowed to leave prison. It was greatly to the credit of all in Northern Ireland that they coped with the unease of this living out of clemency. It can seem to outsiders curious that, having surmounted such an uncomfortably high hurdle, the peace process can appear to be tripped up by what seem to be relatively small obstacles. It sometimes happens, however, that a runner falls in the later stages of the steeplechase (an event rather sadly being expunged from athletics) through exhaustion. The 400-metre hurdler, Alan Pascoe, once failed several attempts to leap a hurdle as part of his lap of honour having just eased over all the hurdles in the race of his life. The cumulative impact of compromise after compromise may lead to a weary individual or community responding with less generosity on a smaller issue. It is important in what follows, therefore, to bear in mind that the ethics of decommissioning or police reform would not be as uneasy without the context of mutual concessions. They would not be necessary or interesting, however, if it were not for the fact that they are part of a greater whole. Seeing the ethical environment in the round may enable us to identify the right action and to refrain from excessive moral indignation at what we see as the main protagonists unreasonably insisting on a micro-matter.

For peace processes around the world and throughout the ages are characterised by unease. It is not at all surprising that releasing prisoners, or forming a government or a cross-border body, or decommissioning or policing, or the right of primary schoolchildren from one community to walk to school past the houses of another community or some other issue will (as the media cliché puts it) 'threaten to derail' the peace train. Politicians and voters will often, perhaps always, be able to claim with some justification to be at the end of their moral tether with the intransigence of 'the other side'. For many, it was immoral in the first place to deal with 'the enemy' and it would be immoral now to make one more compromise. Now is the time to take a stand. Enough is enough. This is the rhetoric of the moral high ground, from where the view seems crystal clear.

To put this in perspective, however, the unease of peace in Northern Ireland is not of the same order as the alternative, the unease of armed conflict. Living in the middle of a conflict is both uneasy and life-threateningly dangerous. War and armed conflict more generally, to include terrorism, pose some of the most troubling ethical dilemmas. Preparations or lack of preparations for war, from appeasement to the building up of deterrent forces with the primary intention of preventing war through to thoroughgoing belligerence, have spawned a huge literature on the ethics of defence policy. The just war tradition is one of the most famous developments of general ethical principles. It comes at much the same level of generality as the Archbishop of Westminster's principles in the case of the

Siamese twins (and there is some merit in comparing the two sets of principles, although a warning has already been given about placing too much store on superficial consistency or inconsistency). War is only justified when it is fought by a proper authority for a just cause, such as national self-defence in response to aggression, when only minimal force is used, subject to proportionality and only in relation to legitimate targets (such as the armed forces of the aggressor). Applying this just war doctrine to particular contexts is, however, yet another problematic exercise. Generation after generation sees new aspects to their dilemmas, as illustrated by the Holocaust, the development of the atomic bomb, the campaign for nuclear disarmament, chemical and biological warfare. Within each generation, let alone between generations, people will in good faith disagree on the application of the principles to a particular set of circumstances.

If the price of peace is some moral queasiness, therefore, many will consider this preferable to the loss of human life and ethical innocence which war entails. Others, however, would rather that the conflict continue than that a compromise should effect a settlement at some cost to their ethical principles. For instance, to pursue the issue which has formed a bridge between the last chapter and this one, releasing prisoners after ceasefires has been one of the most unpalatable developments for many in various peace processes, not only in Northern Ireland. Victims of attempted murders and the families of victims who were murdered could be expected to find this difficult. Of course, victims and the families of victims also found it difficult in the earlier years of the Troubles when the crimes happened, when those guilty of crimes against their loved ones were in court or when it seemed that no one was going to be prosecuted for those crimes. As with the cases of Robert Thompson and Jon Venables, cases were contested all the way through the domestic legal system and on to the European Court of Human Rights. As with the case of Jodie and Mary, anyone in court could see that the judges found the cases troubling. In Northern Ireland, however, there were added pressures on the judges in that they also had to take on the role of the jury in 'Diplock courts' after concerns about the impartiality and safety of jurors. Moreover, judges were themselves assassinated and so those members of the judiciary who survived could be forgiven for thinking from time to time that they were trying people who were connected to those who were trying to kill them.

To give but one example of a case to illustrate the uneasy dilemmas which the judges had to resolve during the Troubles: I wrote an article in the *Irish Times* in February 1992 when Lord Justice Kelly sentenced the double agent Brian Nelson to ten years on five charges of conspiracy to murder and related charges. Brian Nelson was an undercover agent who infiltrated the loyalist Ulster Defence Association and spied on them for the British Army.

Seventeen people were killed by the UDA during the three-year period in which Nelson was acting as a spy, one of whom was the Belfast solicitor Pat Finucane. The army's intelligence unit stated that his work helped in protecting 217 individuals who received death threats. My article began by stating that 'The Brian Nelson affair poses in stark form, a daily dilemma of the Troubles: is it ever justifiable for the authorities to violate the Rule of Law in fighting a "dirty war"? Those who say "no" will be accused of living in a dream world, sacrificing real lives for ivory tower principles. Those who say "yes" will be accused of descending to the level of the paramilitaries, abandoning the moral high ground which separates the lawful from the lawless.' In Lord Justice Kelly's own words, he took 'into account that Nelson gave up a comfortable life in Germany at the behest of the army and with good motivation, not for gain, and with the greatest courage submitted himself to constant danger and intense strain for three years'. Great courage has also been shown by lawyers such as Lord Justice Kelly and Pat Finucane while 'intense strain' has also been the lot of lawyers and their families. Politicians on all sides in Northern Ireland have also faced 'constant danger and intense strain' with the 'greatest courage'. It is worth adding that it is not only those who chose high-profile roles, such as politicians and lawyers, who were placed in such positions. During the Troubles, anyone in Northern Ireland could face an agonising ethical dilemma, as when terrorists forced individuals to drive bombs into security force targets under duress as they held family members captive.

So I have little sympathy for any notion that peace-making and peace-sustaining pose such moral concerns about dealing with enemies that we should wash our hands of the process with the result that we revert to the conflict. When the Troubles were in full spate, there was at least as much moral unease as there is now and it was accompanied by greater suffering than now. This is not to pretend that there is no violence or no injustice now. Nor is it to concede that matters of war and peace should be resolved by a utilitarian calculus, regardless of other fundamental moral principles. Rather, it is to say that the problem usually described as 'dirty hands' or 'extrication morality' needs to be addressed. It is not easy for those who have supported the state to deal with those they have always regarded as terrorists, murderers, subversives, especially if they are on the record as saying that they will 'never talk to terrorists'. Nor is it easy for those who regard the state as the oppressor and who are on the record as never being prepared to have any truck with the state to find themselves negotiating with that state or even taking office within it. Nonetheless, it is right that so many in Northern Ireland have striven to fashion a fair and lasting settlement despite their understandable misgivings about dealing with 'the other side'.

It is immediately apparent that the complexities of negotiating peace, or living in conflict, in Northern Ireland have multiplied from the already difficult case of the child killers which in turn had more variables than the agonising case of the Siamese twins. Those of us who found the case of Jodie and Mary almost unbearably uneasy will therefore come with some trepidation to the Northern Irish Troubles. It is important to understand exactly why the ethical dilemmas of Northern Ireland are so many and why they are so acute by comparison with either of our first two uneasy cases. First, decades of the Troubles have followed centuries of conflict so that the history of respective positions is a factor in a way which did not arise in the case of Jodie and Mary. It has become quite fashionable to talk about ethical duties to our grandchildren and generations yet unborn, for instance in relation to environmental ethics, but arguments about what is right or just in Northern Ireland are also bound up with claims of fairness to generations in the past, and especially to those who died in the conflict or on behalf of one of the traditions or states involved in the conflict. Do we have moral responsibilities to those who in 1916 were battling on the Somme or engaged in the Easter Rising, to those who died for the Crown or for the nation, for Ulster unionism or Irish republicanism? It is easy to dismiss as a negotiating tactic the stance, for instance, that Republican leaders could not surrender their weapons because that would be a betrayal of hunger strikers and others who gave their lives to a shared cause. It is uneasy but necessary, however, to pause and reflect on the implications of too hasty a dismissal of that position. Is the counter-claim that the hunger strikers were wrong in the first place, or that those who died on hunger strike, such as Bobby Sands, would not accept this compromise, or that the current leaders are not really motivated by concern for those who gave their lives to the Republican cause? Are those who dismiss that stance saying that surrendering weapons would be a betrayal but that this is the morally right course of action? Do they portray the surrender of weapons as a victory over republicanism? Usually, negotiators in such processes do strike a position which seeks to make sense of the past, present and future, constructing a narrative that allows a change of direction while claiming it is faithful to the past.

Although, from the Unionist viewpoint, the whole Republican struggle was unethical, although they may well not trust the current leaders with whom they are dealing, although they may find it morally queasy to be dealing with them at all, there may be some recognition that the Republican leaders are grappling with a kind of moral paradox, of the 'ethic-within-the-unethical', when it comes to giving up the armed struggle or compromising with the British state. This is in addition to the prudential or practical difficulties which those Republican leaders have had and continue to have in keeping their leadership positions and their lives, while risking being seen to renege on what they have said and what their fellow-travellers have died for on a journey which now seems to be changing direction to Stormont from its original destination of Dublin. This is the historical context of a problem usually put in philosophy texts as 'extrication morality' or 'dirty hands'. It has some similarities with the moral and practical difficulties facing double agents such as Brian Nelson. During the conflict, the dilemma may have been put more bluntly: is it ever right to act unethically, for example to authorise a murder, so as to maintain credibility with an organisation in order to save others (the double agent's question) or in order to bring the organisation over time to a ceasefire (the leader's question)? Even to put the question in this way is to show why leaders who sue for peace are often regarded as traitors, as turncoats or double agents or Lundys. Once the ceasefires happened, the moral dilemma may have seemed less difficult, but it is still there and it may still explain why some seemingly reasonable compromises are rejected, at least at certain stages.

Of course, there is another explanation for apparent intransigence, namely that the political leaders are using negotiating tactics in a way calculated to maximise what they see as the interests of their supporters. The possibility that the negotiator facing you may be genuinely following the logic of a, from your viewpoint, warped moral and political code or may be trying to outmanoeuvre you complicates your own position. You also have your own historical framework of ethical commitments which may, in turn, seem similarly twisted to the opposing negotiators or contrived for strategic gain. A further complication comes from the uncertainties identi- fied by John Elford. It may be that you know what the others will do if you take such-and-such a step. It may be, however, that you are uncertain. One reason for this may be your distrust of them but another may be your doubts as to whether they can convince their supporters. 'Jumping together' into an arrangement is sometimes possible but that may in turn pose further moral dilemmas because the negotiations then begin to pair off what you may regard as incommensurable actions. If you demilitarise, we will decom- mission our weapons. Yes, but we were always entitled to have military bases and armed police so long as you were attacking us whereas you were never morally justified in terrorism. Oh yes we were justified in defending our people. Oh no you weren't. And so on.

Unease is multiplied, then, by the history and by the uncertainties, such as how others will act in the light of your moral choices or whether their true reasons or position are being disclosed. A further complication is that in these circumstances individuals rarely have the power to make a decision on their own. Politicians have to take colleagues and/or electors with them or at least have some confidence that their risky lead will be followed. I suggested at the end of the first chapter that a happily married couple might in good faith disagree about the ethics of separating Siamese twins when one would die. Imagine how much more unease there could be, therefore, when an unhappy coalition of Unionists has to take life-or-death decisions in the light of the history, their perception that those with whom they are negotiating cannot be trusted and will not deliver on their promises and when there is no consensus among themselves. In this context, it is facile to accuse politicians of lacking moral courage merely because they cannot at a particular time bring themselves as a group of politicians to do what you would do as a single individual.

Once more I have mentioned time. One of the more witty turns of phrase in relation to the Good Friday Agreement is the expression 'Sunningdale for slow learners', suggesting that twenty-five years later we have a settlement which is much the same as that offered when Ted Heath and Garret Fitzgerald brokered a deal. It may, however, be too slick a phrase for our own good. First, Sunningdale did not work because Unionist citizens did not accept the merits of the concessions agreed by negotiators and in that sense it is a warning that the same may be true even now. Second, as with the release of child killers, timing is crucial and it is important to give people the opportunity not to be locked in a time warp, frozen at the point of a murder or a conviction or a denunciation or a deal or the rejection of a deal.

In the summer of 2001, the issues causing most unease appeared to be decommissioning and policing. As the new academic year started at the beginning of September 2001, there were extraordinary scenes in north Belfast as little schoolgirls ran the gauntlet of protesters on their way to primary school. Since unease has accompanied each phase of the Northern Irish struggle, first for peace and then for inclusive and stable government, it is debatable whether the particular occasions for a row are the primary causes or whether they are only manifestations of the underlying distrust and difficulties which have bedevilled progress.

Decommissioning, for example, did not feature as an issue when I lived and worked in Northern Ireland from January 1989 to July 1995. This is not to belittle the issue. Again, times change and something which was not a prominent concern in one era can genuinely become the focal point in another time. It would be a mistake, however, to become fixated on the intricacies of one particular matter without understanding the deeper challenges for moral reasoning in a peace process. Pitching our discussion at that level of generality, it seems to me that there is a link between the causes for ethical concern in the early 1990s and those which seem to preoccupy the early years of this decade. For many of the issues revolve around the same axis: on what terms, if any, should those who use or condone violence in protest against a state be involved in constitutional politics? I put it in that way to emphasise that it is a moral dilemma for those who were earlier committed to the use of violence, as to whether they should have any truck with the state, as well as being a moral question for those usually described as constitutional politicians, as to whether they should now participate in negotiations or government with those they describe as terrorists or former terrorists.

In January 1989, when I moved to Belfast, Tom King was still Secretary of State for Northern Ireland and there was lively debate about the broadcasting restrictions on Sinn Fein and other parties linked to paramilitary groups. From the late 1980s to the early 1990s, the question of who should debate with whom sometimes seemed to be the issue. There were talks about talks among constitutional politicians when Peter Brooke succeeded Tom King. The citizens' movement, Initiative '92, founded by Robin Wilson and myself, provided an opportunity for all-comers, including those subject to the broadcasting restrictions, to exchange ideas on ways forward with the Opsahl Commission. Talking became all the rage, from talks with Sir Patrick Mayhew when he succeeded Peter Brooke, to talks between John Hume of the SDLP and Gerry Adams of Sinn Fein and, we now know, between the IRA and representatives of the British government. My submission to the Opsahl Commission was called 'Lost for Words' and was subsequently published by *Index on Censorship*. In this, I drew attention to the limited and limiting vocabulary which inhibited the search for progress. For the *Irish Times* in October 1993, before the Downing Street Declaration, I wrote an imaginary Adams–Hume document, since no one seemed to know whether there was a real one and, if there was, whether it would ever be published. After the first IRA ceasefire in August 1994, I wrote an imaginary Unionist response for the *Belfast Telegraph*. My aim in all this was to play my part, however small, in creating the moral and linguistic environment in which others could take responsibility for their destinies. In my current day job at Liverpool Hope University College, I have been concerned to create good physical environments and in the wider world there is a whole industry of environmentalists but, as the Chief Rabbi and others have observed, we need also to pay attention to our moral environment. Words as well as images are some of the key features of the ethical landscape which we can shape.

The interaction of words and images in media portrayal of developments in Northern Ireland was at the heart of the broadcasting restrictions, that uneasy issue of the late 1980s which defined, in some ways, a particular phase of the Troubles. To many, the ban on carrying the voices of those associated with supporting paramilitaries was 'half-baked', as it was described by Lord Donaldson, Master of the Rolls, during the ensuing litigation. Some could see, however, that the government was putting the mark of Cain on those who supported the use of violence. Freedom of speech was still being respected to the extent that the image of the speaker could be seen and their words could be conveyed by an actor or by subtitles. Yet the government was interrupting the normal order to send out a signal that those covered by the ban were not participating in democracy on the same terms as 'constitutional politicians' who condemned the use of violence. It was akin to the government health warning on a packet of cigarettes, almost as if a pulsating asterisk in the corner of the screen was a reminder that this person supported violence.

That is perhaps a more coherent way of putting the restrictions than they deserve. Another way of looking at the ban is to say that the Home Secretary of the day, Douglas Hurd, was doing the least that he could while still being seen to be doing something in response to some particular atrocities which had riled the Prime Minister, Margaret Thatcher. The blowing up of a coach carrying soldiers at Ballygawley, followed by the bomb attack on the home of the senior Northern Irish civil servant, led the Prime Minister to insist that something had to be done. Internment would have been the most extreme response. The broadcasting restrictions were a less draconian response. Debate centred on three questions: whether the 'ban' was lawful, whether it was politic and whether it was counter-productive. It is the interaction of all these which often makes a dilemma uneasy. Without agreeing with the semi-ban, however, it is worth noting the sophistication of cutting to the heart of the media coverage of the Troubles. In the modern world, appearing on television is one of the signs of success, even of authority. By making it more difficult for the media to carry interviews of paramilitaries, the government was, in one view, trying to address a perceived democratic deficit. It was countering what governments often see as the media glamourising the use of violence. Of course, one reason why some predicted it would be counterproductive was that another source of power, authority and influence was the perception of being a martyr, which this device fostered. For our purposes, another aspect of the ban which gives pause for thought, even after it was rescinded as part of the peace process, is that it touches directly on a pervasive but usually only latent ethical issue: the question of when to speak and when to maintain silence.

The previous chapter argued that there is a time for silence. This also applies to the peace process in Northern Ireland or elsewhere. The wisdom of Ecclesiastes tells us, however, that everything has its season or time so there is also a time for saying something and a time for taking further action. We need once more that elusive art of judgement to decide when to speak out and when to keep our own counsel. This applies to private citizens as well as to public figures. Robert Kennedy's point applies in all contexts, that individual ripples of hope can combine to make a difference, to make waves. In Northern Ireland, we have been challenged by the poet John Hewitt for 'coasting along' and by the novelist Brian Moore for 'the lies of silence'. We should be uneasy about complacency, about not speaking out at all or soon enough:

You showed a sense of responsibility
with subscriptions to worthwhile causes
and service in voluntary organisations;
and, anyhow, this did the business no harm,
no harm at all.
Relations were improving. A good
useful life. You coasted along.
[. . .]
And all the time, though you never noticed,
the old lies festered;
the ignorant became more thoroughly infected;
You coasted along
And the sores suppurated and spread.
[. . .]
You coasted too long.

We should be grateful to those who have been in Northern Ireland throughout the Troubles working steadily for the common good, helping to advance the causes of peace and justice for more than thirty years. Yet we could always have done more and done it sooner. We have to make tragic choices and there is a human, social cost when we stand idly by or delay. Nor are the responsibilities confined to those living in Northern Ireland. The chief offenders in terms of 'lies of silence' are said by one of Brian Moore's characters in his novel *Lies of Silence* to be those in Westminster who ignored the evidence of injustice before the Troubles' latest manifestation in the 1960s. When I wrote to *The Times* in May 1991 supporting the then Brooke talks against the doom merchants such as Conor Cruise O'Brien, it was pointed out to me that Graham Greene had written to *The Times* in the late 1960s saying that talks were inevitable so why not have them then? He was right, so why did it take another twenty years or more, during which time, of course, unease and tragedy multiplied?

Part of the answer is to do with the 'lies of silence' or the failure to place enough moral and political concern behind the issue of resolving the conflict. Ten years ago, for example, I wrote a book entitled *The Cost of Free Speech*, arising most immediately from my interest in the saga surrounding the publication of Salman Rushdie's novel, *The Satanic Verses*, and in the broadcasting restrictions on Sinn Fein and others. The preface drew attention to the murders of lawyers in Northern Ireland, specifically mentioning Pat Finucane and Edgar Graham. Looking back, this indicates my sense of unease that liberal England was worked up about the broadcasting restrictions and the book-burning stunt by Muslims in Bradford yet did not take risks for peace or mutual understanding and in particular did not support those whose lives were on the line in trying to create a more just society in Northern Ireland.

In first-year law classes at Queen's, I discussed the broadcasting restrictions with a small tutorial group of particularly articulate and sharp first-year law students from a wide range of backgrounds, who disagreed deeply on the ethical rights and wrongs of the law on freedom of expression. One of them was Sheena Campbell, a mature student in her late twenties, a mother and an extremely able participant in these debates. At the beginning of her second year, she was followed from the law library one Friday night to the pub where some other mature students and members of staff rounded off the week and there she was shot dead. As Dean of the Law Faculty, I was called to the hospital and so met her family and friends, some of whom were prominent in Sinn Fein. This was well before the first IRA ceasefire. Before coming to Queen's, Sheena Campbell had stood as the Sinn Fein candidate in the by-election for Upper Bann, which was won by David Trimble, then a lecturer in law at Queen's. At the end of the requiem Mass, the parish priest stepped forward and spoke briefly but movingly to thank those who had come because they knew Sheena Campbell, those who had come because they did not know her but shared her politics and those who had come because, although they did not know her and did not share her politics, they thought that this was no way for a human being to die. Even after the ceasefires, of course, the violence has continued and again we can all be touched by it, as illustrated by the bomb in 1996 in Manchester, near to where I now live, and the Real IRA's bomb in Omagh in Northern Ireland in the summer of 1998. In the latter, a Liverpool Hope student and her mother were among those seriously injured. Suzanne Kelly was at home at the end of her first year on a four-year degree course training to be a teacher. She returned to her studies, graduating on time in the summer of 2001, an inspiration to all, but also one of the many affected by the uneasy twilight world between war and peace in which Northern Ireland has been poised even since the ceasefires of the mid 1990s.

In this context, there is little to commend the option of coasting, of avoiding facing up to our responsibilities for making a difference in Northern Ireland. This has been the easy way out for many on either side of the Irish Sea, on either side of the border, on either side of any peace line and we should hesitate therefore to criticise those, such as politicians and community leaders, who have engaged with the issues, risking their lives and their families' tranquillity. Yet we should all be uneasy about successive obstacles to progress in the peace process and we can all make a difference, without necessarily committing our lives to the search for justice. For example, I began 'Lost for Words' by quoting Václav Havel who observed that 'Important events in the real world . . . are always spearheaded in the realm of words.' In everyday conversations, avoiding the dubious debating moves outlined earlier in this book ('you would say that, wouldn't you, because you're a Catholic/Protestant/Republican/Unionist/nationalist/

loyalist/Irish/British . . .') is a start and introducing more constructive and generous rhetoric is an improvement. For instance, I tried to offer new rhetoric for nationalists and then for loyalists. The first came in the fictional Adams–Hume statement which I wrote for the *Irish Times*. The second came in the fictional Unionist response to the first IRA ceasefire which I wrote for the *Belfast Telegraph*. These and similar attempts to influence the language of the debate got me into difficulties with those who could not grasp that I was imagining what those who actually held the relevant political positions could best say to advance what is now called the peace process, not that I was endorsing or promoting their views. This elementary point, similar to the problems solicitors and barristers have when the media identify them with their clients, made for some amusing as well as unsettling moments. In each case of imagining a new statement of an old position, nationalist or loyalist, I had in mind the secular but moving imagery of Harper Lee's great novel, *To Kill A Mockingbird*, in which the narrator's father, Atticus Finch (played by Gregory Peck in the film version), tells her that if she really wants to understand other people she needs to clamber inside their skin and walk around in it, to imagine how the world seems from their perspective. Moral imagination, like ethical judgement, is needed if we are to craft a better world. By trying to spell out the best possible presentation for the nationalists and loyalists to put to one another, I was engaged in a long-hand version of the short-hand approach which most law students would take to any uneasy case. It took me years, but in tutorials law students are expected to cover the ground in a nano-second, racing in their minds through the best way of putting alternative arguments, before adopting a position in response to a hypothetical case.

Before suggesting, then, what we should be doing in Northern Ireland now, when the problem appears to be decommissioning or policing, it is important to trace how the language of progress has emerged. This has a value in terms of understanding Northern Ireland but also as an example of a slow-motion replay of the mental scanning which goes on in arguing about hypothetical or real uneasy cases. On the particular issue, my ideas were but one set of thoughts, some of which have surfaced in speeches and documents by the politicians whereas some have not found favour. I would like to think, however, that they at least gave citizens a foretaste of the rhetoric to come in politicians' talks, declarations and agreements, thus helping to create some of the space in which others took courageous risks for peace. My imaginary Adams–Hume document, first published on 14 October 1993 and thus written in life before the Downing Street Declaration, reads as follows:

If the IRA were to take the first step and if nationalists of all persuasions were to set aside what we see as our rights in the cause of harmony, would others have the courage to take the other necessary steps to achieve a lasting, just peace? Republicans believe that the root cause of the conflict here is the British presence. Republicans share with all nationalists the belief that the right to self-determination lies with the people of the whole island of Ireland. Both republicans and nationalists acknowledge, however, that unionists claim a right of those in the six counties to determine all our futures. Our differences on the rights-based arguments should not prevent imaginative ways forward. One possibility is for us all to set aside our perceived rights and to focus instead on what would be right to do. It is not always right, not always pragmatic, not always generous, to insist on one's rights even though one continues to believe in and cherish them.

Republicans are confident that all the people in the North and throughout the island, of whatever tradition, could work together if 'British neutrality' became a reality rather than one of a number of fictions which [the] British government use as and when it suits them. It is not merely the setting of what republicans regard as an artificial unit of the six counties for any border poll which distorts the ability of Irish people to determine their own destiny. Republicans believe that there is also a series of handicaps placed on them, such as a network of restrictive laws and economic subsidies to the unionist community throughout the century. Given these distorting factors, republicans would not regard even a simultaneous poll in all 32 counties tomorrow as an exercise in the genuine self-determination of the Irish people. It is no wonder, then, that the border poll in the North alone 20 years ago was boycotted by nationalists. A regular commitment to testing opinion as people experience working together in an atmosphere of genuine British neutrality, however, would go a long way to encouraging republicans to set aside our right and agree to abide by the results of, say, five-yearly polls.

It has been 25 years since the latest round of conflict here grabbed international headlines. As so many other conflicts around the world have seen dramatic developments in recent years, nationalists hope that all parties here will consider bold steps.

The British army acknowledges that the IRA could continue its campaign indefinitely. Suppose, however, the IRA were to decide instead to take a risk for a just peace. Other stages of any such process could be marked by generosity from republicans if there were others who would be prepared to respond in the same spirit.

What would those responses be? This is not a matter of establishing preconditions, but rather imagining a sequence of events which might follow a dramatic move by republicans. Were others to consider these, then republicans could call on the IRA to suspend the armed struggle *sine die*.

The subsequent steps would be a matter for discussion, but we have in mind that the British government should keep its promises (from the Mayhew Coleraine speech in December 1992) of withdrawing both troops and restrictive laws given a cessation of violence; that loyalists should stop their murder campaigns; that as many as possible of the powers currently exercised by Stormont should be operated by local politicians under a system which gives communities an equal voice; that the European Convention on Human Rights should be incorporated into the domestic laws of the whole island, along with legal recognition of nationalism, as well as unionism; that there should be effective guarantees of the equal rights of all and appropriate arrangements for the phased release of all imprisoned as a result of the conflict here; that there should be new North–South institutions to reflect our identity; that there should be a new accord between the Dublin and Westminster governments; that those governments and American friends of Ireland could invest in the creation of job opportunities on a fair and equitable basis; and that there should be a commitment to frequent, regular polls, North and South, on the constitutional question as the people of the North experience working together.

In those circumstances, we could all envisage the next quarter of a century witnessing a process of creating the climate in which genuine self-determination can proceed and so there could be a just and lasting peace arising from a cessation of violence.

This proposal is not premised on 'joint authority' or any other particular form of administration. Nor would it necessarily mean that a united Ireland or a complete British withdrawal would come about soon or in 25 years or ever.

If people were to decide, without influence from Britain and with the experience of working together, to have a border (whatever that might mean in the Europe of the 21st century), then that would be the current outcome of the exercise of self-determination. Unionists cannot expect an eternal guarantee of a Westminster link since it is in the nature of self-determination that those taking control of their own lives may opt for independence at some point.

Equally, nationalists cannot expect that at any moment there will be an agreed new Ireland. What we can expect is that if republicans and nationalists put their rights to one side, others might respond with similar courage and generosity of spirit.

I commented that this might have been too weak for Sinn Fein or for the IRA, or that it might have been too demanding for Unionists. It deliberately fudged some detail but would be well received internationally. I concluded that it might represent the highest moral ground to which the Republican movement, guided by the nationalist Sherpa John Hume, could climb with the oxygen of generosity.

My imaginary pluralist Unionist document, published on 30 September 1994 and thus written in advance of the loyalist ceasefire, was written as a response to that oxygen of generosity in the aftermath of the IRA ceasefire on 31 August 1994. My concern was that Unionist self-esteem needed consolidation before parity of esteem could be envisaged. My suggested line for Unionists ran as follows:

The Union is between those who cherish citizenship of the United Kingdom. It is a union with the values, rights and principles of the state, such as freedom under the rule of law. The UK is a multi-national state, a multi-ethnic state and a multi-faith state. It is moving all the time to a more inclusive, pluralist celebration of diversity. Unionists should move with their state, not reluctantly as the lesser of two evils but positively, taking the lead in devising ways to give practical expression to the pluralist ideal.

Within Northern Ireland, the oft-quoted phrase of a Protestant parliament for a Protestant people was a regrettable reaction to the Southern cry of a Catholic state for a Catholic people. The proper counter should have been 'pluralist institutions for diverse people'. Unionism ought to be about a pluralist governance of a pluralist citizenship. It should not be about one group dominating another. It should not be anti-Catholic. Indeed, as properly understood, the desire to be citizens in a pluralist state is the political belief of many Catholics here and in Britain. Likewise, there must be no anti-Irishness among unionists. In one sense (albeit a sense sadly undermined by republican hijacking of Irishness), anyone born here has an Irish aspect to their identity.

This vision of citizenship in a pluralist state is open to those who feel both Irish and British. It is also open to those whose background makes them uncomfortable with the term 'British' but who nonetheless find citizenship in the pluralist UK not unattractive (the unionism which dare not speak its name). It is open to those who are proud to be from Northern Ireland. It is open to those who are proud to be British. What is more, it goes some way to explaining what it means to be British. It is not about maps, it is not about exclusivist demotions of a nation, it is not a matter of romantic myths, but nor is it about gaining power. It is about citizenship, the political structures of a state and ensuring through checks and balances that those with responsibility do not abuse power but do respect diversity.

The republican map image approach, in contrast, seems to say that one land mass equals one nation equals one people equals one state. Unionists look at maps, land, sea, peoples, nations and states very differently. Unionists see an archipelago, a constellation of islands off the mainland of Continental Europe. Adapting John Donne, unionists could say that no island is an island in itself.

This is not to say that geographical ties are irrelevant. Unionists share with others in these islands a sense of place, of locality, of affection for where they were born and raised, for where they and their families and friends have built a life. Unionists must oppose any form of ethnic cleansing.

Thus, unionists agree with the Pope's recent condemnation of all kinds of nationalism in his blunt addresses to Catholic Croatia. The conflict here is between a political approach of nationalism and a political approach which rejects nationalism. Unionists have a coherent political philosophy which runs counter to nationalism but is not a mirror image of it.

It would be wrong, however, to ignore the deficiencies of unionists within Northern Ireland or deficiencies in the government of the UK in always living up to the best pluralist traditions and ambitions of the state. For the most part, the UK state has reacted stoically to the threat of subversion and violent terrorism restricting rights only when absolutely necessary and with a sense of proportion. There have, however, been lapses from the highest standards, apologies are owed and apologies should be given. The responsibilities of successive governments are not simply for their direct rule years but in creating impossible structures in the Stormont years and not overseeing the consequences; in short, for not governing.

Within Northern Ireland, unionists must apologise for any anti-Catholic bigotry, whether arising from fear of the unknown or fear of instability or fear of the disaffected or fear of disloyalty or not from fear at all but just from plain prejudice. Whatever the cause, there is no excuse for any and every failure to treat all-comers as first-class fellow citizens.

Apologising for past wrongs and drawing a line under the past are easier said than done, especially for those on all sides who have lost family and friends in the conflict or who have endured years of living under threat or who were never personally responsible for decisions or who have always personally disavowed the violence carried out allegedly in their name. There is always somebody better placed to apologise. People wish to draw different lines under the past, just as they wish to draw different lines of statehood on the map. Nonetheless, unionists must summon up the courage to say that they are sorry for the wrongs done in their name. The oxygen of generosity can provide the atmosphere which we all need on the ascent to a better tomorrow.

Citizenship of the union confers both rights and duties. As far as rights are concerned, politics has been seen here for too long as a zero sum game – if 'you' win, 'we' lose. A pluralist vision, however, should be confident enough to say that when we enrich our society by promoting the rights of any section, we all win and that when we restrict the rights of any section, even if we feel we have to do so temporarily because of security, we appreciate that we all lose.

As for duties, and lifting that line under the past for just a little longer, allies in the wider world do not forget that when the call came to defend pluralism across Europe during the Second World War, many people from Ireland, North and South, volunteered to fight fascism. Without making any gibes about the neutrality of the Republic, a sense of duty (rather than conscription) inspired many to defend their own and other states against Hitler's brand of nationalism and quest for ethnic purity. That spirit was all of a piece with this account of pluralism.

Unionists can also be proud of the role played by people here in building up the UK economy by industrial successes in an earlier era. Having contributed in such a way, there is no shame in benefiting from the advantages that have flowed from membership of a large and strong economy and from the principle of taxing equally across the UK and supporting the disadvantaged equally across the UK. Nonetheless, there is a real desire on the part of many people, whether currently unemployed or in work, from all backgrounds here to seize the opportunity to make an enterprising economic contribution once again.

Thus, on no side is the relationship between local unionists and fellow citizens of the UK simply a matter of selfish strategic or economic interests. The union transcends all these concerns. Understandably, people here have turned in on themselves in recent years to the point where the unionist contribution to building up the UK needs to be reinvigorated. The legal system of Northern Ireland could, for example, be the pace-setter within these islands for incorporating a charter of rights, based on the European Convention.

The logical consequence of this re-vision of unionism is that it should be open to such debate about what forms of governance can be adopted within this part of the state or across its borders, especially if hostilities cease in terms of internal violence and external territorial threat.

Within the UK, homogeneity has never been a requirement of the union, as evidenced by the different arrangements worked out in relation to, for example, Scottish law and the Welsh language. Outside the UK, it is self-evident that common Irish and UK membership of the European Union across the UK's only land border raises all kinds of potential for co-operation, so far stymied by the Republic's territorial claim and republican paramilitary abuse of the border.

What might be called the external constitution of the UK has developed apace in the post-war era which is why all can look forward with confidence to incorporating some of the external safeguards into our domestic law through a charter of rights. A new rhetoric of pro-portionality, parity of esteem and subsidiarity needs to be explored and harnessed to the task of creating inclusive ways forward which guard against abuse.

Unionists should not be misled into constructing their own political philosophy as a mirror image of nationalism. They should not cling simply to the principle of consent, important though that is. Nor should they succumb to the line that the strength of unionists is in their numbers and their geography. The strength of unionism ought to be in the quality of its argument, the attraction of such a pluralist vision and the actions taken to develop citizenship in a pluralist state. The union is an aspiration and an imperative to work for a society in which all those who wish to be citizens can flourish.

It is for others to judge whether any of this has helped but a parallel process can be undertaken by anyone concerned with any uneasy ethical challenge. Imagining the rhetoric needed for a way forward may in itself help to create the space for some accommodation of seemingly conflicting viewpoints or for some new thinking. Northern Ireland is by no means the only ethical/political problem where the underlying issues are in part to do with self-respect, self-awareness and respect for the other. Finding ways to express these notions can in itself help to achieve the preconditions for a resolution. In the particular context of Northern Ireland, coherent explana-tions of nationalism and unionism were necessary for self-esteem before parity of esteem could realistically be addressed.

In Northern Ireland, not only was progress bedevilled by all of the dubious debating ploys outlined in the first chapter (you would say that, wouldn't you, because you're a Catholic or you're a Brit; if you give in to 'them' on this, they will end up taking 'that') but a variation on the theme of argument by definition made the development of more constructive vocabulary all the more difficult. This was the tactic of tainting words with the guilt of association. If 'they' used the phrase first, it must be a trick. In an acute form, this accusation can work even if it is mistaken so that one team or another can come to resent a phrase because someone has told them that the other team used it first, although in truth it was their own team who invented it. In this Humpty Dumpty world, even one of the most able and positive of politicians, Sir Reg Empey, almost torpedoed a vital concept, the obscure history of which it is therefore worth considering.

Parity of esteem is 'not only politically expedient – it is theologically correct . . . a natural consequence of a biblical insight', according to the Methodist minister, the late Revd Eric Gallagher, one of the great peacemakers of Northern Ireland. The phrase 'parity of esteem' is usually traced to Sir Patrick Mayhew's December 1992 seminal speech in Coleraine. His use of the expression in turn owed something to the Second Report of the Standing Advisory Commission on Human Rights (SACHR) on religious and political discrimination and equality of opportunity in Northern Ireland, which spoke of equality of esteem some two years earlier in June 1990. The Ulster Unionist politician, Councillor (now Sir) Reg Empey, wrote a critical article in the *Belfast Telegraph* on 17 August 1994 attacking parity of esteem, attributing it to the New Ireland Forum of 1984. This article at least caused me to refresh my memory of the Forum's Report but I could not find the expression in that document. So I set off on a paperchase. The first reference to parity of esteem in this Northern Irish context which my personal research yielded was in the 1975 Report of the Constitutional Convention, where it was invoked by the Rt Hon. David Bleakley of the Northern Ireland Labour Party in the context of North–South relations. I would welcome news of earlier sightings.

It may be that some of the politicians in Northern Ireland have been around so long that they almost forget what they or others have said, only to retrieve from their subconscious a variation on a half-remembered theme. The normally reliable and constructive Reg Empey, for example, was a member of that Constitutional Convention in 1975 where the phrase was mentioned, but two decades later he had come to think that the phrase 'first surfaced in the report of the New Ireland Forum in 1984, chapter 8. The terms were used in the chapter which dealt with joint authority. This tells us . . .' Since the phrase is not there, however, it tells us that his memory was playing tricks. Far from parity of esteem being a nationalist plot, the earlier surfacing in the convention a decade earlier than Reg Empey remembered was very much in the Unionist context of suggesting that the Republic should esteem the North by moderating its territorial claim, whereupon the North could esteem the South by playing cross-border neighbours. Another member of that Constitutional Convention who personally used the phrase 'parity of esteem' in its deliberations in 1975 was Oliver Napier of the Alliance Party. Like David Bleakley, he went on to chair the Standing Advisory Commission on Human Rights which duly invoked 'equality of esteem' in 1990. Incidentally, David Trimble and Reg Empey were both members of the Constitutional Convention for the Vanguard Party. By the mid 1990s, Reg Empey and Dermot Nesbit were, with myself, members of the Standing Advisory Commission on Human Rights. In the subsequent talks, Empey and Nesbit were two of David Trimble's most trustworthy and able lieutenants. Grappling with concepts, as well as cases, which you find uneasy is part of the process of peacemaking and peace-building.

Some Republicans were equally sceptical of the concept of parity of esteem, believing it to be an attempt to impose a purely internal settlement. Together with those who thought that it spelled disaster for the Union, that might seem to have presented an insuperable barrier to the concept flourishing. Although the rhetoric might change, however, this idea is at the centre of uneasy ways forward. Indeed, this was seen prophetically in the 1975 context in which it was used by the Northern Ireland Labour Party (NILP), in the Report of the Convention at paragraph 147:

> The NILP recognises the need to look beyond the frontiers of Northern Ireland and to develop good relations with neighbours. But it stresses the need for realism; there is a price to be paid for North/South co-operation. In particular, the Irish Republic must not lay claim to the territory of the North and must acknowledge the right of the Ulster people to determine their own destiny. Equally, the North would recognise the value of co-operation, between equals, with the South. Such parity of esteem is essential for progress, but once it is established Irish people should find no difficulty in working out agreed forms of contact, beneficial to both parts of the island.

Whatever its provenance, parity of esteem is a concept whose value to ethical debate is not ruled out by ambiguities in the phrase or by differences in how it is interpreted. There are many concepts on which we can unite but of which we have different conceptions. We are all in favour of justice, for instance, but we believe it points to different answers to specific questions. Thus, while the cynics will say that parity of esteem is a phrase which bridges all kinds of political divides simply because it is meaningless, another more positive way of putting almost the same point is to say that it is helpful because it is open to many different interpretations. Not surprisingly, then, the expression was criticised as confused, some saying it favoured nationalists with others believing it was window-dressing for an internal, Unionist approach. Nonetheless, the ideas behind the phrase began to acquire a popular currency.

Those elected to the 1975 Constitutional Convention used the term parity because there was then much discussion of parity in relation to financial matters, but it may be that the religious origins of the word (good dictionaries will point towards the sense of parity among the apostles) had a role to play. Certainly, esteem is a word which can be traced back considerably further than the New Ireland Forum, at least to the prophet Isaiah. Esteem is the opposite of contempt. Many Republicans and loyalists seem to value respect, at least from within what they see as their respective broad families of nationalism and unionism but also from those who purport to exercise authority over them. This is not at all surprising or undesirable. On the other hand, it is not at all surprising that it is difficult for those people, often themselves vulnerable and fearful of change, in the 'mainstream' to show respect to those who have seemed to condone the use of violence to intimidate them.

To respect someone is not to agree with them, nor to condone their aims nor the means they employ or themselves condone. Likewise, to tolerate someone or some way of life is not to endorse it. Indeed, if one agrees with X, one is not tolerating X. Toleration only comes into play when one finds X repugnant but decides nonetheless not to use any means at one's disposal (such as prohibition by the criminal law) to curtail X. If tolerance is the essence of liberalism, then it is not the self-professed liberals (for whom 'anything goes') who are the tolerant ones. Since they do not find X (whatever X might be) objectionable, they never have the chance to exercise the virtue of tolerance. It is those who initially are appalled by X who might choose tolerance. (For X, please substitute a variety of phenomena from homosexuality to racism, from nationalism to unionism.) Respect is an attitude which goes further than tolerance, although tolerance is itself further than many of us are willing to go, and again it does not depend on agreement with the X factor.

What respect or esteem needs, in my opinion, is some religious or secular underpinning which prizes people in all their diversity. A secular humanism could perhaps provide such an approach but for many people in Northern Ireland there is a religious imperative which was again expressed and exemplified by Eric Gallagher:

> The quest for social justice is the logical conclusion and implication of loving my neighbour as myself. That means that I will not only be party to but that I will positively advocate my neighbour enjoying the same rights and privileges that I do, that I will work to see social and political structures which give him and her that entitlement. That will entail a flexibility and accommodation on and from both sides that knows nothing of an Ourselves Alone or Not an Inch philosophy.

Once we have imagined a positive case for nationalism and one for unionism, parity of esteem begins to come into its own as a bridge between the two. For inherent in the versions of each of the positions – nationalism and unionism – which I have imagined is a recognition that progress depends upon respecting and cherishing diversity. There is a natural temptation to rush towards a particular point of detail and say that diversity and parity of esteem mean that some demand must be met, for example in relation to policing. Yet it matters how we argue about parity of esteem, not merely what we ultimately decide. Indeed, unless we approach the discussion in the right spirit, it will be self-defeating. A shouting match about mutual esteem seems a contradiction in terms. Moreover, we must focus on the right level of abstraction if we are to apply the concept helpfully. There is a danger in going straight to using the concept to demand from others specific concessions about policing or decommissioning without having shown a willingness to show the underlying respect which the concept presupposes.

My argument so far in relation to the Northern Irish peace process is intended to bring us to the following propositions. Peacemaking can be ethically uneasy, but the alternative of war or armed conflict gives a moral imperative to making uneasy choices. This is more complex than the admittedly difficult cases of, for instance, medical ethics, principally because so many people are involved, there is so much history, there are so many nuances of position, individuals can exercise far less control than they can as patients, proxies for patients or doctors, and leaders are in the ethically uneasy position of edging those who elect them towards new positions. The peace process has something in common with the issue of releasing child killers and indeed changing attitudes to prisoners facilitated later stages of the peace process. Uneasy choices in the cause of peace require moral imagination. A proper understanding of contempt, respect and esteem is not easy. In all this, language is important, as are symbols.

Given these complexities, developments in Northern Ireland will serve not only as important in their own right but also as a surrogate for other dilemmas of uneasy politics, uneasy economics and uneasy community relations. Is it right to join the euro or to send troops to Macedonia, to subsidise the farming industry, to promise not to raise taxes when public services such as health and education seem under-resourced, to turn away refugees or asylum seekers, to allow racial tensions to spill over into violence? All these questions can be addressed in the light of an ethical framework for judging whether developments in Northern Ireland are fair.

The way I favour of testing our intuitions in such uneasy cases is to play a variation on a game devised by the doyen of American political philosophers in the post-war era, John Rawls. He talked of imagining what we would decide under a 'veil of ignorance' in the 'original position' in four phases of the development of a just society. In the first, the principles of justice are formulated. Then there is a constitutional convention to apply those principles to the task of establishing a system of government. Third, laws are promulgated. Fourth, they are applied. If the Downing Street Declaration is to be regarded as the result of the first phase in relation to Northern Ireland and the Good Friday Agreement is the second, then arguing that the principles in these documents are abstract and do not reveal the answers to the next stages is to miss the point of theory which is necessarily abstract. Theory tries to express complex truths in simple commanding principles. In the words of Rawls, 'The deeper the conflict, the higher the level of abstraction to which we must ascend to get a clear and uncluttered view of its roots.'

In a book about uneasy ethics, it will come as no surprise that I am going to vary Rawls' theme by constructing what I will call an unoriginal position. Imagine what you would choose as the principles to guide Northern Irish society, deciding in your own self-interest but without knowing what your self is, whether you are Catholic or Protestant, nationalist or loyalist, British or Irish, male or female, unemployed or rich, police or policed, victim or perpetrator of violence, bereaved or convicted prisoner. A difference between Rawls' original position and my unoriginal position is that his veil of ignorance prevents the parties from knowing which society they will be in, of which generation, or anything about the specifics of the opportunities and problems faced by people, or of the probabilities of being rich or poor, whereas those in the unoriginal Northern Irish position need to know all the significant interpretations of the conflict and the support they command and likely reactions to any initiative.

This difference is justified because a standard criticism of the Rawlsian original position is that it has a built-in bias in favour of the risk-averse, whereas a peace process needs to take risks. Instead of Rawls' term of a veil of ignorance, a better metaphor for this unoriginal position is a device which enables us to see more clearly, from a variety of vantage points, as with the adjustment to the Hubble telescope in space a few years ago or a remote control unit enabling us to switch channels. Instead of Rawls' linear sequence, which seems to take us from Downing Street to Good Friday to Patten and the Policing Act in the third stage and then to policing 'on the ground' if we ever reach the fourth stage, I prefer to consider these stages in cyclical mode, contributing to a multidimensional reflective equilibrium. On my approach, we test not merely our principles against the unoriginal position and vice versa, we test our principles of justice against the constitutional structures, the law and the practice. In the world of Northern Ireland, we run through the sequence in particular areas of public life, such as fair employment or policing or decommissioning and report back to the first stage before we can make a grand run through the sequence across the totality of relationships.

What we are doing in all this, to translate from the secular Rawls to the language of the Catholic tradition, is exploring what it is to build up the common good. It is not surprising to me, therefore, that when the Northern Irish Catholic bishops, in their August 2001 statement, welcomed the two governments' implementation plan for reforming the police service in line with the Patten Report's proposals, the brief exposition of their position invoked the key phrases of justice and the common good several times. In the document's sixteen sentences, the phrase 'the common good' appears five times. The flavour is given by this example:

The challenge of the Gospel, reflected in Catholic social teaching, places the legitimate and urgent pursuit of justice within the broader context of concern for the common good and the task of reconciliation. We have continually held that the creation of a Police Service that is 'professional, effective and efficient, fair and impartial and free from partisan political control' is an essential part of the common good and a just demand in any society . . .

Of course, one can disagree with the bishops' judgement as to whether the latest implementation plan measures up to the standard of the common good, or the unoriginal position, or any other touchstone. Sinn Fein, for example, has done just that whereas the SDLP and the Irish government have endorsed the revised proposals. These are disagreements on the *application* of the principles which ought to govern fair policing, but at least a consensus seems to have been reached on the higher level of abstraction, the values put in quotation marks by the bishops, which are taken from the Patten Report: 'professional, effective and efficient, fair and impartial and free from partisan political control'. We do seem to have come a long way since those days, only a decade ago, when Sinn Fein were subject to broadcasting restrictions, for now there is not only a Sinn Fein Minister for Education in a six-county administration but the only barrier to a Sinn Fein member of the legislative assembly sitting on the Policing Board is Sinn Fein's own reluctance to accept the revised implementation plan.

It is perhaps not surprising that this makes many Unionists and loyalists, together with many police officers, distinctly uneasy. Far from the oft-quoted line that 'peace comes droppin' slow', peace has come far too fast, from this perspective, so that the real point of tension is not the detail of more than one hundred recommendations. The deeper issue is whether those who have only recently turned to constitutional politics and who have still not persuaded their paramilitary wing to decommission their weapons, should be entitled to participate in democratic decision-making. This provides a good example of where a counter-intuitive religious ethic can prove its worth in contrast to secular rationality. The parable of the labourers who came late to the vineyard nonetheless being worthy of their hire and of equal pay was something which I could not fathom before my time in Northern Ireland. The parable, however, can be read as making sense of this uneasy case. While others resent the latecomers to the democratic fold, generosity of spirit demands that they now be eligible for their full entitlement. The Gospel according to St Matthew (ch. 20) puts it thus:

Now the kingdom of heaven is like a landowner going out at daybreak to hire workers for his vineyard. He made an agreement with the workers for one denarius a day and sent them to his vineyard. Going out at about the third hour he saw others standing idle in the market place and said to them, 'You go to my vineyard too and I will give you a fair wage.' So they went. At about the sixth hour and again at about the ninth hour, he went out and did the same. Then at about the eleventh hour he went out and found more men standing round and he said to them, 'Why have you been standing here idle all day?' 'Because no one has hired us,' they answered. He said to them, 'You go into my vineyard too.' In the evening, the owner of the vineyard said to his bailiff, 'Call the workers and pay them their wages, starting with the last arrivals and ending with the first.' So those who were hired at about the eleventh hour came forward and received one denarius each. When the first came, they expected to get more, but they too received one denarius each. They took it, but grumbled at the landowner. 'The men who came last,' they said, 'have done only one hour and you have treated them the same as us, though we have done a heavy day's work in all the heat.' He answered one of them and said, 'My friend, I am not being unjust to you; did we not agree on one denarius? Take your earnings and go. I choose to pay the last-comer as much as I pay you. Have I no right to do what I like with my own? Why be envious because I am generous? Thus the last will be first, and the first, last.'

Much of the posturing over decommissioning and policing can be seen as those who regard themselves as having laboured all day in the vineyard of democracy grumbling about generosity being shown to those who only came at the eleventh hour. They could respond, however, by pointing out that it was only at the eleventh hour that they were called, that their ability to make a contribution was recognised. Or they can look at the parable the other way round and say that they have been labouring in a different vineyard and it is only at the eleventh hour that others have come to join them. The parable teaches us a lesson which is difficult to explain in secular terms. It clearly comes, however, from the same flow of ethical thought which Cardinal Daly offered at the beginning of this chapter where he spoke of the impact of compassion in our treatment of prisoners.

Generosity is uneasy. It can be too easily underestimated and devalued. For example, in the run-up to the Downing Street Declaration, it was too easy for some to tell others to 'go the extra mile' for peace. After a particular phone call from Bill Clinton to John Major, some sections of the media seemed to think that this injunction, said to have been offered by the President to the Prime Minister, was Bill Clinton's own turn of phrase. For a jogging president, an extra mile does not seem so far to go. Those with a firmer knowledge of the Scriptures will recall that somebody else had expressed a similar, but significantly more onerous, idea almost two thousand years ago. Jesus's injunction was to go two miles with the person who asks you to accompany them for one mile. That is indeed an extra mile but it could also be put in the form of go twice as far as you are asked. I followed this expression through the media prelude to the Downing Street Declaration with some particular interest because I had referred to the phrase four years previously at an inter-Church conference in Northern Ireland where I had quoted Hans Küng:

> The Christian message [says] that renouncing rights without expecting anything in return is not necessarily a disgrace: that Christians at least should not despise a politician who is prepared to make concessions . . . a renunciation of rights without recompense can constitute the great freedom of the Christian: he is going two miles with someone who has forced him to go one. The Christian who lives in this freedom becomes critical of all those – on whatever side – who constantly protest verbally their peaceful intentions, who are always proffering friendship and reconciliation for the sake of propaganda, but in practical politics are not prepared for the sake of peace occasionally to give up obsolete legal positions, to take a first step towards the other person, publicly to struggle for friendship with other[s . . .], even when this is unpopular.

The spirit of this approach is incorporated into my accounts of nationalism and unionism. Incidentally, the direction in which you are heading makes a difference as well as how far you go. The Report of the Constitutional Convention of 1975 reveals that Robert (now Sir Robert) Cooper, then of the Alliance Party and subsequently of the Fair Employment Commission, took issue with the vacuous use of the expression that Northern Ireland was once again at a crossroads. He observed that the task was much more difficult than that suggested by this phrase. The crossroads had been reached many years previously and the wrong turn taken. The task now was to retrace our steps, make up lost ground and move forward in the right direction.

How we have come to this point in the road, to even the limited, halting progress which Northern Ireland has witnessed in the last decade, is worth more reflection. The thrust of my argument so far has been to emphasise that we all have responsibilities and that we can all generate hope through our words and actions. Nonetheless, those in positions of political authority have extra opportunities and challenges of leadership. Some courageous leadership has been shown on all sides. Peter Brooke, for example, praised Gerry Adams's courage and the risks taken by John Hume and David Trimble for peace led to the Nobel Peace Prize. Irish and British leaders such as Albert Reynolds and John Major also deserve great credit for their boldness and imagination. Although some of the leading politicians have featured in Northern Ireland throughout the Troubles, such as John Hume and Ian Paisley, it is plausible to argue that a newer wave of leading public figures may have had something to do with the recent progress, either directly or symbolically. I am thinking of the contributions made by Tony Blair, Bill Clinton and David Trimble in their detailed involvement, together with the symbolism as head of state of the election of Mary McAleese as President of Ireland.

Blair, Clinton, Trimble and McAleese have one factor in common which may explain the Third Way, beloved of modern political leaders. It is not to do with presentation or policy, style or substance. It is, rather, a mode of thought. Indeed, it may be so much a part of their way of approaching issues that the politicians themselves do not realise its significance. The link is that the political thinking of all four is moulded, whether they like it or not and Tony Blair claims that he did not, by their university experiences as students of the law. Their approach to uneasy politics or ethics is rooted in university law tutorials. Three of the four are married to former law students. All have friends in the law and in legal education. Two of them became law teachers at university and David Trimble taught Mary McAleese. Tony Blair is not only married to Cherie Booth QC but is the son of a law lecturer and is surrounded in government by other former law students whose survival and/or promotion sometimes baffles observers, for instance Jack Straw, Stephen Byers, Geoff Hoon, Lord Irvine and Lord Falconer QC.

Of course, other politicians such as Lord Hailsham and Margaret Thatcher have qualified at the Bar, but neither of them studied law at university. They studied classics and chemistry respectively. What is most relevant to my argument is not the practice of law but the cast of mind formed by academic seminars, tutorials and moot courts. This links Clinton, Blair, Trimble and McAleese. They are all veterans of the uneasy case, the hypothetical, the link to crime and punishment, the testing by reference to theories of justice, the application of principles to facts across the whole gamut of human activity.

In other words, Tony Blair and other 'Third Way' politicians think in the way that a law student is encouraged to think – committed to assessing issues on their particular merits by a process of formulating and weighing reasons across a range of seemingly unconnected topics, rather than striving for some ideologically determined set of coherent outcomes. This is not to say that Blair always puts the arguments in this form in his public performances. He famously uses the spin of a politician and the public has expectations of old politics which include hearing some appropriately ideological rhetoric. Nor does the Prime Minister always adopt the policy which this law student reasoning process yields. He, like David Trimble, has to judge how far he can take his party and voters. My point is, however, that the instinctive mode of reasoning of these Third Way politicians is that of a proto-judge, which can be explained in large part as arising from this common factor many world leaders share of absorbing undergraduate legal reasoning.

There are ironies here. First, it is difficult for many observers to move beyond the assumption that 'thinking like a lawyer' is a bad thing precisely because it has acquired a bad name by linkage with a certain kind of lawyer-politician's approach. Second, politicians are thinking like lawyers just as constitutional change is bringing law to the centre stage in this country so that the key shapers of our society in this century will be leading judges, among whom will quite rightly be numbered, I predict, Cherie Booth QC, whose elevation to the Bench is delayed but not ultimately precluded by Tony Blair's current role.

Bill Clinton's legalistic playing with words during the Monica Lewinsky saga, his verbal ingenuity devoid of any moral anchor, is a classic example of what cynics expect from lawyers. There is, however, a more noble line of legal discourse, exemplified by the courageous US Supreme Court in the 1950s which stood up for the rights of minorities against the prejudices of the majority in a way no US politician, subject to re-election by that majority, had ever done. So there are at least two visions of legal thinking – the one regarding it as slippery wordplay, the other as a rational, serious attempt to subject complex problems to a process of controlled argument. In neither case, however, is it driven simply by an ideology, as we have been led to believe that politics should be.

The assumption behind right-wing and left-wing politics could be described thus: left-wingers have a pattern theory of justice, believing that the cake should be sliced fairly and that the role of the state is to ensure such a division or pattern of distribution; right-wingers, however, have a historical view of justice that allows those who have acquired the cake to keep it on the grounds that it would be unfair, tyrannical and unworkable for the state to attempt to create and hold fast to a pattern by taking some of one person's share and giving it to another person. When Tony Blair and Mary McAleese were undergraduates on either side of the Irish Sea, the American philosophers Rawls and Nozick were writing along these lines, the former arguing for a pattern, the latter for freedom from the attempted imposition of a pattern.

This is thought to be the stuff of politics – lawyers in the UK have traditionally only tinkered at the edges of these great debates. Law students and commentators from outside the law often suppose that judges decide cases in a certain way because of background prejudice and (warped) theories of justice. As rich, white, male, middle-class, middle-aged, public-school, Oxbridge types (just like Tony Blair), judges are assumed to be right wing (just like . . .?). All such stereotyping shows, however, is that students or commentators who think this way would not themselves, at that stage, make good judges. Judges disagree with one another on major cases (that is why the disputes get to the appellate courts and have split decisions, such as Law Lords 3–2 in the appeal by the Home Secretary against the decision on the tariff for Venables and Thompson), even if they share the same background. Tony Benn is even more privileged than Tony Blair but they do not have identical political views. Even if they did, it does not necessarily follow that their political views would triumph in a legal setting.

Rather, the history of law on both sides of the Atlantic shows that judges are more capable than most of us can claim to be of putting to one side their own prejudices, of changing their minds, of evaluating cases on their merits, of being driven by a commitment to the best argument rather than to a previously determined ideological outcome. As law students, Blair, Clinton, Trimble and McAleese would have been encouraged to think through the arguments which advocates would put on each side of an argument. Then they would imagine the best answer that a judge could discern in the light of such advocacy. Having looked at a hypothetical problem in contract one day, it would be tort the next. Ideological consistency between the tutorials would not have been prized by their tutors. Indeed, the teachers could not have known, and would not have cared, what was being said by their students across the full sweep of topics. What would have counted would have been the quality of analysis, given the cut and thrust of argument on the particular question of the moment. Law tutors are, however, wont to put their pupils on the spot and expect not only an imaginative but a decisive way forward. This education has some claim to be a good training for government.

In my experience, first-year students tend to reveal their ethical intuitions when asked to make such a snap decision. A contract case may revolve around inequality of bargaining power or whether a promise is always to be honoured. A medical law case may concern euthanasia or abortion. The moral hunch which is first voiced is then questioned and the student becomes adept at defending the answer which first came into their mind. When pinned into seemingly having to accept bizarre answers to absurd hypotheticals in order to maintain consistency with this initial premise, the student may buckle or may find a creative third way between their first thought and the tutor's or a fellow student's withering criticism.

Applied to politics, this is the Third Way. It does not easily conform to a right/left/middle categorisation because it is not driven by an overarching vision of preferred outcomes. On the other hand, it is not simply immoral or amoral pragmatism. There may well be a cluster of values underlying the thinking of the law student, the judge or the politician. Tony Blair, for example, seems to have an Aristotelian/natural law affinity with virtue theory in which various values, rather than one overarching idea such as utility, underpin morality. There will certainly be judgement calls on the consequences of alternative policies which each will have to make. Furthermore, there are questions about when it is right for which institution of government to proceed in a 'Third Way', given the increasing complexity of the constitution.

Indeed, this is the most significant feature of the new or forthcoming order. The constitution is being transformed so that arguments can be evaluated by those best placed to weigh them in the balance – devolved assemblies in Northern Ireland, Scotland and Wales, regional agencies in England, arguments about a reformed House of Lords and a new electoral mechanism for the Commons, freedom of information for all and a Human Rights Act to reserve fundamental concerns to the court of reason.

This is not to claim that Tony Blair or anyone else will always choose the ethical or rational way forward according to the balance of arguments. Of course, he will sometimes allow sentiment or self-interest or party interest or tradition to outweigh the merits. Watch, for example, the unfolding story of electoral (non-)reform. Nor is it my claim that he *presents* his ways forward in this manner. He will for a time still dress them up in the rhetoric of old politics and he will always spin them to suit his party's re-election prospects. As the media and the electorate become more sophisticated, however, all these political institutions will behave more like courts, weighing arguments on the merits. This is not necessarily a good or bad development. This model is not really 'like a lawyer' so much as really 'like a law student'. Indeed, this is what one would expect from a quartet of political leaders who have not plied the trade of legal practitioner for any length of time so much as moved between the worlds of legal education and politics.

Of course, even if they are not rich legal practitioners themselves, they know people who are. The law student mentality and circle may explain the transatlantic phenomena of Tony's Cronies and the Friends of Bill and Hillary. Law students who proceed to live and work with other lawyers find it second nature to have a lifestyle of relative privilege while representing minority/disadvantaged interests. This is perhaps why Tony Blair seems at ease with a Bernie Ecclestone or a Rupert Murdoch and bemused by allegations that this hobnobbing with the rich and powerful distances him from the people who voted for Labour. Tony Blair and his 'cronies' such as Lord Falconer QC, the pal he ennobled and brought into government first as Solicitor-General, then as everything, and Lord Irvine, the Lord Chancellor, move in very rich circles not through inherited wealth but through having been paid a fortune for their professional ability to argue.

It may be that this minor insight into the Blairite Third Way can help to identify why 'stars' with a background in the study of law, from Jack Straw to Stephen Byers, rise in the present government – or to explain how some 'stars' have held their place in the firmament for so long. It may be that it simply confirms cynical assumptions that law students are a self-selecting group of intensely ambitious people whose political ascendancy is not influenced by their choice of undergraduate study.

It is not only easy to accuse politicians of self-interest, it is easy to accuse them of inconsistency. As I have observed throughout this book, however, this is itself a problematic argument. It is not to lawyers 'inconsistent' that they represent different interests in different cases or argue 'inconsistent' points in different circumstances. This is not 'ignoring principle' in favour of unfettered pragmatism. Rather, it is adopting a particular principle, that of participating in a forensic process which edges society forward by considering the best possible arguments for alternative stances before adjudicating so that what is perceived to be the better argument wins. As we move more towards a court-based constitution, then whether or not this is the Third Way, it will soon be our way.

If this explanation of legal reasoning in hypothetical cases is the model for *process* in the Third Way, the key word for me in the *substance* of political thought and action ought to be the virtue of 'hope'. The difference between hope and a feeling of hopelessness is the deepest difference between the 'haves' and the 'have-nots', the included and the excluded, the privileged and the disadvantaged. Hope is what the socially excluded are excluded from, which is why the Catholic Church and others are so concerned to include the marginalised as part of the common good.

In this book, I am trying to stimulate readers' reflections on uneasy cases in a number of ways, from exploring hypotheticals and pointing out flaws in debating ploys to drawing on Church statements and testing intuitions by imagining what we would regard as fair in the unoriginal position. My own conclusions on the uneasy cases of these first three chapters could be put thus: offering hope to at least one of the Siamese twins, to the killers of James Bulger, to the people of Northern Ireland, are the options which appeal intuitively to me. I test those hunches by reference to what I regard as a humane and wise tradition. I try to listen to, and understand, counter-arguments, even if I do not always acknowledge them at the time. When I have not committed myself, and sometimes even when I have, I revise my opinions in the light of this process. If asked, I offer advice behind the scenes and sometimes can still be persuaded to do so in public. I enjoy attempts by students to wrestle with these dilemmas and I try to do my bit when the opportunity presents itself in terms of public service. Balancing these roles with family life and responsibilities at work can be uneasy.

In all this, I have some sympathy for a fictional character who was lambasted by one of my predecessors as Professor of Jurisprudence at Queen's University, Belfast, Professor William Twining. He castigated C.P. Snow for creating in Lewis Eliot an academic lawyer who never seemed to teach or research. Having failed at the Bar, Eliot had been found a sinecure as a Cambridge law don and, says Twining, 'There for most of the next ten novels he lives the life of a humane and cultivated participant-observer of academic, political and social life. During the whole sequence there is scarcely a mention of his opening a book, entering a library or putting pen to paper.' Yet there are many worse fates than being described as 'a humane and cultivated participant-observer of academic, political and social life'. For even his arch-critic, Twining, is conceding that Eliot is a socially responsible, or at least a socially engaged, law don. High technology now spares many a dedicated online teacher and researcher from some of those physical tasks. More importantly, fascinating as a novel would be about the minutiae of entering libraries or putting pen to paper in the days before our desktop computers connected us to the legal world, there is ample evidence in Snow's novels to indicate that he understands academia and that Lewis Eliot does work. It is just that Snow's understanding of academia is not Twining's and that Lewis Eliot's notion of work is not Twining's. For example, Snow sums up the dons in *The Sleep of Reason* through the observations of this former academic lawyer, Lewis Eliot, at one of the university court meetings. Once the sixth item on the agenda is reached, even an impatient chair cannot proceed swiftly for it is entitled 'Extension to Biology Building':

> The voices round me didn't sound as if they could have enough of it. The UGC! Architects! Appeals! Claims of other subjects! Master building plan! Emotions were heated, the voices might have been talking about love or the preservation of peace. Of all the academic meetings I had attended, at least half the talking time, and much more than half the expense of spirit, had been consumed in discussions of building. Whatever would they do when all the buildings were put up? The answer, I thought, though not that afternoon, was simple: they would pull some down and start again.

This passage has much in common with modern campus comedies such as Malcolm Bradbury's *Cuts*, several novels by David Lodge and Andrew Davies's television triumph *A Very Peculiar Practice*. Indeed, it has much in common also with my experience of everyday life in higher education as I have taken great delight in knocking down buildings and walls during eight years of fun at Liverpool Hope. C.P. Snow knew more about the academy than Twining seems to think. More seriously, as hinted at in the phrase 'preservation of peace', Lewis Eliot has a sense of perspective because his skills as an academic lawyer had been deployed in wartime and thereafter in *The Corridors of Power*, the title of one of the novels in this sequence and a title which, together with Snow's forty-year-old lecture on *The Two*

Cultures, is a phrase which, for all his alleged weaknesses as a writer, C.P. Snow has bequeathed to us. Eliot sums up the social responsibility of lawyers by serving in the war and thereafter not in an ivory tower but in the corridors of power.

The term 'third way' struck a chord with my recollection of the approach of my law tutors, especially Joseph Raz. I remember commenting at the time to my fellow tutees (one of whom is now a QC and one a partner in a leading firm of solicitors in the City) that every week's work seemed to reveal two lines of thought, two analyses of the case law or the concept for discussion, but that in the tutorial our teachers would always produce a third way through the reading. Anticipating what that might be became the way to undertake the week's work and that is how the craft is handed on from one generation to the next. Contrary to popular belief that lawyers are boring and mechanical, this endless ability to find a third way forward is a working out of the creativity which is central to our work and on which Professor Ken Robinson has written so inspiringly. Given the opportunity, we can transfer these skills to our working lives beyond law or, for that matter, politics. In true C.P. Snow fashion, for example, I have tried to find a third way around a number of property developments during my six years as the head of an academic institution.

We have opened, for instance, a second campus for the creative arts in Everton, a disadvantaged part of the city of Liverpool. Our £17 million project has been based around the St Francis Xavier church and the old school building next to it. This site in Everton was the exact scene of a famous riot in 1901 which led to a leading case on freedom of expression and assembly, *Wise* v. *Dunning*, in which Pastor Wise was represented by F.E. Smith, later Lord Birkenhead, the first Lord Chancellor to run into difficulties over expensive wallpaper. Gerard Manley Hopkins, the poet and Jesuit priest, had served as a curate in the parish in the 1880s. Pastor Wise was denouncing the role of the Jesuits outside St Francis Xavier church and then in the city centre. This case still has a relevance for the Parades Commission, Drumcree and associated issues in Northern Ireland. One hundred years on, the scene of the *Wise* v. *Dunning* saga had become run-down, but creative ways forward have been found to bring new hope to a community no longer divided by religion yet hitherto deprived of access to higher education. What does it profit a community to have no disturbances of the peace if there is no opportunity or aspiration for meaningful self-expression? Hope is an ecumenical foundation and our re-establishment in the midst of social exclusion is a small marker of Liverpool's progress in the twentieth century from sectarianism to ecumenism. Our origins in the centre of Liverpool, incidentally, date from the middle of the nineteenth century when the Sisters of Notre Dame established a teacher training college for women opposite the poorhouse (where the Catholic cathedral now stands) so that the Irish refugees who fled from the famine might have the hope of education for their children.

This autobiographical excursus was intended to bring us full circle from reflecting on the ways in which any individual can try to shape their language and thinking about a conflict to the possibility that it might influence others and thereby perhaps create space for more exalted public figures to find a dramatic way forward. This in turn was my reason for reflecting on why it is that in confronting an uneasy ethical dilemma we can sometimes reach for a third way. Noticing that so many of the more significant figures shared a cast of mind also shaped by tutorial discussion of hypotheticals, I have begun to offer an explanation of the Third Way in politics. Before returning with this analysis to contemporary events in Northern Ireland, and in later chapters revisiting the Third Way, there are two further detours to note.

The first is to emphasise that I am not saying that only jurisprudence tutorials prepare 'ordinary' citizens or extraordinary politicians for resolving uneasy cases. Other subjects have their own ways of training the mind and engaging us in ethical reasoning. Moreover, some of the leading figures in the Northern Irish peace process did not benefit from university education at all but have clearly brought their own intelligence to bear on the same problems with great insight. Equally, I might add that some of the great lawyers did not study jurisprudence at university or did not go to university at all.

The second is to pay tribute to the American leg of my own travels around uneasy cases, in particular to the book *Tragic Choices* by Guido Calabresi and Philip Bobbitt. They have a different target and they come from a different perspective in that their primary focus is on pan-society decisions, such as the allocation of scarce resources or of risks. Organ and blood donation would be an example of the former. The draft, conscription to the armed services, especially in the Vietnam era, was a prime example for them of allocating risks. Their methodology was more of an economic analysis, exposing the choices which face a society. This is in contrast to my interest in how we as individuals either make decisions, in the Siamese twins' case, or contribute to the climate in which those with more power take decisions, in the cases of releasing child killers and promoting peace and justice in Northern Ireland. Nonetheless, there are obvious parallels and inspirations in their compelling account of how societies change their approaches over time. They think this is because values conflict and so society can only come to terms with itself by obscuring the choices or changing from time to time the selection methods by which the choices are made. Even those of us who would disagree with some of their premises or conclusions can learn from their commitment to exposing starkly the choices which confront us and to analysing rigorously the alternatives. Their last words are worth recording:

We do not live in the timeless days of a dog or sparrows. As we become aware of what we, as a society, are doing, we bear responsibility for those allocations that will be made as well as for what has been done in our names. If one understands more than before for having read this essay, one can still appreciate that tragic decisions need be made and are not the easier for the understanding.

We began our consideration of uneasy ethics by considering a host of hypotheticals raised in the case of Jodie and Mary, since when I have been claiming that the issues of what to do have become even more complex as we have explored the release of child killers and the progress of the Northern Irish peace process. In paying tribute to the support given to the last of these by Quakers from within and beyond Northern Ireland (especially the support offered to Initiative '92 by the great Quaker charities), it is worth noting nonetheless the Oxford philosopher Stuart Hampshire's marvellous contrast of innocence and experience, which takes Quaker and Catholic approaches as opposites:

> Consider an early Quaker meeting house with freshly whitewashed walls, rather worn and polished benches and handrails, and no pictures or representations of any kind, no altar, no decoration, no centre to the room and no raised dais, no designated spaces for rituals and sacraments. As soon as you open the heavy oak door and step inside, you are aware of stillness, purity of outline, and cleanness, of the absence of distractions and encumbrances, of the invitation to quiet reflection . . .
>
> It is easy to see why men and women who met here would be inclined to turn away from moral complexities and from ambiguous situations, and why they would become pacifists and conscientious objectors. Their conception of the good was a vision of simplicity, whiteness, straightness, uprightness, cleanness, of sweeping away anything contaminated or corrupted or squalid . . .
>
> The opposed conception of the good, associated with experience, can be illustrated by . . . the corridors, ceremonial rooms and chapels of the Vatican, a storehouse of works of art and monuments from the Church's often turbulent history . . . The Church has lived through innumerable wars, periods of exile, negotiations, unwanted compromises, embarrassing alliances, distressing manoeuvres and secret betrayals.

An irony in this beautifully drawn, insightful contrast is that Catholicism is often portrayed in contemporary Britain as being simplistic on ethical issues. To some extent, this is because the media tend to focus on sexual ethics, partly because the media tend to identify Catholicism with moral majority campaigning groups rather than the more sophisticated analysis of

123

bishops and partly because the Church's teaching is simple and clear-cut on some of these issues. I used the term 'contemporary Britain' deliberately because contemporary Northern Ireland presents a different picture. The media tend to portray groups there much more in Stuart Hampshire's terms so that the Catholic Church is seen to be operating with moral complexities and ambiguities, compromising in embarrassing company, whereas the Protestant community is portrayed as seeing issues in black and white, if not always in the Quaker mode of pacifism. Both teams are seen as believing in certainties, but Protestants are perceived to read texts and contexts in straightforward ways while Catholics are thought to pursue subtexts with some worldly experience or cunning.

This can be dismissed as gross stereotyping, but one aspect of it which deserves attention is that in talking in this way we have slid easily from the nationalist/loyalist rhetoric of political positions to religious terminology of Catholic and Protestant. For years I argued unsuccessfully that the two governments and the major political parties were misguided in polarising communities by blurring these distinctions, reducing everything to two block votes of Protestant/loyalist and Catholic/nationalist. The powers that be prevailed, however, in their preference for establishing two teams rather than reflecting the shades of grey which arise from multiple identities. Even so, it is obvious that even an individual who is proud to be nationalist and Catholic or loyalist and Protestant may attach different weight to those aspects of their identity. Labelling underestimates the complexity of multiple identities within individuals and communities in Northern Ireland.

The beginning of Northern Ireland's 2001–2 school year brought a tragic but classic illustration of these points and of the wider issues raised by uneasy cases. Each morning, primary schoolgirls have been running the gauntlet of Protestant residents as they enter their primary school gates at Holy Cross, Ardoyne, in North Belfast. Vast numbers of police with riot shields, supported by the army, have been needed to protect the girls and those accompanying them. Even so there has been verbal abuse, spitting on the girls and violence against the security forces. The local Protestant residents know that this plays badly in the world's media but they see the issue in black-and-white terms, they believe that the schoolgirls are being used by Republicans to make a point and they are determined to make their stand. The normal Orange Order, loyalist, Protestant refrain of 'traditional route' does not seem to convince them, when applied to the schoolgirls' right to use the shortest route of the public highway to enter their school by the front gates.

It is impossible to understand the politics or ethics of this dispute without some sense of the wider history and context of the Troubles in Northern Ireland and of the halting progress of the peace process. Decommissioning or the details of the policing reforms are not, in themselves, the whole story. If we try to put the fundamental question as 'How should we behave towards one another?', those adults who seem to be directing bile or even a blast bomb at little children would wish to add riders, 'How should we behave towards one another when the other is trying to use children to make a political point?' We are back to the challenges posed by having to choose language and tone in order to frame the question. If some of the rhetoric of the first chapter is used, again we will meet claim and counter-claim. To the point that 'Surely we can agree that it is not in the best interests of children to be insulted by adults while on their way to school?' will come the riposte 'I would not use my children to make a political point when there is a safe, uncontested, alternative route to the school, but it is those parents who have the responsibility to look after the best interests of those children and they are the ones who are exposing their children to the consequences of their choices.' And so on and so on.

The Protestant protesters see the issue as clear-cut, that they are being intimidated by nationalists/Republicans/Catholics and that they have decided to take a stand. Access to the school should not be through what they see as their part of the area, past their houses. They know that the vast majority of those watching them via the media regard this as perverted reasoning. First, the schoolgirls themselves are not at fault. Second, their right to walk a traditional route is the classic cry of the Protestant community over its parades, for example at Drumcree. The marching season's controversies are over exactly the same issue in reverse, that Protestants demand the right to walk traditional routes even though those areas may now be inhabited by Catholics who feel the march is intimidatory. Third, even if both these points were wrong, the protesters would still not be justified in insulting and attacking either the schoolchildren or those who are escorting them, whether relatives or security forces.

Notwithstanding these obvious arguments against their course of action, the protesters seem mesmerised by their insistence on being in the right and they seem to be revelling in the fact that the world does not agree with them or sympathise with them. They have attracted attention to their cause but it is not seen as their plight. Meanwhile, the parents of the schoolgirls could take the safe, back route into school and save their daughters the trauma and risk of harm. Some see it in the crisp terms of a simple issue where they are in the right, but more see it as complex. Some parents are uneasy about what to do. On the one hand, the analysis above leads to the conclusion that their daughters have the right to go to school by the shortest route, through the front gates. On the other, the best interests of the children during their first week at school might be better served by a quiet arrival by the back gate. Then again, is that in their best longer-term interests, if they 'give in' to the protesters? Moreover, how will it be seen by harder-line parents and community or political activists? Will the families who took the easy route have an uneasy life because they will be tarred with the gibe that they did not stand up to be counted? As in our discussion of proxy decisions in medical ethics, it is easy for a parent to confuse their best interests with those of the child and those of the community. One analysis here might be that it is in my child's best interests to follow the back route but it is in my best interests to show solidarity and in the community's best interests for the 'other' community to be shown in the world's media as attacking the schoolchildren. This is not that different, however, from the dilemmas which have faced all parents throughout the Troubles as well as during the 'peace process'. This is the messy world of what Hampshire calls 'experience', where distressing actions may be taken and embarrassing compromises may be made. It is the world of unease. The Judaeo-Christian tradition has much to offer this world, ranging from the wisdom of proverbs, rabbinical stories and New Testament parables through to respect for unique individuals, solidarity with communities and pursuit of the common good of hope.

Within that broad band of ethical thinking, there are several noble lines, such as the Jewish emphasis on family, education, community and hope, and the Quaker commitment not only to pacificism but to peacemaking as illustrated by their charitable works and commitment to progress in Northern Ireland. While respecting those and other religious traditions, I have in this book focused on my own denominational background. Catholicism is too often treated by others, especially the secular media but sometimes also devout people of other denominations or faiths, as if it were illiberal, obsessed with sex and unprepared for shades of grey. In truth, it provides a rounded, coherent, challenging ethic. It will shortly be coming to a court near you, partly because the Human Rights Act inevitably means that submissions of the quality of the Archbishop of Westminster's will be needed in a range of cases in defence of the marginalised, partly because the Act requires judges to have particular regard to freedom of religion and partly because human rights reasoning needs the underpinning of a philosophy of the common good. Catholic approaches to the issues which we have been discussing (and which have not included sexual morality) need to be applied to what Hampshire calls 'moral complexities' and 'ambiguous situations'.

This tradition does accord primacy to authentic, well-informed conscience. This cannot be equated with accepting that anything goes, that truth is relative. Anything can be forgiven, if there is true repentance. It is our responsibility to work away at applying our philosophy to uneasy cases, to improve our skill and sensitivity in the art of judgement. In *Veritatis Splendor*, Pope John Paul II wrote that if the idea of a universal truth about the good, knowable by human reason, is lost, inevitably the notion of conscience also changes. Conscience is no longer considered in its prime reality as an act of a person's intelligence, the function of which is to apply the universal knowledge of the good in a specific situation and thus to express a judgement about the right conduct to be chosen here and now. Instead, there is a tendency to grant to the individual conscience the prerogative of independently determining the criteria of good and evil and then acting accordingly. Such an outlook is quite congenial to an individualist ethic, wherein each individual is faced with his own truth different from the truth of others.

In *Fides et Ratio*, the Pope proceeded to a call for action from philosophers, theologians and others in response to these insights. For philosophers, the message of this latest encyclical is that

it is undeniable that this time of rapid and complex change can leave especially the younger generation, to whom the future belongs and on whom it depends, with a sense that they have no valid points of reference. The need for a foundation for personal and communal life becomes all the more pressing at a time when we are faced with the patent inadequacy of perspectives in which the ephemeral is affirmed as a value and the possibility of discovering the real meaning of life is cast into doubt. This is why many people stumble through life to the very edge of the abyss without knowing where they are going.

Almost every week in Northern Ireland, we are said to be at the brink, staring into the abyss. A recent variation on the language of the slippery slope and of the abyss was a recent Secretary of State's condemnation of the Ardoyne protesters as taking the 'path to barbarism'. Whether or not we are on the brink, if we are to find where it is we stand, to arrive where we started and to know it for the first time, a starting point can be reflection on the cases which make us uneasy, so long as we approach them in the right spirit. This is explained later in *Fides et Ratio*, when theologians are urged by the Pope to remember some words of St Bonaventure, who invited readers to recognise the inadequacy of 'reading without repentance, knowledge without devotion, research without the impulse of wonder, prudence without the ability to surrender to joy, action divorced from religion, learning sundered from love, intelligence without humility, study unsustained by divine grace, thought without the wisdom inspired by God'.

My variation on that theme is to suggest that what Northern Ireland has seen during the peace-and-justice process at its best is a mixture of imagination, hope and unease. In a collection of essays on Christian socialism, Paul

Boateng MP, now a Westminster Cabinet minister, took as his inspiration the idea that St Augustine had said that Hope has two lovely daughters, Anger and Courage. Anger at injustice must be accompanied by the courage to make a difference. Such a combination, together with imagination in our language and vision, may allow unease, in Northern Ireland and beyond, to be accompanied by hope. Indeed, it is this sense of anger and courage, of unease and hope, which characterises the release of prisoners, with which this chapter began, and other challenging elements in the peace process. The anger can be directed at the prisoners, or at their crimes, or at those who led them, or at God or at other humans for the lost lives of their victims. Even at times when the peace process appears to have stalled, the courage of releasing those who committed serious crimes, and the courage of their victims' families, stands as an astonishing act of hope.

4

Ethics in a Spin:
A Byers' Market?

The fall from power of Stephen Byers, a minister at the cusp of the interaction between government and business, is an uneasy illustration of how trust can collapse in modern public life. Government ministers can come to be regarded, fairly or not, as dishonest. Business leaders can come to be regarded, fairly or not, as greedy. When those who are highly paid to run the railway business are seen, fairly or not, to put their bonuses ahead of passenger safety and when the minister responsible for transport is seen, fairly or not, to intervene incompetently and dishonestly, it might not seem surprising that public confidence collapses. Yet the Labour government's self-perception was that it came to power to restore public confidence in honest, sleazeless behaviour by politicians, that it was there to challenge corporate greed and that its strength was in its ability to shape perceptions by media 'spin'. Hubris may have overcome the government as it then lost its leading practitioner of sophisticated presentation, Peter Mandelson, twice, before Stephen Byers followed him in 2002 on to the backbenches.

The significance of this for uneasy ethics begins with the understanding that ethics or morality is about what is right or wrong, what ought to be done or ought not to be done, what is good or bad. In the previous chapters, concepts which contribute to the positive sides of those contrasts have been explored – equality, justice and mercy. On the negative side, we could simply point to opposites such as inequality or injustice, but these last two chapters take a different approach. In the final one, we will look at some of the worst behaviour imaginable and consider whether it can be understood and countered by recognising it as evil. In this chapter, the subject matter is a mass or mess of behaviour which is not as abhorrent but which still seems wrong or bad or disgraceful. Part of our unease may be because we have not analysed with sufficient rigour exactly what, if anything, is blameworthy in these actions by public officials and business executives. Greed is sometimes the accusation levelled at business and incompetence the claim against both ministers and some executives. Incompetence may be so culpable as to merit censure and greed can clearly be seen as a vice, but there are other aspects to people behaving badly in public office. Dishonesty and deception, for example, may be the precise sins which annoy us in a particular incident or sequence of events.

Baroness (Onora) O'Neill, in her 2002 Reith Lectures on 'A Question of Trust' claims that, 'Deception is not a minor or marginal moral failure. Deceivers do not treat others as moral equals; they exempt themselves from obligations that they rely on others to live up to.' She thinks that the drive towards transparency is misconceived since it is 'likely to encourage the evasions, hypocrisies and half-truths that we usually refer to as "political correctness" but which might more forthrightly be called either "self-censorship" or "deception"'. In some cases, we come to dis-trust a minister or public official or business executive. In some, we describe the minister as dis-graced. Understanding precisely what troubles us in the story of Stephen Byers will take us through an introduction to business ethics and the ethics of public life. While it is important to be exact in identifying what is claimed to be wrong in any such behaviour, an overall term can be used to cover the multitude of sins. In short-hand form, what we object to in some ministers and executives, as well as in one another in less public life, can be described as 'acting in bad faith' or acting, in a word, 'badly'.

Yet these phrases such as 'behaving badly' or 'acting in bad faith' are rarely considered. To some, they can be too mild for actions which are betrayals of private or public trust. To others, they can be too strong for actions which are negligent or incompetent rather than malicious. They need to be placed carefully on a spectrum. Moreover, we should apply the terms to a wide range of activity instead of assessing Mr Byers in isolation. Hence this chapter begins with some ministerial comparisons before broadening out to consider other sectors of the economy. Was the fiasco of the railways handled unusually badly when seen in such company as government or business calamities concerning party donations, the e-economy or foot-and-mouth?

In the 1997–2001 Labour government, Stephen Byers was a rising star as Minister for Schools, then a member of the Cabinet as the Chief Secretary to the Treasury and finally Secretary of State for Trade and Industry. After the general election in June 2001, he became Secretary of State for Transport. One stormy year later, at the end of May 2002, he resigned from the government with his credibility exhausted. As one of the Prime Minister's closest and most loyal lieutenants, this was an extraordinary turn of events, especially as his mistakes seemed to be all of a piece with the Prime Minister's own approach to the overlap between government and business. Moreover, all around Mr Byers, the government and big business seemed to be making an even greater hash of a series of economic disasters without attracting such opprobrium. Yet Mr Byers was the one who lost his own closest adviser and then his own job through losing the confidence of business, the media and his colleagues in government.

Even the self-sacrificial device of resigning did not achieve the intended effect of halting attacks on his reputation, as it was soon revealed that another adviser had sent incriminating communications by email, trying to establish whether campaigning rail crash survivors who were making life difficult for Mr Byers were Tories. A more common view, however, was that it was Mr Byers who had made life difficult for himself, some would say because the Prime Minister and he were behaving in exactly the way for which, when in opposition, they had criticised the Tories. Or, to put the point in another way, it could be said that they were struggling to adjust to being in power, especially to the demanding scrutiny which rightly comes, in a democracy, with authority. A theologian might ponder whether there is scope here for the expression 'fall from grace' to describe Mr Byers' departure from the government. My own heretical view, however, is that Mr Byers and his special adviser, Jo Moore, were somewhat unfortunate to lose their jobs, especially at a time when there were more calamitous sagas in the mismanagement of the economy by government and business. The Byers' fall from power, or from grace, or just from popularity, needs to be understood not because it reveals the essence of business ethics but because it has elements which both contribute to and distract from a balanced understanding of good management, whether of the railways, the country, big business or small business.

It is instructive to compare and contrast the progress of another government minister, Estelle Morris. She started at the same time as Stephen Byers, one step behind him as a more junior minister in what was then the Department for Education and Employment (it had been the Department for Education and Science until the 1997 general election). When he was promoted out of the department, she was promoted to take his place as the Minister for Schools. When the Secretary of State for Education throughout the 1997–2001 government, David Blunkett, became Home Secretary after the 2001 general election, Estelle Morris was promoted to the Cabinet, taking his place as the Secretary of State, while the department had yet another name change, to the Department for Education and Skills. In October 2002, she resigned with great dignity, saying that she was not up to the strategic task of managing such a wide-ranging department. She emerged with considerable praise from fellow politicians and the media, even among those who had been criticising her for a series of difficulties, such as the doubts about A-level marking that summer and the failure to reach literacy and numeracy targets which both David Blunkett and she had highlighted.

Ministers come and go, as do business leaders and football club managers. Loss of confidence in or trust of a minister is behind some departures but usually in relation to their ability to secure good results. Sometimes, as in the case of Stephen Byers, the media and the public seem to doubt what the minister says. Estelle Morris's departure was different. There is an analogy between Kevin Keegan and Estelle Morris in resigning because they thought that their jobs, as England soccer manager and Education Secretary, were so important that others should take over who could make more of a success of the roles. Kevin Keegan soon reappeared as a victorious club manager at Manchester City and no doubt Estelle Morris, who was a school pupil only a few hundred yards from that club, will return to the front line of efforts to improve schools. The case of Stephen Byers was different for two main reasons. First, even their worst enemies acknowledged that Kevin Keegan was committed to football and that Estelle Morris was committed to education, whereas Stephen Byers did not seem to be quite that engaged with his series of briefs in government. Perhaps unfairly, some critics illustrated this by reference to the fact that he was not able to drive yet was Secretary of State for Transport. Second, Mr Byers seemed determined to hold on to office, whereas Kevin Keegan has shown more than once that he will walk away from posts on his own terms. Estelle Morris defended her difficult position to the point where political commentators and insiders were confident that she could survive, before bowing out just when she did not have to do so. Although there are differences between the cases of Byers and Morris (or Keegan), the suspicion remains that some high-profile jobs, at least in some periods, are almost impossible to carry out successfully given the scrutiny of the media and the interested public, such as voters, shareholders, supporters, customers, pupils and their parents, students, teachers.

This is not to deny that there may have been failures of judgement. Indeed, the main reason why Mr Byers' story seemed to many observers to be emblematic of business and government ethics 'in a spin' is that one of the most image-conscious of ministers kept repeating mistakes which undermined credibility, just as the wider government (indeed, the most image-conscious of governments) kept repeating mistakes which made it look untrustworthy and improperly beholden to business interests. From its first election in 1997 to its second electoral success in 2001, Mr Blair's New Labour Party seemed to rely on murky funding. In particular, the Bernie Ecclestone, Lakshmi Mittal and Richard Desmond donations to the Labour Party were all perceived as influencing government actions. The suspicion grew that the government had lost touch with the very basic ethical principle of honesty. Whether or not the government *is* routinely dishonest, the *perception* that it is fast and loose with the truth is enough to undermine the civic virtue of trust. Given that the government is so dedicated to its own image, there is some bewilderment at the way in which the scandals and elementary mistakes keep being repeated.

Stephen Byers and Tony Blair might seem an odd couple to get into difficulties over the relationships between business, government, truth and conflicts of interest. They have already been identified as archetypal former law student devotees of the Third Way. It might seem to be a counter-argument to that analysis of the Third Way that Mr Byers' legal background could not save his ministerial career. On the other hand, the person brought into the Cabinet on his departure, Paul Boateng, was yet another lawyer and it may be that the Third Way law tutorial mode is related to the problem which Tony Blair, Lord Falconer, Lord Irvine, Stephen Byers and company seem to have with the unrelenting public scrutiny of their decisions. For there are three clues in the last chapter's analysis of lawyers' culture which can cause difficulties for anyone who treats political and business settings as if they were law tutorials.

First, the point was made that barristers place much store on not being identified with the views of any client. It is understood within the law game that they will argue for or against the same person or point in different cases. The arrogance of a legal culture assuming that lawyers' past links do not influence their current decisions was punctured by the fuss over Lord Hoffmann's conflict of interest in the Pinochet case. He did not think it necessary to disclose his connections to Amnesty International who intervened in the case about whether General Pinochet should be extradited. There is something of Lord Hoffmann's approach in the Prime Minister's incredulity that anyone could think the acceptance by the Labour Party of £1 million from Bernie Ecclestone or £100,000 from Richard Desmond or Lakshmi Mittal or £50,000 after £50,000 from the chief executive of a biotechnology company could possibly influence his government's decisions. Second, the Clintonian delight in word games plays well in tutorials but can come across as disingenuous in the public domain. Third, consistency across different areas or over time is not prized, or even known, in a world of different tutors for different subjects, but the political and media worlds are much more demanding arenas.

In opposition, Tony Blair had made much of 'sleaze' on the part of fringe players in John Major's government and party, even though Mr Major himself was widely accepted as the epitome of integrity. Almost as soon as he came to office in 1997, however, Mr Blair exempted Bernie Ecclestone's Formula One racing industry from a ban on tobacco advertising – thus allowing Mr Ecclestone to continue receiving millions of pounds through sponsorship – without mentioning that Mr Ecclestone had donated £1 million to the Labour Party. Thereafter, a wide range of characters expected to influence Mr Blair's government in a way which he would have de-nounced had his political opponents been implicated in such relationships. Supermarkets supporting the development of genetically modified crops, the Hinduja brothers looking for passports and Lakshmi Mittal trying to take over the manufacture of steel in Romania all seemed to be well received by the government.

In 1997, the Prime Minister recognised that his links to Bernie Ecclestone, and the secrecy surrounding the donation, could have seriously damaged his political health, hence his response was to claim that he was 'a pretty straight sort of a guy'. Within four or five years, however, the Prime Minister had become more blasé. Labour was widely denounced, not least by other Labour ministers, in 2002 for having earlier accepted £100,000 from the pornography entrepreneur, Richard Desmond. Even if the donation should have been accepted at all, there was particular cynicism about the gift and its acceptance during the period when Mr Desmond's attempt to take over the Express Newspaper Group could have been blocked by the government in the person of the hapless Stephen Byers (when he was Secretary of State for Trade and Industry). Mr Byers gave another misleading answer to Parliament on the process by which the bid was approved, creating the impression that he was simply following established practice and the advice of the Office of Fair Trading in allowing the takeover. The truth was that the Office of Fair Trading, as it subsequently made clear, did not make any judgement about whether Mr Desmond was a fit and proper person to own a national newspaper but only looked at the implications for competition. The Prime Minister gave a similarly disingenuous answer on the same topic in a high-profile television interview with Jeremy Paxman. The Prime Minister created the impression that there could be nothing wrong with the Labour Party taking money from someone who was judged to be such a fit and proper person. It was, however, Mr Byers, when he was at the Department for Trade and Industry, who made that judgement – after Mr Desmond had donated the money. The department was subsequently forced to admit that it had not investigated, for instance, the hard-core pornographic websites run by Mr Desmond.

At the same time as the Railtrack mess, in the autumn of 2001, the government was embroiled in another scandal. Lakshmi Mittal wished to take over the state's steel industry in Romania. He had donated a substantial amount of money to the Labour Party. The British ambassador to Romania drafted a letter for the Prime Minister to sign which strongly supported Mr Mittal at a crucial stage of the negotiations. The ambassador's girlfriend worked for a British firm of solicitors involved in the deal. Lakshmi Mittal is an Indian citizen. Downing Street first tried to pretend that his firm was a significant employer of British citizens as it sought to explain the Prime Minister's intervention, that the Prime Minister would not have known of the donation at the time when he signed the letter and that he just signed, unaltered, a letter which was put in front of him. The facts were different, but that was expected by almost every observer since we have become accustomed to government prevarication bordering on deceit in these circumstances. Somewhere in Downing Street, someone vetoed use in the draft letter of the word 'friend', either on the ground of inaccuracy or to prevent undue influence or to distance the Prime Minister from any subsequent difficulty. Those are three possible explanations which vary from the commendable to the prudent, veering towards the ethical. Even so, the government mentality or incompetence is such that they had to adjust their story to concede that the draft had been altered. The facts are that Mr Mittal's company, LNM Holdings, was registered in the Dutch Antilles, a tax haven. It has 125,000 employees of whom 91 are based in the UK. It secured this contract, with Mr Blair's help, against the interests of Welsh steelworkers, and the company spends considerable sums of money supporting policies in the USA which also work against the interests of what remains of the British steel industry. Daily revelations emerged about the company's support from New Labour, for instance in securing a European loan. Once more, the spectre loomed of influence and connection supplanting merit. The government seemed angry that anyone should question its integrity, yet conflicts of interest require, in a democracy, exactly the vigilance which opposition parties and the media were showing in the Ecclestone, Desmond and Mittal stories.

Individuals or governments can be forgiven relatively easily for an *isolated* mistake. A *pattern* of behaviour, however, is often taken to be different. If big business (or the trade union movement) seems to influence Labour (or the Conservatives) through donations, or if embarrassing emails emerge regularly, confidence in the integrity of the government is undermined. This may not be fair. The fact that the government repeatedly takes money from business figures, tries to conceal the links for as long as possible and makes decisions in favour of those businesses does not mean that its behaviour is unethical. It may be, but the mere repetition of an action does not automatically make it immoral. The pattern of behaviour may be one not of immorality so much as of overlapping spheres of activity where the same people or corporate bodies will come into contact with one another. This may well give rise to conflicts of interest but they could be managed. We are rightly uneasy because these are difficult issues, but we need to reflect on the individual merits of the cases rather than assume malfeasance. Of course, sympathy for the Labour government on this is bound to hover around zero because they chose to pontificate on ethical matters – Mr Blair, in opposition, attacking John Major's party for similar 'sleaze' and Mr Cook, when Foreign Secretary, proclaiming an 'ethical' foreign policy. Again, however, the fact that Labour was pious and unwise does not necessarily mean that it (or its predecessors in government) has acted unethically.

Whether or not higher education is a business, similar points could be made in that realm. The media reported that the Prime Minister's eldest son, Euan Blair, had been offered a place at Trinity College, Oxford, whose President, Michael Beloff QC, is a distinguished barrister well known to Euan's mother, Cherie Booth QC. Euan Blair went in the end to another university, Bristol, where there is also intense competition for places. While this is none of our business, it was fair. If Euan Blair's grades did not quite match Trinity's offer, he was shown no favour.

Yet Trinity and Bristol were embroiled in an increasingly ferocious media and government debate about the ethics of university admissions. Trinity had already featured in a row over the rejection of another 2001 applicant when his father (a former student at, and major donor to, Trinity) sulked publicly. Meanwhile, Bristol became hero or villain for trying to reverse its reputation as an independent school haven through rejecting some of the best-qualified candidates from that sector to secure instead those from state schools judged to have the right potential. Substituting privilege for race as the ground of contention, much could be learnt about the ethics of student admissions from the American universities' experiences of affirmative action in the 1970s.

While there are almost bound to be networks of contact between universities and schools or families, however, this does not mean the decisions are necessarily corrupt. The head of a college may know the parent of two applicants, one as a donor and/or alumnus, the other as a work colleague and/or friend. It is still possible for the college to decide fairly for or against each of the applicants and for there to be no undue influence caused by the connections, not least because it is unlikely that the principal would be involved in admissions. Accusing colleges or applicants of unethical behaviour is especially misplaced when based on ignorance of the details of applications. Moreover, the fact that other government ministers had atttacked Oxford and school choices in the Conservative leader's family does not justify political or media mischief-making at the expense of a son of the Prime Minister.

Whether we are discussing political donations or university admissions, it does not follow that an individual or a government is acting immorally just because it looks as if there might be a conflict of interest or because they have (however cheaply or inadvisedly) criticised others on similar issues. It is possible to make donations to political parties with integrity just as higher education is awash with applicants and decision-makers who act with integrity. Ill-informed criticism too often elevates dissatisfaction with a decision to supposedly moral indignation about the process. At the risk of being accused of naivety, my advice would be to hesitate before accusing others of acting unethically in these circumstances.

Similarly, failing to learn the lesson of the permanence and 'leakability' of emails featured throughout Mr Byers' difficulties but does not of itself amount to immorality. On the afternoon of 11 September 2001, one of the most infamous and tasteless emails in history was sent by Jo Moore, the political adviser to the Secretary of State for Transport, Stephen Byers. She urged the Department of Transport to 'bury' bad news in the aftermath of the attacks on the USA. Mr Byers' office contacted Railtrack that afternoon. The department was eventually overwhelmed by its own bad news as the Railtrack saga unfolded and Stephen Byers was described with increasing frequency as 'beleaguered'. When it appeared that the civil service press officers were having to take action to prevent Jo Moore repeating the advice of bringing out bad news to coincide with the funeral of Princess Margaret on 15 February 2002, the 11 September 2001 row was revived. As Downing Street became embroiled in the departmental disputes, both Jo Moore and the director of communications at the DTI, Martin Sixsmith, were said to have lost their jobs. It transpired that Jo Moore had not on this occasion sought to 'bury' bad news and that Martin Sixsmith had not resigned. The furore illustrated, however, that when special advisers or press officers become the story, their jobs are at risk. This is something which those attracted to the roles presumably understand, at least given the mounting evidence.

There are three layers here. Whether or not someone of influence should leave their job if they are unable to do it without attracting bad publicity is itself an ethical question. The original row, on the other hand, could be seen in a different light, for infamy or tastelessness in email sending is not necessarily unethical. Most fundamentally, the substance of public decision-making is an ethical concern. Here, the government finally calling a halt to public subsidy of what seemed to be an incompetent Railtrack had many positive aspects. If the government struggled to cope with the foot-and-mouth crisis, its own incompetence in that saga and in failing to make the railways run on time does not automatically amount to having acted immorally. Transport safety is more obviously an ethical matter. Although there are, therefore, ethical as well as economic and political aspects to decisions on government intervention to subsidise one industry or to withdraw subsidy from another, they are complex and not to be confused with sympathy or popularity. Nobody would expect public sympathy for the email sender or victory in popularity contests for chief executives who used redundancies in the circumstances of 11 September to cover other corporate (perhaps managerial) mistakes while continuing to receive their own huge remuneration packages. Yet advisers are expected to maximise good news and minimise bad news while business managers are expected to prioritise the pursuit of maximising profits or, in difficult times, of minimising losses. It is possible to argue that, unpleasant as it may be to be (or to be caught being) opportunistic in the aftermath of the 11 September attacks, people might be failing in their duties if they did not take swift action.

Rewards and risks come from tragedies as well as from the human joy of events such as jubilees. It was salutary to see a letter in the *Guardian* on 1 January 2002 suggesting that newspaper editors properly 'exploited' the tragedy of 11 September 2001 by adding pages and selling more copies. The writer asked whether it was time to stop berating Jo Moore for her similar attempt to react swiftly in the interests, as she saw it, of her employers. Similarly, if one business closes, or runs into difficulties, that may make life easier for another corporation. Reacting quickly to, or even anticipating, a competitor's withdrawal is not ghoulish. Using up moral energy on the wrong matters is itself profligate. Rather than worrying about Jo Moore, we should save our ethical concern for her minister, Stephen Byers. Even then, it is important to acknowledge that his judgement was contingent upon a complex set of facts and that even a crass decision need not be an immoral one.

Admittedly, the government is the risk absorber of last resort so that politicians, advised by the civil service and rightly subject to a vigorous, free media, should be held responsible for the tough decisions which they have to take when Railtrack or the rural economy are at risk, even if the decision is that it is a matter for a regulator or for the market. Nowadays, ministers' freedom to manoeuvre is restricted by European Union rules designed to maintain a free market, but they still have enough discretion to make or break companies through sending signals. The lesson of Railtrack is that the arrogance of managers reduces the space in which ministers will work to perpetuate a struggling company. Just as in other ethical contexts, we should beware the easy use of the claim that government is being inconsistent, as between foot-and-mouth and Railtrack. Different departments were involved in the different messes and the context of the wider world had changed, quite apart from the fact that the election had taken place between the two sagas' denouements.

In September 2001, the government lost patience with railway management and refused to release any more subsidies to Railtrack, with the result that the company could not continue to trade. Neutral observers might have thought that shareholders could have anticipated this outcome, given the public furore over poor service, followed by the Hatfield tragedy on 17 October 2000 when four people died in a crash which happened on a piece of track known by Railtrack to be broken, then the 'overreaction' of widespread 20 mph speed restrictions and consequent delays, and finally government anger at Railtrack's decision despite all this to pay shareholders a dividend and senior executives substantial pay and bonuses. What seemed to surprise the shareholders was that Railtrack was not renationalised but rather was taken into railway administration. This was seen as a device to stop them receiving the compensation which would have followed the government compulsorily acquiring their property rights. In contrast to those affected by the foot-and-mouth epidemic, stockholders bore the loss from the seemingly more remote risk materialising of their shares becoming worthless.

The story of Yates and Simpson on the mountain, mentioned in the Court of Appeal's consideration of the Siamese twins' case, may be a better analogy to this saga. The government had done its best to guide Railtrack to safety but eventually had to look after its own interests and cut the rope (of public subsidy). When Stephen Byers took Railtrack into administration on 5 October 2001, Railtrack's shares were £2.80. It seems that Byers received legal advice that £8, the average price for the preceding three years, would, under European law, have been the relevant figure for compensation if the government had chosen to renationalise. This was said to have implications for the government's private finance initiative (PFI), schemes in which private investors are expected to take risks over government policy in supporting the building of, for example, hospitals or schools or prisons. Why would anyone trust the government after the Railtrack saga? Well, no investor in their right mind would trust the government before or after Railtrack if by trust we mean rely on a consistent approach. We are back to the essence of risk. As Nigel Harris observed in *Rail* magazine: 'The pundits, financial advisers and city institutions who howl so loudly do so, I suspect, partly to mask their own embarrassment, for they have been guilty of passing several clearly-sighted signals at danger.'

Railtrack was brought into existence by the Conservative government in 1996 with the primary aim of privatising the railways for ideological, political reasons. In 1997, the new Labour government had as an overriding political objective the avoidance of raising taxes (to distinguish itself from Old Labour) and therefore stuck to an economic policy which restricted public investment in the railways. Then rail-users/voters grew dissatisfied with the service and the government switched its focus to ensuring that the railway system enabled trains to run on time. The next change in priority came when crashes, which many saw as a direct result of the three successive priorities of privatising, economising and timetabling, scared the government into adopting yet another new main objective: safety.

Confused, vague or rapidly changing objectives rarely make for good business or for good business ethics. Two further causes of calamity were the non-alignment of executive incentives with any of these aims and the non-alignment of shareholder interests with any of them. In the case of the former, executives had salary and bonus arrangements which paid little or no attention to any of the changing priorities even though linkages would have been easy. In the case of the latter, shareholders ignored the short-term messes, perhaps in the mistaken belief that there were two reasons why their investment pounds would be matched by government/taxpayer subsidy pounds. First, they might have thought that short-term media and voter/ user pressure would encourage the government to throw public money at any problems. Second, they might have thought that the government's long-term interest (some would say obsession) with private finance initiatives for public services meant that the government would never cut Railtrack's lifeline of public subsidy. In October 2001, they found out that they were wrong on both counts. On the first, the attacks of 11 September meant that the media were not really putting pressure on any other element of government action. On the second, the Prime Minister's all-consuming interest in the same matter, the prosecution of the international 'war on terrorism', meant that the long-term credibility of the government's courting of private sector investment had temporarily lost the attention of its main champion.

The attacks of 11 September may have had another, subliminal, effect in bolstering Stephen Byers' resolve to take action. The risk of subsidising poor management in transport, especially where safety was compromised, became markedly less attractive after 11 September. There had been crashes before and after privatisation, of course, but the sequence of Southall in 1997, Ladbroke Grove near Paddington in 1999 and then Hatfield in 2000 was salutary. At the same time, 11 September meant that Mr Byers would be reluctant to use public funds to compensate share-holders. First, the money could be put to better use in improving safety directly through investing in the track. Second, less public money would be available as the war against terrorism would use up government reserves. So 11 September could have clarified for Mr Byers that he needed to take action promptly and he needed to do so without wasting public funds, especially on compensating shareholders who might well have bought shares at a low price expecting renationalisation to yield them a profit.

The issues discussed in most applied philosophy discussions of business ethics can seem remote from the everyday experience of a worker in a company. The intricacies of the statutory regime around the privatised railways may be even more abstruse. Almost everyone can recognise, however, from their own working lives the danger of the weaknesses in communication and coordination which seem to have contributed to the tragedy of the broken rail at Hatfield. Understanding the sequence of events also explains why it was Hatfield, rather than the even more tragic accident at Ladbroke Grove, which played such a part in bringing down Railtrack. Thirty-one people died and 425 were injured at Ladbroke Grove when an inexperienced driver went through a red light. A year later, a trainee driver was at the controls at about the maximum speed of 115 mph at Hatfield when the train came off the rails. The condition of the immediate cause, a broken rail, had been a matter of concern since 1998. If the right level of management had known what other parts of the company knew, then a 20 mph speed limit could have minimised the risk of a serious accident while repairs were effected. Indeed, there were three attempts to repair the particular stretch of rail in the weeks before the crash, which each failed through human error, such as delivery not being possible because the new rails had been sent on the wrong kind of train which therefore could not unload them without causing other problems.

Now these kinds of delays and errors are endemic in many people's working experiences. In most cases, the result is a dissatisfied, perhaps lost, customer; in some industries, however, the outcome can be a loss of life. These matters ought to be the stuff of business ethics. The enemy of responsible management of a business is not only the idle or self-absorbed executive who does not take action demanded by safety, but also the employee or customer or observer who cries wolf so often that a real danger is ignored. In other words, as responsible workers, we should not run the line that lives are at risk unless we really think they are. When warned by a responsible worker, those who have the authority to take action should put safety above the demands of bonus arrangements (which might, for instance, be lost if the lines are closed for repairs). At more senior levels within a company, the bonus arrangements should not be structured in such a way as to compromise safety. Staff goodwill and good communication needs to be fostered at every level so that what one part of the company knows will be conveyed to those others who need to know.

Stephen Byers was moved after the 2001 general election from the Department of Trade and Industry to Transport, which was seen as a demotion or, at best, a transfer sideways, perhaps because he had failed to answer the deep questions about when government should intervene in industry. Unfortunately, he immediately faced the same question in the context of the railways, the most uneasy of settings. The quandary for the government as a whole, though Stephen Byers could not be blamed person-ally, is that if it was right for the government to withdraw support from Railtrack in October 2001, threatening jobs and shareholders, why did the government not intervene earlier, in the interests of safety or travellers' comfort and service? The government's limited role in a regulatory age, however, might well be more subtle. There is a respectable argument that the government should have left this to the regulator. Unless it wished to persuade Parliament to change the legislation surrounding the regulator and the rail industry, the government should have shown the supreme resolve, of refraining from intervention, even in the face of Railtrack's mismanage-ment. The most obvious, but by no means only, reason for this is the remoteness of the possibility, on all known form, that the government could add rather than subtract value from the enterprise of establishing a safe, efficient railway network.

To the extent that we can explore business and government ethics through the fall and fall of Stephen Byers, readers may gravitate towards answering the uneasy practical question: what would you have done at each stage of the story? The uneasy *ethical* question, however, is significantly different: how do you decide in any particular case whether Mr Byers, or anyone else, is merely acting incompetently or is acting immorally? To put his series of decisions in perspective, some control group of decisions needs to be considered. Since Mr Byers was only one decision-maker among many, it is reasonable to compare his difficulties with other contemporaneous problems involving business disasters and misguided government intervention. It may be that our moral indignation is misdirected at Mr Byers if his mistakes are contrasted with even more serious corporate and government failings. Lord Nolan's Committee on Standards in Public Life set out seven principles of selflessness, integrity, objectivity, accountability, openness, honesty and leadership.

Whether we are addressing macro or micro questions of business ethics, the problems in the new millennium are not to do with a shortage of authoritative statements of ethical principles. From the Nolan guidelines for government to banks' instructions to traders, there are plenty of norms. Rogue trading or rogue governing happens not only when the ethical principles are unclear but where the simplest, clearest rules are not applied or monitored properly. To take another disaster from 2002, Allfirst, the Allied Irish Bank subsidiary in the USA, which employed the rogue trader John Rusnak, was not oblivious to business ethics. They issued to Mr Rusnak and similar employees an exemplary set of six principles:

- Am I being fair and honest?
- Are my intended actions legal?
- Will my action stand the test of time?
- How would my action look in the media and in public?
- Will my actions damage the reputation of the organisation?
- Is anyone's life, health or safety endangered by my action?'

These are good guidelines for government ministers as well as for foreign currency traders. They apply also to those working in small and medium enterprises right through to big businesses. Asking the right questions, however, is not enough. Complacency in checking on the upholding of such principles seems to have been to blame for Allfirst then losing half a billion pounds. Mr Rusnak earned what is by banking standards a modest salary of $85,000 a year and was one half of a two-person team which brought in about $10 million a year from foreign exchange deals. It seems more extraordinary, therefore, that he should lose the bank $691 million before his managers noticed, than that the high-flying Nick Leeson should bring down Barings. Particularly after the Leeson saga, the risk of a rogue trader might have been expected to be high on the list of concerns for the banking industry. Yet on the very same day in February 2001 as Allied Irish Bank made its statement about Mr Rusnak's losses to the stock market, the Centre for the Study of Financial Innovation published its annual 'Banana Skins' survey of the major risks identified by two hundred senior bankers, which placed rogue traders at twenty-four out of thirty. In the immediate aftermath of Barings, the rogue trader risk had been placed fourth (1996) and third (1997), but as the Centre's co-director observed in his report: 'Some banana skins come and go, some are hardy perennials. The top 10 since 1996 charts the changing concerns. The rogue trader, so troublesome in 1996 and 1997, has completely disappeared.'

The bank's six principles are even simpler and clearer than the Archbishop of Westminster's five principles for the Siamese twins' case. There may be some overlap between the bank's six guidelines but it was probably better to err on the side of spelling out variations on ethical themes rather than to strive for the most concise formulation. What the banking industry was meant to have done in addition, however, was to minimise the risks of another Leesonesque rogue trader losing such large amounts by a combination of control mechanisms. Some of these were routine managerial systems and checks, some were technological devices, but the fundamental safeguards are an understanding of the psychology of rogue traders and eternal vigilance. The failure of Allfirst or Allied Irish to apply these four elements consistently, or in some cases at all, has an uncanny parallel (as we shall explore in the next chapter) to the failure of the USA, Britain and other Western governments to apply consistently basic techniques to forestall the spectacular terrorism of 11 September 2001. If you intend to stop major terrorist attacks, you must use the best management systems at airports, you must use technology to identify risks (e.g., through tracking currency flows or airline passenger movements), you must understand the psychology of the potential perpetrators and you must guard against boredom or complacency. Indeed, if you see a risk dropping down the bankers' charts, that is a signal to review your controls.

Although the language of Allfirst's six questions seems simple, the discussion of the Northern Irish peace process shows that there may still be an element of being 'lost for words'. To take the first Allfirst principle, one which was also crucial to the Byers' saga, it may not be enough to state that honesty is the basic virtue, or even to have elaborate mechanisms for monitoring it, if we mean different things by the simple word. There are some signs that the word is being devalued and some that it is being used in different senses. In terms of 'honesty' being downgraded as a meaningful word, it has become commonplace for people to say, 'To be honest' or 'To be perfectly honest' when there is no more honesty in the revelation which follows than in the rest of their conversation. Meanwhile, soccer pundits are increasingly using 'honest' in a related, proper, historically attested but slightly different sense. The Liverpool and England soccer striker, Emile

Heskey, is routinely described as an 'honest' player. This is not a reflection of his refreshing reluctance to dive or act (in contrast to the Brazilian Rivaldo's infamous faking in the 2002 World Cup where he pretended to have been hit by the ball in the face) in order to get opposing players into trouble. It is instead a comment on his willingness to run selflessly backwards and forwards in the team's cause, rather than to conserve his energy for a showcase opportunity to score. 'Honesty' in the sense of 'hard-working' has a respectable lineage. I suspect, however, that there is an unintentional pincer movement on the moral force of the word 'honesty' by these two developments. On the one hand, people are becoming accustomed to using 'honesty' as a meaningless precursor to meaningless observations. On the other hand, they are becoming acclimatised to equating hard work with honesty. One could imagine the Prime Minister saying, 'To be honest, Stephen Byers was an honest worker for the government.' Yes, but did he tell the truth to, or did he mislead, Parliament? Everyone is honest in the 'to be perfectly honest' sense and Stephen Byers was honest in the Emile Heskey sense of being hard-working, but he might not have been honest in the relevant sense of truth-telling at various points in the Railtrack/Department of Transport saga.

Mr Byers did not seem to accept that he had not been telling the truth. Nor, which is not quite the same, was he prepared to admit that he had misled Parliament or the wider public. The latter refusal to accept the obvious was particularly mystifying. Perhaps he was deterred by what he saw as the consequences of any such admission or perhaps, in a related point, by the way in which fault has become implicit in those phrases. There is no doubt that Stephen Byers literally misled Parliament when he told MPs that Martin Sixsmith had resigned and literally told Parliament something which was not true. This is not quite the same, however, as *intending* to deceive Parliament. Mr Byers may have thought that the statement was true or that it would be fulfilled within minutes. More culpably, he may have thought (mistakenly, as it transpired) that announcing that the resignation had happened would put more pressure on Mr Sixsmith to turn Mr Byers' wish into reality.

As for whether Mr Byers was unethical or incompetent, a different example of the distinction is provided by the coincidence (if it was a coincidence rather than yet another attempt to 'bury' news) of his departure happening just before the major celebrations for the Queen's Golden Jubilee. Looking back from the vantage point of the triumphant jubilee weekend in June 2002, it might seem that the tone of unease for government in the new millennium was set by the Labour government's hubris over the Millennium Dome and their inability to organise a party to celebrate the turn of the millennium. Yet most of New Labour's embarrassment at the Dome was at worst an example of incompetence, rather than of immorality.

If the Hinduja brothers were encouraged to make a donation to the project in the belief that it would help their passport/citizenship applications, that would have been unethical. That apart, however, the Dome could be judged merely a folly, badly executed, unless it is thought that the hubris which led the government to waste millions of pounds of taxpayers' money takes the venture into the realm of immorality.

If the new millennium started badly for the government with the Dome fiasco, things got worse a year later in the run-up towards the general election, beginning with the foot-and-mouth crisis which indeed delayed the poll to June 2001 from Labour's preferred date at the beginning of May. Disasters continued through to the resignation of Stephen Byers from the government. Even so, it would be wrong to imagine that the only corporate- or business-and-government horror stories during this period were in the UK. In the USA, for example, the rogue trader story was not even the most notorious corporate disaster of the same period, that 'honour' going to the Enron and Andersen saga. Moreover, on both sides of the Atlantic, there were corporate meltdowns which could not be attributed to the shortcomings of government. They turned instead on bad judgement by managers and shareholders, often behaving recklessly in taking risks.

For example, 2001 saw Marconi shares in freefall month after month, the biggest loss of shareholder value in British corporate history, with the associated bad news of widespread job losses. If we take the period from the peak of the foot-and-mouth crisis to the last days of Railtrack, Marconi's half-year loss from April to September 2001 was approximately £5 billion, or £27 million a day. This is worth considering as a control mechanism to temper any impression that it is only when government is involved, or when a rogue trader strikes, that business is thrown into confusion. In the case of Marconi, a company shed share value inexorably without government intervention, yet stakeholders failed to arrest the extraordinary decline in share value. The disciplines of the market seemed paralysed as the senior figures at Marconi held on to their jobs for months in the face of mounting evidence that their strategy of moving from being a conglomerate with a specialism in weapons, in the days when Marconi was GEC, to focusing on telecommunications in the mobile phone age, had destroyed Marconi's expertise, competitive advantage and reputation. Not only profits and share value but also jobs were lost.

In the switch from what some had regarded as an immoral industry – armaments – into the more anodyne communications industry, Marconi had accomplished the extraordinary feat of acquiring an even worse reputation for acting badly. In particular, there was widespread unease at the way in which pay and bonuses continued to flow to the executives who sacked workers, especially given the fact that the mistakes were the executives' own strategic errors. Within a year, the chairman, Sir Roger Hurn, the chief executive, Lord Simpson, and his heir apparent, John Mayo, had all departed. This does seem to have been a story of business mistakes, free from government interference, but this does not necessarily bring it into the category of disasters in business *ethics*. A business is a complex enterprise with responsibilities to a range of interested parties, including shareholders, customers and employees. It largely falls to the senior executives, especially the chief executive, other executive directors, the chair and the non-executive directors to determine how these duties will be balanced, yet there can be a conflict between the executives' self-interest and the interests of the other stakeholders. If the executives are set on a strategy of repositioning which is leading to short-term losses, the possibility of drama turning into corporate tragedy seems obvious in hindsight. Each day, it becomes more difficult for the executives to justify the direction in which they are taking the company but also to admit their mistakes and to take remedial action. Non-executives and/or shareholders would, in traditional business theory, call the executives to account. In practice, confidence in the underlying strategy or in the previous successes of the leading figures may have clouded the judgement of those who could have ousted the senior executives.

Any government can be a fickle friend for chief executives of major corporations. One moment the government can be lionising Bob Ayling, the former chief executive of British Airways, appointing him to supervise the development of the Millennium Dome. The next he can be out of favour and indeed out of a job. Shareholders may consider that more attention should be paid to the day job by those who are paid to manage major businesses. Even so, of course, managers who focus exclusively on their day job may not be able to improve a company's performance indicators. For the last quarter of 2001, a year after Bob Ayling had departed, his successor Rod Eddington had to report that British Airways suffered its worst trading period in history, with an operating loss of £187 million, worse even than during the Gulf War a decade before. About a quarter of the BA workforce left in the six months after the 11 September attacks. Moreover, other international airlines such as Swiss Air collapsed altogether in the aftermath, having been subsidised to the hilt by a national government. Nevertheless, the beginnings of BA's problems are often traced to the Ayling era and summed up in the conclusion, however unfair, that once executives are distracted by government, the business may suffer. The reverse also applies. Any corporation or chief executive can be a fickle friend for governments. Tony Blair seems to have believed that his being sympa-thetic to the businesses of Bernie Ecclestone or Lakshmi Mittal, who had handed over seven- and six-figure sums respectively to the Labour Party, should be viewed by the public as unconnected to their donations. Lakshmi Mittal's global activities soon began to be examined by the media with the result that the government's reputation was further tarnished.

On the American side of the Atlantic, the new business century began with the serial collapse of Internet companies in the year 2000. The dot.com/dot.con saga has at least caused some to look again at incidents which their schooldays' study of history may have included, such as the South Sea Bubble of 1720 and the similar Dutch tulip story of the 1630s. Most investors knew that the claims about South Sea trading were extravagant or fraudulent but really did want to get rich quick and so seized the opportunity on the principle, as one of them put it, that 'when the rest of the world is mad, we must imitate them in some measure'. As Internet companies were floated in the final years of the last millennium, the same phenomenon was at play. It did not seem to matter to many investors whether the business was sound. The question was whether the market would think it was sound. Or, to be precise, whether other investors would think that other investors would think that it was sound enough for others to want to invest, with the result that the price would rise and so the original investors could sell at a profit. John Cassidy draws attention to this in his book, *dot.con*, by quoting the words of John Maynard Keynes half a century earlier, comparing the stock market to a newspaper photographic beauty contest where the winner is the reader who selects the most popular combination of the choices sent in by all readers: 'It is not a case of choosing those which, to the best of one's judgement, are really the prettiest, nor even those which average opinion genuinely thinks the prettiest. We have reached the third degree where we devote our intelligences to anticipating what average opinion expects average opinion to be. And there are some, I believe, who practise the fourth, fifth and higher degrees.'

The folly of such speculation, divorced from any attempt to understand the real-world prospects of the nascent companies, seems obvious (with the benefit of hindsight). Yet the capitalist system seems, in the long run, to thrive on the freedom to make (or lose) money in such a way. Those who call for investors to show more responsibility can seem pious and/or other-worldly. It is part of most ethical traditions, however, to warn that rights entail duties. Moreover, in the short run, even self-interest should serve to warn investors of the risks of following the herd at times of frenetic, bordering on manic, stock-market activity. Before coming to any moral judgement, it is important to trace the way in which the herd instinct takes over the market and to understand what happens when reality dawns. Again, John Cassidy's study is invaluable. He traces the difficulties facing Mary Meeker, Morgan Stanley's key executive, who realised that these stocks were being overvalued but who floated along in the bubble until she burst it. If she refused to work for an Internet start-up, another bank would and as they made huge profits, Morgan Stanley would look foolish (in the short run) through missing out on fee income which would go to its rivals and her position would be untenable. The context in which she worked is clear from an interview given by one of her bosses, Joseph Perella, the head of Morgan Stanley's investment banking department, to John Cassidy in 1999:

> The people buying Internet stocks don't think they are buying Morgan Stanley, American Express [i.e. companies with a track record of achievement and profits] . . . There has been a fundamental shift in American capitalism. Previously, venture capital was a private game. Now, the public is willing to fund the growth of companies that are almost start-ups. Basically, the public is saying, 'I want to own every one of these companies. If I'm wrong on nineteen and the twentieth is Yahoo! it doesn't matter. I'll do OK.' That's job-creating. That's wealth-creating. Yes, it is a lottery, as Greenspan said, but it's also fundamental to the evolution of this country.

The Greenspan referred to by Perella was Alan Greenspan, the powerful chairman of the USA's Federal Reserve, America's central banker. He knew that the Internet stocks were overvalued, using the phrase 'irrational exuberance' in December 1996, but took more than three years before acting to raise interest rates so as to check the herd instinct. His reluctance to act was ideological . . . His reference to a lottery was as follows: 'What lottery managers have known for centuries is that you could get somebody to pay for a one-in-a-million shot more than the value of that chance. In other words, people pay more for a claim on a very big pay-off, and that's where the profits from lotteries have always come from. So there is a lottery premium built into the prices of Internet stocks.'

There is ethical unease in some quarters at lotteries, for this very reason. Marketing lotteries as charities is one response. This does not address the fundamental concern of those who regard the UK National Lottery, for example, as akin to a tax on the poor for the benefit of the rich, in that poor people may spend more than they can afford, a company (Camelot, so far) reaps huge profits and skilful lobbying rather than need seems to be able to attract project funding. Even if what Alan Greenspan described as the 'lottery principle' was acceptable for the odd pound or dollar, especially when some of the money went to a good cause, it overheated the economy when applied to Internet stocks and shares. If individual investors bet all their spare money, or money which was not really spare, on Internet start-up businesses, they were set to lose the lottery and be crushed when the herd turned round and stampeded in the opposite direction. Whereas the Nasdaq index peaked in March 2000, Friday 14 April 2000 saw the biggest Nasdaq fall since the crash of Monday 19 October 1987, a Black Friday to echo Black Monday. For almost a year and a half, the dust failed to settle. The American economy was in decline despite several interest rate cuts.

One hundred thousand jobs were lost in August 2001. Then the attacks of 11 September compounded the end of the Internet boom era, undermining confidence, pushing the markets down still further and putting online developments into perspective. Airlines and other major businesses were accused of using the excuse of an expected downturn in the world economy to make thousands of employees redundant so as to cover their own executive level mistakes.

The American corporate disasters were not all to do with the Internet or the attacks of 11 September. In the same period as Mr Byers was being roasted in the British media, at the end of 2001 and the beginning of 2002, the American energy company Enron and its auditors, Andersen, were engulfed in controversy, as major misreporting of corporate performance came to light. In November 2001, Enron announced that it had overstated its profits by more than £600 million over the previous four years. The share price plummeted from $90 to less than $1 and the company filed for bankruptcy, the largest American corporation ever to do so. Senior executives had cashed in share options worth millions of dollars earlier in the year, before the public announcement. They seemed to have benefited from the questionable accounting in which they had engaged. Their employees, however, lost jobs and pension security. Attention naturally turned to the auditors: what were they doing in condoning, or not identifying, what seemed to be the parking of debts in offshore partnerships? The collapse of faith in auditors matched the share-price dive when it emerged that the auditors were busy shredding Enron-related documents. What about regulators and ultimately politicians? Nobody was surprised to learn that Enron and the auditors had connections to the British and American governments. The chairman of the Press Complaints Commission, Lord Wakeham, turned out to be a non-executive director of Enron, having arrived at that position through a similar role in one of the privatised British utilities, Wessex Water, which had been taken over by Enron. What about the Enron executives themselves? When Clifford Baxter, the former vice-chairman, was found shot dead in his car at the end of January, it was assumed that he had committed suicide in advance of Congressional hearings, even though he was thought to have been one of the whistle-blowers, uneasy at the company's practices.

Any observer would be uneasy at such a saga, from any vantage point. Anti-globalisation campaigners have long since been arguing against the takeover of the world by corporations. Where their subtext has seemed to be a generalised distaste for profit, they can be dismissed as antediluvian. Where they have focused on environmental concerns, they have attracted more sympathy. Where they have warned about the corrosive effect of unethical corporate behaviour, they turn out to have been right. It was no surprise to the campaigners, or to most voters, that Enron had sponsored the Labour Party and had succeeded in persuading the new Labour government to renege on its manifesto commitment to impose a moratorium on gas power stations. The manifesto promise had been given to protect the jobs of miners, since the Tory enthusiasm for gas power would be at the expense of the coal power stations. Successive trade and industry ministers, Peter Mandelson and Stephen Byers, were convinced by Enron. US files, released in 1999 under their freedom of information laws, suggested that 'Prime Minister Blair has recently intervened to water down the moratorium proposal'. The chairman of Enron Europe was awarded a CBE. Along the way, Peter Mandelson decided not to refer Enron's takeover of Wessex Water to the Monopolies and Mergers Commission, which is how Lord Wakeham became a non-executive director of the Enron empire. New Labour had been difficult to trust on corporate matters since the new government was revealed as having accepted a £1 million donation from Bernie Ecclestone. Virtually all cynicism having been exhausted, and the Tory Lord Wakeham being implicated, the Enron/Andersen saga did not seem at first to taint Labour ministers in quite the way that the more modest Hinduja cash-for-passports or Hamilton cash-for-questions rows had derailed the careers of prominent politicians.

The auditors, Andersen, had been in a similar position some time before. Margaret Thatcher had effectively banned Andersen from government work because they were the auditors for the DeLorean sports car company which failed spectacularly in Northern Ireland, wasting millions of pounds of public subsidy for its Belfast factory. As the government sued Andersen for £200 million, the auditors were effectively ostracised throughout the dozen years which remained of Conservative government, both under Margaret Thatcher's leadership and then John Major's premiership. Andersen therefore provided free researchers for Labour when it was in opposition, working, for example, on its windfall tax on utilities. The free work seemed to have been rewarded when the DeLorean litigation was settled for about 10 per cent of the claim immediately Labour took office and Andersen began to take on a considerable amount of government work. Andersen was commissioned, for instance, to write a report on Private Finance Initiative. Andersen was enthusiastic, offering figures which the Prime Minister regularly quoted to demonstrate the advantages of PFI. Andersen reaped its reward when it regularly received the commission to handle PFI schemes. It was only when the Enron saga attracted the attention of the British media that much notice was taken of Andersen's sudden ubiquity in life under Labour, as contrasted with its exile under the Conservatives. Once the link was made, however, the media began to see conflicts of interest everywhere.

It is the failure of the intelligent people at the centre of these debacles, from Ecclestone to Mittal and from Marconi and dot.com to Enron, to learn from their first mistakes which is especially puzzling. Other government ministers, public officials and private sector investors, speculators, shareholders and managers were all repeating their own and their predecessors' mistakes throughout the period in which Mr Byers has attracted so much attention. Even those of us who do not equate the repetition of such errors with unethical behaviour must be perplexed as to why lessons are not learned. One explanation is that much of the decision-making came at around the same time, whereas the discoveries came at longer intervals. While it seems as if the second or third should not have happened given the first set of revelations, the decisions had already been taken. Another explanation is more simple: that even leading figures in business and government have bad judgement. A third account would dwell on the role of the media, arguing that it is the vigilant scrutiny which is the crucial factor. The lesson which people in the media spotlight need to learn is that there is no hiding place, whereas their first instinct seems to be to carry on as before but to put more effort into keeping their actions secret. This is futile, but that is a difficult lesson to absorb.

An easy solution might be for the government not to get so involved in business matters. For the government is more often in the wrong when it intervenes than when it allows the market, or even foreign governments distorting the market, to determine the outcome of a business venture. In the uneasy world of politics, however, the government cannot distance itself in such a clear-cut way. This is so even in an era of regulation, in which not only does the government not own what used to be public utilities but it has even, on the surface, abdicated to independent regulators the role of referee. Events have shown that, when it matters to government, the regulators can be swept aside in much the same way as can the executives of a utility, as illustrated by the exchange between Tom Winsor, the rail regulator, and Stephen Byers, the Secretary of State for Trade and Industry, once the latter had decided to take Railtrack into railway administration. Byers left Winsor in no doubt that the government would not let the regulator block this manoeuvre, as Tom Winsor explained in evidence to the House of Commons Transport Sub-Committee. There was a device available to Winsor, an interim review of access charges, designed for the very circumstance of Railtrack getting into financial difficulties, but Byers told him that the government would table emergency legislation to prevent him using this means of directing money to Railtrack. Winsor warned that this would undermine the private sector's confidence in investing in other utilities. This is much the same argument as the case against using railway administration rather than renationalisation. Individual ministers do not tend to last long enough to worry about such long-term considerations and Mr Byers was unlikely to face them personally since he had already been moved from the Department of Trade and Industry to this transport brief.

A better response from Railtrack or Mr Winsor would have been to have called Mr Byers' bluff by starting an interim review and seeing whether the minister could succeed in persuading Parliament to pass any such trump-the-regulator emergency legislation. Railtrack managers, however, unlike the regulator, did not seem to have the will to fight the government's decision.

In summing up a bad year for business and government interventions in business, commentators did not dwell on, or in many cases even note, ministers' contrasting approaches to agriculture and the railways, no doubt to the relief of government. Railtrack shareholders did not attract widespread sympathy since rail-users saw themselves as the secondary victims of Railtrack's management, with the primary ones being those injured in rail accidents. Shareholders came a distant third, if they were victims at all. There was some sense that the farming and food industries were to blame for the foot-and-mouth epidemic starting and that the government were to blame for not controlling it swiftly. Overall, however, the public were not encouraged by the media to think of these sagas as connected, ethical dilemmas. They do, however, raise uneasy questions about the morality of risk and reward as well as about the ethics and efficacy of government intervention or non-intervention in an era of regulation rather than nationalisation. Nor were they isolated ethical questions in the contemporary economy.

It is difficult to predict whether, or afterwards to explain why, one uneasy ethical dilemma will become a cause célèbre while another will seem to disappear from media view after a day or two in, so to speak, the *Sun*. There is something of the herd instinct at play which is a phenomenon worth exploring in its own right for insights into business disasters and business ethics. Quite apart from the literal sense in which herds were involved in the foot-and-mouth crisis, my contention is that the herd instinct is behind so many seemingly irrational aspects of these business sagas, such as the dot.com boom and bust, Marconi's flight from the unfashionable but profitable business it knew (weapons) to the fashionable but unprofitable business in which it floundered (telecommunications/mobile phones), the relentless media focus on Railtrack and the courtship between New Labour and the corporate world. These herds have, however, respect for, or fear of, the leader, which increases the danger for others. If Sir Richard Branson of Virgin Trains, or the Prime Minister Tony Blair, is untouchable, for whatever reason, then the hunters will take aim at the next most prominent hide. Hence the media gamekeeper, Lord Wakeham, was almost bound to be poached, if not by Enron then by some other saga, as was the Prime Minister's most assiduous gatekeeper, Peter Mandelson, as was the rail network's least glamorous element, Railtrack.

A parallel process can be seen in the herd instinct on moral dilemmas, where modern media are also responsible for quickening the pace. Instant and continuous information and comment often seem to be overwhelming judgement in the sphere of ethics, especially at its intersection with the sphere of business. The temptation, if it all seems too complicated, is to stop exercising independent judgement and follow instead the herd which is heading towards Byers, Mandelson, Baxter, Wakeham or Meeker. Within hours of a development, all known commentators have committed themselves to opinions in the media. Thinking individuals, however, are entitled to reserve judgement and to change their minds. Anyone taking stock might begin by taking out their moral compass and assessing the direction in which they want to go. Of course, the four points of the compass may be unattractively labelled with Railtrack at one point, foot-and-mouth at another, Marconi at a third and Enron/Andersen at the fourth. Care must be taken, therefore, whichever route is chosen and care involves adequate preparation against the herd which is ready to gore Andersen, Enron, Lord Wakeham and the Labour government. The relationships between politicians and business leaders can seem so embarrassingly self-seeking that there is little sympathy when they lay themselves open to claims of acting unethically. It may be, however, that when so many businesses, causes and lobbyists are involved in sponsoring political parties, the possibilities of decisions being determined by a single interest are diminished. In a world in which almost every major business seems to be buying influence, it is not so clear that any individual business will get the government policy which it wants because of this cash-(or consultancy-)for-favours mentality. As explained in the last chapter, the roots of so many New Labour characters in the legal world may have a curious part to play. Tony Blair, Cherie Booth, Lord Irvine, Jack Straw, Stephen Byers and other legal figures come from a world in which a barrister or a firm of solicitors or even a judge can take it for granted that their appearance for or against a business or cause in one context has no impact whatsoever on their participation or judgement in another case. On a daily basis, lawyers convince themselves that they are making judgements on the merits of the instant case with no undue influence carrying over from personal connections or past involvements. The wider world sees matters differently.

Some of us are naive enough to accept that New Labour ministers, including the Prime Minister, changed their minds on gas power stations because they had never really thought through their initial stance until Enron and co. put their counter-arguments. The fact that doors were opened for Enron because of their sponsorship of New Labour was a necessary but not sufficient condition for the decision going in their favour. The coal-mining interests and others who had lobbied for the original proposal already had the access which the big corporations only acquired after the election. Although it would be a cleaner world in which politicians did not accept significant sponsorship from business or unions or individuals, it does not follow that the only factor nowadays in a government decision is who has given the politicians what. Lord Hoffmann's Amnesty past was not a material fact in his judgement on General Pinochet. Other Law Lords without such a background came to the same conclusion. Nor is it a bad thing for judges to have committed themselves to human rights pressure groups, just as it is no bad thing for politicians to listen to those affected by their decisions, including miners and energy executives. Ultimately, therefore, the issues surrounding undue influence should not be allowed to submerge the ethical questions about the substance of the decisions themselves. If we allow parties to be funded in these ways, we must expect conflicts of interest. Alternative funding or more transparency in disclosure is needed rather than rushing in a herd to condemn the politicians. In Northern Ireland, official announcements about quango appointments now include statements about political activity and remuneration from other public service, e.g. X is also the chair of her local branch of the Y party and receives £5,000 p.a. for serving on the Z Commission. Similarly, announcements could easily be made which detailed the meetings between ministers and interested parties, from business executives to pressure groups, and listed the donations from those who had been met.

If all conflicts, or potential conflicts, of interest were identified, that would not turn uneasy dilemmas into easy decisions. It would still be difficult to decide whether to subsidise farmers or to stop subsidising Railtrack. The ethical framework of an economy which allows the Internet bubble or Enron/Andersen accounting to destroy lives would not be immune from criticism just because we knew the conflicts of interest every time bankers or journalists or entrepreneurs indulged in media hype over dot.com shares or every time Enron or Andersen met a government minister. Most of the dot.com collapses happened within the law and the Enron accounts appear to have been filed in accordance with the law. The ethical questions are to do with risk, consent and what might be called the morality of insightful trading. Insider trading is criminal on the basis that it is immoral to benefit from knowing something through your insider position which is not known to the general market. Yet profit often follows shrewd decisions which are based on superior insight into what is going to happen next. Should the person who has a better understanding of the market in, say, antiques tell the seller that the price will soar before buying at a snip?

Confusing your own interests with someone else's or with the wider community's is an issue with which medial ethics has had to contend, as a subset of the doctrine of informed consent. Consent is a concept which has been subjected to detailed analysis in medical ethics but not so much in business ethics. In the 1980s, I predicted that medical law would eventually develop a doctrine of informed consent that answered six questions, which could be recast as follows:

- Does the patient have the capacity to consent?
- If not, who should act as proxy and on what criteria?
- If yes, is the patient deciding voluntarily?
- If yes, does the patient understand the risks?
- If yes, does the patient understand the alternatives?
- If yes, is there any reason of public policy to override the consent?

Many uneasy ethical judgements come, in medical contexts and beyond, when the answer to the first question is negative and the decision-maker is answering the second question by making a judgement allegedly in someone else's interests. In medical law and ethics, the question arose almost immediately in the case where the authorities sought the sterilisation of a mentally handicapped seventeen-year-old young woman. Professor (now Sir) Ian Kennedy and I wrote an article in *The Times* entitled 'This rush to judgement', over which the Law Lords pored (and to the title of which Lord Hailsham, then the Lord Chancellor, objected). The Law Lords rejected our concerns and authorised the sterilisation, although it is still possible to doubt whether decision-makers in this case or in other cases are very good at separating different influences. The law in this country sets the criterion as the 'best interests' of the patient. Common sense suggests that decision-makers confuse the best interests of the patient with their own best interests or the community's best interests. Life might not be as stressful for those who have to care for the mentally handicapped young woman if she cannot become pregnant and the community would not have to bear the costs of bringing up any child, but it is not clear that her own best interests are being served. If she was at risk of rape before the sterilisation, for example, she remains at least as vulnerable after the decision. The difference is that she will not become pregnant and society will not have to worry about a baby.

Of course, all decision-makers will claim that they are judging what to do in the patient's best interests and almost all will genuinely think that they are doing so. This does not mean, however, that they are right. Parents, politicians, teachers and business executives all take decisions every day which they similarly believe are guided by the best interests of those for whom they are responsible. Nevertheless, observers may suspect that the decision-makers confuse their own interests and the community's interests with the interests of the person on whose behalf the choice is being made. Enron's executives no doubt justified their accounting practices on the basis that inflated profits would be good for the company. Marconi's executives were following a bold strategy that they convinced themselves was in the best interests of their company. (Funnily enough, they were mimicking the investment strategies of those who lost their money in the Internet bubble, preferring the business they did not know.) Politicians have an infinite capacity to persuade themselves, and quite an ability to persuade voters, that they take decisions in the best interests of others when the common factor appears, to the cynical, to be their propensity to decide in a way which favours their own careers.

Even if we set all that aside, however, there is room for genuine disagreement on what is the best way forward for, say, Britain's railways or rural industries. Although business ethics seems, on the surface, to be about restraining greed, another way of understanding it is as an articulation of assumptions in order to clarify different perspectives on values and on facts or consequences. In the British cases under discussion, it is not so much greed or value conflicts which cause unease as disagreements on the fundamental aims and on the prospects of achieving those aims by different methods. If anyone knew how to make the railways run on time at no extra cost and with no risk of crashes, everyone could be persuaded to support their preferred course of action.

Similarly, the unsatisfactory handling of the foot-and-mouth epidemic was a result of changing and/or selfish objectives prevailing. The overwhelming interest of the government was to hold the election on their planned date, 1 May 2001, and to win comprehensively. Their first priority, then, was to stop the spread of foot-and-mouth. Culling seemed to be the decisive way forward so culling it was. Vaccination did not commend itself as sufficiently robust. After all, if there were no cattle or sheep left, foot-and-mouth would have to stop. Almost immediately, problems multiplied. First, there were not enough government or other vets to carry out the cull in sufficient numbers in the time available. Second, disposing of the carcasses was itself an environmental hazard which provoked hostile reactions from the voting public. Third, the epidemic was spreading. Fourth, the resulting bans on travel in rural areas undermined the tourist industry. Fifth, it became clear that voting would itself be affected, so reluctantly the date of the election was delayed, thus negating the point of the original decision to proceed with culling. Compensation for farmers seemed the decent corollary to the determination to cull.

The dominance of the election in the thinking of government therefore prevented the proper ethical and economic debate from ever taking place within Whitehall or Westminster as to who should bear the loss, given that the agricultural and food industries had pursued policies which courted the risk of foot-and-mouth, a risk which had materialised only decades before. Neither the media nor Parliament held the government or the farming industry to account. Pre-election fever, and ineffective opposition, meant that public money was handed over to farmers in exactly the way which

Railtrack executives and shareholders expected for their industry. There was no experience by the public, however, of any incompetence by farmers whereas the railways provided travellers and journalists with daily horror stories. Moreover, the combination of another election triumph and the disaster of 11 September changed utterly the politics and economics of public subsidy during the course of 2001. Railtrack shareholders were caught like dot.com investors as the bubble burst. The illusion of online start-ups flourishing forever was matched by the illusion of railway-line hold-ups being tolerated for ever.

If we insist on comparing the economic and ethical arguments for public subsidy of farming and railways, value for money is an obvious test. Expectations might be another element although this panders to the lingering view, even after Margaret Thatcher's enormous impact on politics and economics, that the government should step in when all else fails, that compensation should be paid to support the rural economy or that subsidy should keep the railways running on time or that employees in some industries should be protected from unemployment by government intervention. Another related survival of the pre-Thatcher era is the moral unease in some quarters at the whole idea of others earning high salaries, making profits and boosting share value. From such a perspective, an employer's primary moral duty is to provide employment for its staff. This was superseded in successful companies by a focus first on share value and profits and now on customer service. Some commentators have not caught up with either wave of change. Margaret Thatcher exploded the old model in terms of both economics and politics, showing that the discipline of the market could improve customer service whereas nationalised industries tended to be inefficient, benefiting employees but not serving the interests of customers or taxpayers. Many of those who lost that economic argument, however, have indulged themselves in a sustained moral sulk.

The churches are particularly prone to being uneasy with profits, share value, mass redundancies and fat cat salaries. Internationally, the churches were at the forefront of calling for Third World debt to be dropped as a way of marking the millennium. Bishops tend to be uneasy with the world of big banks and corporations. Church of England bishops, for instance, only receive modest stipends and expenses themselves yet they are discomfited by predictable media criticism of any perceived extravagance, such as living in palaces or employing drivers. One of the distinguishing features of forays by bishops and other moralists into business ethics is the underlying sense of not respecting business, indeed doubting its fundamental values. In contrast, there is usually an admiration for the medical profession's technical skill, even if there are doubts about its abilities in communication and moral judgement, among those who participate in medical ethics.

Amid the complexity and harshness of the intersection between commerce and government, a particular subset of the many ethical questions which arise concerns risk-taking, feather-bedding and consistency. Should taxpayers' funds have been used to compensate farmers for known, if remote, risks to their businesses materialising during the foot-and-mouth epidemic? Should they have been used to compensate Railtrack shareholders who took the risk of investing in a poorly performing company which relied on public subsidy continuing? Should they have been used to compensate the airline industry for the risk materialising of downturns in business following the 11 September attacks?

After all, one of the reasons why businesses and shareholders sometimes make spectacular gains is that they take risks. Windfall taxes by the New Labour government could be regarded as penalties imposed on some of the more successful risk-taking companies, but generally shareholders are left to take the benefits of their gambles. Should they not therefore run the risk of failure or calamity? Otherwise, where is the risk? Several dot.com ventures failed during the same period without calls from those who risked their money for government to reimburse them. The difference in the cases of foot-and-mouth could be that government policy had contributed to difficulties. Or it could be said that there was a greater public interest in supporting airlines after 11 September. A cynical view is that foot-and-mouth preceded, indeed delayed, the general election whereas Railtrack was only dealt with robustly after the election, possibly under cover of the distractions caused by the events of 11 September.

Indeed, it used to be at election time that the government's role in the economy was most openly discussed as a matter of ethics in the macro sense, in that elections used to be fought on such moral lines as the choice of higher or lower taxes. Old Labour seemed to make a moral virtue out of higher taxes, the implication being that it was somehow worthy to yield up more income for government to redirect towards public services and the amelioration of the conditions of the most disadvantaged. Margaret Thatcher's emphasis on lower taxes was portrayed by her opponents in politics, the media and academe as the elevation of selfishness above ethical duty. She was convinced, however, that such reactions reflected not only bad economics but also bad moral reasoning. Her view was that it is immoral for the state to take from individuals any more of their money than is absolutely necessary for defence, public order and essential public or social services. Individual citizens would flourish more if they had more control of their own destiny. Moreover, the state has shown itself to be inefficient in managing businesses. Privatising them brought in, from this view, the disciplines of the market (although, as the events described in this chapter demonstrate, these constraints are themselves of questionable reliability). New Labour has tried more self-consciously to locate Thatcherite economics on the high moral ground, but both Labour and Conservative parties in opposition have fought the last two general elections on the ground that they would not increase the taxes set by the party in power. This process of calling a truce on the good old election arguments about the level of taxation leaves it to the Liberal Democrats to run the Old Labour line that higher taxes can take us to an even higher moral plane, with their commitment to put an extra penny in each pound on income tax in order to fund better education services.

The Labour–Conservative consensus on not disturbing the voters' disposable income (at least not through the headline income tax method) gives rise to a classic case of unease. Many of those who vote for the new economics and ethics of lower taxes are still embarrassed about doing so. They cannot believe their luck that they are allowed to keep a bigger percentage of bigger salaries than in the Old Labour era and have politicians tell them that this is both good for the economy and good for the soul. Of course, one of the reasons why income tax can be kept low is that other methods of tax have increased over the years. 'Windfall' taxes on utility companies seem to attract little hostility. Indeed, those who are embarrassed about low income tax may be pleased that those corporations which are making big profits are being targeted instead.

The role of Andersen in this regard has already been mentioned, but here it is worth pointing briefly to the psychology and ethics of the 'windfall' element, in contrast to the hubristic assumption that tax or subsidies are a right. As was observed in the first chapter, arguing relentlessly for 'consistency' between, say, subsidising farmers and the railways is a questionable approach. Different circumstances merit different treatment. Taking 'windfalls' for granted is, however, a risky approach for government or industries. The best legacy of Margaret Thatcher was her attempt to rupture the mentality which assumed that state handouts would subsidise inefficient state-run industries. Her solutions did not always work. Several of the privatised industries seem even worse and the habit of complacency and dependency is so ingrained that it bounces back very quickly.

What is needed is simplicity, clarity and robust efforts to add value within a framework of values. Although the moral unease surrounding business is compounded by the complexity and multiplicity of the interested parties – the stakeholders – a simple answer can usually be found even to conflicts of interest between the stakeholders, so long as the decision-makers are not overawed by closeness to power, patronage and influence. The value of a firm such as Cadbury, which makes and sells chocolate bars, is not to be measured by the resale value of its machinery added to the cost of the chocolate ingredients it happens to have on its premises. The real value is in the brand and the endless creativity which the company shows in developing its markets. Investing in people and in the brand, as well as in chocolate and machinery, are all required for the company to flourish. Deep down, some critics of business confuse the corporation with the physical chocolate and machinery. Some think that the current employees, rather than consumers or past or future employees or shareholders, should be the primary concern of the company. Cadbury and Rowntree were founded by Quaker families with a strong moral sense, exemplars of the independent-minded, dissenting tradition mentioned above as the antidote to, or perhaps the vaccine against, the herd mentality. The firms have been generous developers of social infrastructure in their immediate localities as well as supporters of wider good works through spin-off charities. The many interested parties have complementary but also to some extent competing claims as to whether any pound or million pounds of revenue should be invested in a pension fund, or in better facilities for staff, or in a goodwill gesture to former staff or in marketing or in protecting the company's intellectual property through legal actions or in research and development of new products or in supporting research into urban regeneration.

Sir Adrian Cadbury has explained how his grandfather addressed an uneasy dilemma of business ethics:

> In 1900 Queen Victoria sent a decorative tin with a bar of chocolate inside to all of her soldiers who were serving in South Africa. These tins still turn up today, often complete with their contents, a tribute to the collecting instinct. At the time, the order faced my grandfather with an ethical dilemma. He owned and ran the second-largest chocolate company in Britain, so he was trying harder and the order meant additional work for the factory. Yet he was deeply and publicly opposed to the Anglo–Boer War. He resolved the dilemma by accepting the order, but carrying it out at cost. He therefore made no profit out of what he saw as an unjust war, his employees benefited from the additional work, the soldiers received their royal present, and I am still sent the tins.

Sir Adrian goes on to observe that the problem would have been less easy to resolve if Cadbury had been a publicly quoted firm where shareholders could well have been in favour of both the war and making a profit from the order. In this prize-winning essay, he also notes that the interests and preferences of all 'shareholders' or 'employees' may not be the same. Hence the complexity of an ethical conundrum for a business can be multiplied even in a company which has a clear, easily understood business and moral framework such as a chocolate-maker with Quaker foundations. Of course, success is a factor. Whereas a successful company such as Cadbury can maintain harmonious relations between its stakeholders, an unsuccessful company such as Railtrack or Marconi will find the tensions unbearable. Government intervention has also become more complex in the intervening century since Queen Victoria and the Boer War. Government took more and more direct control only to retreat in the 1980s.

Business ethics on the large scale of Marconi, Railtrack and Enron or, more positively, of Cadbury is difficult for many to apply to their own working lives in smaller enterprises, perhaps facing more mundane challenges. There may be some relevance, therefore, in my own experience as a chief executive at Liverpool Hope University College. Hope is a not-for-profit higher education institution with some 7,000 students, 700 members of staff and a turnover of £30 million p.a. From September 2003 I become Vice-Chancellor of Leeds Metropolitan University. Leeds Metropolitan University is a bigger enterprise with 37,000 students, almost 3,000 employees and a turnover of £110 million p.a., one of the largest universities in the country. Leading and managing any higher education institution is not as perilous as performing the chief executive role on the high wire or trapeze of Marconi, Railtrack, Enron or Anderson but managers in higher education have to operate in a context which has many of the features, albeit on a smaller scale, of the bigger, more commercial world. Higher education in the United Kingdom is a microcosm of the intersection of the private and public sector economies, where random changes in government and quango policy are a considerable risk. My day job therefore involves me in a mini version of some of the ethical dilemmas which arise in this chapter. Certainly, higher education is subject to many regulators and quangos. To name a selection, the Higher Education Funding Council for England, the Teacher Training Agency, the Quality Assurance Agency, Ofsted, UCAS and HESA all have an input. As the accounting officer, ultimately to Parliament, for public funds, I have to take a particular interest in how accounts represent activity, as audited during my time at Hope by PricewaterhouseCoopers. Hope was affected in a small way by foot-and-mouth, as the restrictions on movement in the countryside posed problems for our residential outdoor activity centre in Wales and our requirements that certain students complete fieldwork modules before graduating. Every year, my salary is published, by the *Times Higher Educational Supplement*, in a league table of the pay of heads of institutions, usually accompanied by criticism of 'fat cat' salaries. The *THES*'s annual attack on vice-chancellors' pay was especially vigorous in 2002. The leader was headed 'OVERPAID AND TOOTHLESS – FAT CAT V-CS MUST GO'. It began: 'The amounts vice-chancellors are now being paid is outrageous . . .' and went on to explain that

High pay and perks might be justified if vice-chancellors were responsible for the success or failure of major enterprises. But they are not. Thanks to their and their predecessors' pusillanimity, they in fact preside over what are, in effect, branch officers of a nationalised industry. Through the funding councils, the government tells them what to do and how to do it. They are hemmed in by guidelines, targets, thresholds and frameworks, subjected to quality reviews and audits, and have student numbers and fees dictated by head office. Should they try to exercise leadership within their institution, perhaps by proposing some different way of doing things, they can expect votes of no confidence, rejection by senates and academic boards and protests from students to governors.

When I took up the role as chief executive of Hope in 1995, on returning from Northern Ireland, both the main political parties in England were sparring on higher education but they agreed not to make an issue of it in the forthcoming general election, appointing a commission chaired by Sir Ron (now Lord) Dearing to report just after the vote. This was an elegant way of playing for time, although it caused planning blight. In June 1997, Labour won the election and the Dearing Committee prepared to publish its report that summer. The first bizarre development was the government's rejection, even before the report was made public, of the central Dearing recommendation on financing higher education. Instead, the Labour government removed maintenance grants and required students to pay tuition fees. The second substantial policy shift by the government was that all institutions had to become involved in widening participation among students from relatively excluded groups and areas, whereas elite universities had previously concentrated on research and elite students. This seemed to conflict with the first step, since those from the poorest backgrounds were the most likely to be put off higher education by the resulting debt. It also made life more competitive for Hope which had focused on widening participation for 150 years. The government's third measure which affected Hope was to implement a variation on a minor Dearing recommendation on university college titles, changing the understanding to the exact opposite of the historical position, so that now an institution needed degree-awarding powers to be called a university college whereas traditionally it signified that the institution prepared students for degrees from a high-quality partner such as the University of London or, as in the case of Hope, the University of Liverpool. These three moves amounted in combination to a triple whammy against a church college of higher education with a 150-year track record of opening up access, such as Hope. The government's attack on church colleges which had hitherto had no need of their own degree powers was completed by the government having frozen the process of applying for such powers pending a review. By 1999, that review had still not been concluded and when we forced the government's hand, through litigation, they had made the process much more difficult. In 2002, Hope became the first institution in the country to succeed in securing our own degree powers and therefore qualified for the new university college title under this more stringent test. In January 2003, the much-delayed White Paper on higher education conceded that this should be enough for a full university title.

In such circumstances, life as a manager in higher education is much affected by the policies or whims of government in addition to the stiff competition of the marketplace. A constant influence ought to be the mission and values of the institution itself. As a church university college, for example, Hope has governors, trustees and other stakeholders, especially staff and students, who are accustomed to articulating the high standards of ethical behaviour which they expect. Even colleagues who do not subscribe to the Christian mission in church colleges are quick to invoke the Christian foundation if they consider that any managerial act is 'un-Christian'. 'Christian management' is in this sense equated (quite mistakenly, in my view) with 'weak management' as in the line used by one or two when called to change their ways, 'I thought this was a Christian institution.' Not only church colleges but also specialist institutions, for example in the creative and performing arts, have the advantage of a clear mission and distinctive niches in British higher education.

With that comes the perennial challenge of deciding whether to embrace other activities which more generalist universities such as Liverpool or Leeds Metropolitan undertake. A senior Marks & Spencer executive, a fellow participant in a management training session, convinced me in 1995 that sometimes institutions have to move beyond their distinctive positions in order to survive and compete. His example was the struggle to convince the Marks & Spencer board to stock tinned tomatoes to deter customers from going to Sainsbury's. Both stores had all the other ingredients for cooking pasta and sauce. If Marks & Spencer had insisted on no tinned foods, given their expensive niche marketing of themselves as providing fresh and/or high-quality food, they would have lost customers to their rivals. As a church college which originally trained teachers, some of the modern subjects might have seemed far removed from the core mission of Hope, but business studies, for instance, was introduced in the late 1990s and recently received 24/24 from the Quality Assurance Agency's subject review. A second lesson from that same experience of management training was the need for those leading change to affirm the past while explaining the changed context which requires changed approaches. This is both essential and demanded by fairness to one's predecessors and all involved in the earlier life of an enterprise, from businesses to universities to charities and beyond.

Higher education institutions face the issues of this chapter even though they are, in this country, not-for-profit organisations. For example, universities and colleges are required by quangos to manage risk in a way which many academics find burdensome. There are some obvious performance indicators, such as quality ratings, financial health and student numbers. The collective might of traditional university vice-chancellors, however, seems to have been directed at escaping from what they regarded as the onerous external quality control of the late 1990s. Similarly, the NHS and universities are both implicated in some of the recent difficulties over doctors which have led to inquiries and changed practices from Bristol to Alder Hey in Liverpool. The health world had moved on from my account of the principles to the question whether anyone had been checking rogue researchers or doctors. Any weakness in controls leads, belatedly, to a loss of trust (in more than one sense in the NHS context) and an outbreak of control mechanisms. Higher education or medicine or law cannot, therefore, afford to be condescending towards bankers, auditors, regulators, the media and business more generally. All professions and walks of life need to move on from establishing ethical principles to ensuring that they are practised, monitored and reviewed with vigilance, a point with which this chapter will end.

The governing council of Hope has held vigorous debates about such aspects of business ethics as debt, information technology and marketing. As might be expected of a church institution, there is a degree of scepticism in some circles at each of these. Should Hope, as a church college, encourage students to become indebted as a result of government policies on the funding of higher education? How can the university college discourage irresponsible use of the Internet? Should Hope let word of mouth be the recruitment methodology or is it becoming for a church institution to engage in active marketing of the opportunities it can offer prospective students? Certainly, there have been times when Hope has refrained from popular activities undertaken by competitors (and from means of financing them, such as lottery funding) out of respect for the ethical stance of some governors, but my own view, to take just one of those questions, is that debt or borrowing is not in itself immoral. Debt which is out of control is different from managed debt such as mortgages. Student borrowing is a good investment in their futures. At its crudest, this is shown by the value added to earning capacity by graduating. At its best, education in the round reinforces values as well as adding value and is therefore priceless. As for institutional borrowing, if universities only invest in improved resources when reserves have been built up to cover the full cost, then one generation is paying for the facilities which will be made available to the next generation. A balanced approach is rather to aim for a mix of three elements (accumulated reserves from the surpluses of previous years, current income or hypothecated grant for the project and borrowing to be repaid during the enjoyment of the facility) to be invested in the learning environment. An imbalance may be forced on an institution (e.g., because it does not have the reserves but has an excellent project, or because it has the offer of a government or European grant which demands match funding) but spreading the risks and benefits over generations of students is to be preferred.

The distinctiveness of Hope includes a preface to the risk-management policy in which the presidents of Hope, the Archbishop and the Bishop of Liverpool, outline a theology of risk, including the importance of risk-taking. Achieving a balanced view of risk is a challenge, especially given the tendency to blame others when risks materialise or accidents happen. For example, it has become fashionable to describe the story of the bursting of the 'dot.com', bubble by using the phrase 'dot.con' but this is a misnomer. Internet investors, like Railtrack investors, were not conned. They simply took risks and made bad judgements in the desire to make money which was their undoing. There is a difference if they were misled, as perhaps in the case of Enron, by reliance on worthless auditing, but 'investors' in Internet companies or Railtrack were not, by and large, investing in order to create or distribute wealth or value through the service or product. They were not passionate about the business in the way in which a higher education institution expects its stakeholders to be. Rather, they were guessing that the stocks would rise and they would reap a financial reward. Their judgement, therefore, was crucial, both to invest initially and to hold the stock. While the workers in a company receive money for the contribution they make daily to producing the goods or services, the investors are being rewarded for supplying funds. The individual investor's decision can take a few seconds but the worker's efforts can continue for years. In these circumstances, therefore, crying unfair as an investor is strange since it is no more unfair or fair when the price goes down as when it goes up. There would not be a reward if there were not a risk.

Are risks moral? Is luck moral? Is it right to let some risk-takers face the consequences of their judgements unaided but to intervene in support of others? How should we balance the interests of different stakeholders in a commercial enterprise, for example customers, employees, suppliers and shareholders? Is it right for chief executives to have massive pay increases while their mistakes lead to redundancy for other staff? There are many variations on these questions in business ethics, often with an environmentalist stance: is it right to exploit the natural resources of one part of the world to benefit another, or to secure the comfort of this generation at the expense of the health of the next? These questions could be deconstructed in many ways. The chief executive may be benefiting from a huge pay increase but this should be a decision by a remuneration panel of non-executive directors in the light, if they are performing their functions properly, of meeting performance indicators. The corollary, in a risk-sensitive economy, should be that chief executives run the risk of losing their positions if their risk-taking does not add value to their companies. The Chicago economist, Professor Milton Friedman, was one of the inspirations for the approaches of the Thatcher and Reagan governments. He claimed that the responsibility of managers is to 'make as much money for their stockholders as possible'. He judged that so-called corporate social responsibility takes the stockholders' money or the consumers' or the employees'. Of course, a lesson from the Ecclestone and Mittal stories is that some corporate donations can benefit the company. In Northern Ireland, we have been challenged by the poet John Hewitt for 'coasting along' and by the novelist Brian Moore for 'the lies of silence'. These are the key issues for social responsibility. We should always be uneasy about complacency, about not speaking out at all or soon enough. Hewitt understood the cynical dimension to corporate giving or networking.

> You showed a sense of responsibility
> with subscriptions to worthwhile causes
> and service in voluntary organisations;
> and, anyhow, this did the business no harm,
> no harm at all.
> Relations were improving. A good
> useful life. You coasted along . . .
>
> And all the time, though you never noticed,
> the old lies festered;
> the ignorant became more thoroughly infected;
>
> You coasted along
> And the sores suppurated and spread.
> [. . .]
> You coasted too long.

Through risk-taking, corporations can do great good and can cause great harm. The USA, for instance, has been understandably traumatised by the tragedy of some 3,500 people dying in the 11 September 2001 terrorist attacks on the World Trade Center. We know that 2,500 people were killed in Bhopal, India, in 1984 through an accident at a chemical factory without the West showing anything like this outpouring of grief. Domestically, Railtrack has experienced meltdown after four deaths in the Hatfield derailment when it had survived the Ladbroke Grove crash which caused so many more deaths. Risk is not, therefore, something which can be coldly calculated with each potential lost life representing a known cost. Risk-taking and risk management are arts. The displacement of risks, when they materialise, is another distorting factor which is often discounted in the calculation of costs. Indeed, a good definition of influence, as in networking with government, is the ability to deflect the cost of risks. The infamous

Arthur Andersen study of the PFI programme, for instance, gave the Prime Minister the figure he wanted, that the twenty-nine schemes they surveyed in 2000 would yield on average a 17 per cent saving for the taxpayer. In practice, of course, the mutual admiration society of New Labour and Big Business passed the risks to the taxpayer when corporations made a mess of these initiatives. For example, Siemens installed a new computer system for the Passport Agency under a £120 million contract. Their private sector know-how managed to *increase* the waiting time from eleven to forty-one days at, for example, the Liverpool passport office in a single year, between May 1998 and May 1999. Although the contract would have entitled the government to penalise Siemens, New Labour did not wish to antagonise the particular firm or to dissuade others from bidding for similar PFIs or to admit failure. As a result, the taxpayer paid for Siemens' incompetence. George Monbiot's conclusion has a familiar tone:

> We should not, perhaps, be surprised that private projects are likely to be more expensive than comparable publicly funded ones. Borrowing money costs companies more than it costs government, as companies are less credit-worthy than nation states. Companies, unlike the state, can also expect to make a robust profit. According to the accountancy firm and PFI advisers Chantrey Vellacott, health consortia hope to make between 15 and 25 per cent a year from privately financed hospitals.
>
> As a result, the Private Finance Initiative will, in the long term, add substantially to the public sector borrowing requirement. At the end of 1997, an unlikely row broke out between two of the most staid of Britain's financial institutions, the Treasury and the Accounting Standards Board. The Board was concerned to ensure 'that Parliament is not misled over the extent of the payments it is committed to make in the future'. Some projects, it claimed, should really be counted against the borrowing requirement. Otherwise the Private Finance Initiative, the board maintained, could be viewed as what accountants call 'an off-balance sheet fiddle': a debt hidden from public view but which the government would eventually have to pick up.

That was written in the year 2000. In 2002, Enron was caught out in this same manoeuvre which the British government expected to finesse past the public in pursuit of its PFI obsession. Ask not for whom the bell of risk- or buck-passing tolls. It tolls for thee.

This leads inevitably to questions about who guards the guardians of the public interest: should the government allow bankers and auditors to regulate themselves or should there be tighter public control to guard against the reporting of bogus profits and deals by rogue traders? One reason why we are uneasy at such questions is that we have no clear sense as to what the purpose of government involvement in business might be. A more fundamental reason, however, is that we have no clear sense as to what the purpose(s) of business might be. The most basic explanation of mass unease is that many businesses themselves seem to have no understanding of their own purposes.

In contrast, the first chapter did not have to dwell on doctors' doubts about the point of an operation to separate Siamese twins. Some disagreement on the point of punishment is, however, behind the complexity of the issue in the second chapter, just as in the third chapter, the contortions of the Northern Irish peace process are in part due to vagueness as to what interested parties will accept by way of compromise. In the case of business, one assumption is that the purpose is to make a profit. Observers are rarely sure as to why this is the case and the profit motive sits uneasily with a more natural assumption that the point is to provide the goods or services which the business offers or more generally to satisfy the business's customers. At various times in the struggle between employees and trade unions, on the one hand, and managers on the other, it has sometimes seemed as if companies exist primarily for the workers or the executives. Shareholders are also said to be the main people in whose interest a business should be run. This is usually interpreted as taking us back to the profit motive on the (equally questionable) assumption that shareholders' interests are synonymous with profit. When no clear priority emerges, all 'stakeholders' are invoked. So far, this simply shows confusion as to what the economic purpose of a company might be. It does not even begin to answer the question whether any of the purposes would be ethical.

The Internet start-up phenomenon complicated matters still further. Since these companies were loss-making, their market valuations were hardly likely to be based on profit. Rather, it was the prospect of a distant profit which was said to justify the high value placed on their stock. They were gambling on creating 'market share' by heavy investment in marketing. Since they therefore lost a substantial amount per item sold, an unsurprising problem faced them: the more their turnover grew, the bigger their loss. At some point, presumably as other companies (which were running the same optimistic line to their potential investors) collapsed, they would be able to raise their prices and capitalise on their market position. That moment would never come, however, if they ran out of cash themselves and so many dot.coms never made a profit before being taken into receivership.

It was not only the private sector 'new economy' firms, however, which entered the new millennium with no clear sense of purpose. Although the doctors knew what they were doing in the Siamese twins' operation, the National Health Service, and the old public sector in general, has been under attack from all sides, including the Labour Prime Minister Tony

Blair. Reform is vital and, according to the Prime Minister, those who oppose reform are 'wreckers', a term previously associated with Stalin's approach to those who disagreed with him. Yet high-profile failures in the privatised former public sector, such as the railways, hardly give confidence that such reform will do anything other than 'wreck' the NHS. The government seems committed to the Private Finance Initiative as one way to bring private money into public services. Andersen, the firm which features so badly in the Enron saga, is trusted by the Prime Minister and the Chancellor when it concludes that PFI projects are good value for money. Andersen, however, benefits from PFI projects. Their sister company, Andersen Consulting, was behind the farce of a new National Insurance computer. Once again, the government wrote off most of the private company's liability for its mistakes. The upshot is that private companies do not really take the much-vaunted risk of the market but do take the profit when they are funded by the taxpayer for public works which are financed partly through loans which could be negotiated at a cheaper rate by the Treasury. The same companies advise the government that this makes economic sense. Our economic and ethical unease should be profound for the simple reason that this behaviour by government and the private sector is both uneconomic and unethical.

Many of the economic and ethical disasters of recent years are immorality tales, then, involving blatant conflicts of interest or confusion over the purposes of the enterprises. There have always been such conflicts and confusions, however, so is there anything distinctive in the new era which accounts for a greater unease? It may be that the answer is something to do with instantaneous media coverage of the business and government worlds.

The simple conclusions which I would draw from this millennium's series of corporate and government disasters begin with the need for a different type of adviser. Jo Moore has become a symbol of a certain kind of adviser, focused on securing good media coverage for her minister and (with conspicuous lack of success) on minimising bad publicity. There are other kinds of special advisers – the majority – who specialise in policy. There does not seem to be a single special adviser in government, however, of the kind which is needed, namely an adviser on ethics. In particular, ministers need to be told by somebody who is not beholden to them when they are at risk of acting unethically. By the time the official guardians come into play, such as the Permanent Secretary of a government department or an ombudsman or standards commissioner or committee, the absence of such advice can be fatal. When the traditional civil service, special advisers and Her Majesty's opposition all fail to check ministers, then the media are (in between elections when the electorate has an opportunity to pass judgement) the last influential champions of the good and the right. Nor is business in a better position than government to make ethical judgements.

Again, consultants are likely to be brought in by companies to advise on change management, branding, marketing or fashion but not on ethics. Consignia, the corporate artist formerly known as the Post Office with another world-class brand in the Royal Mail, became a joke epitomising what sceptics see as the futility of brand identity consultants. Likewise, British Airways' difficulties are often timed from the decision to paint its aeroplanes' tail fins with modern artistic designs instead of its traditional British flag. This is not to say that there is anything inherently wrong in rebranding. The new brand of 'Hope', for example, captured the mission and values or the soul of an institution which needed a new identity as three founding colleges had been merged into one. It is not always so clear that businesses which are not merging should invest in rebranding. In some cases, turning to advisers on business ethics, or developing in-house expertise, would be better value for money than calling in external brand consultants.

The second priority, beyond a focus on ethics or values which would seek out independent moral advice, should be to understand the purpose of the enterprise in which the corporation or the government is engaged. Confusions over the purposes of business in general or a business in particular have contributed to the difficulties highlighted in this chapter, as have confusions over the distinction between a regulator and a government minister.

The third concern for business ethics must be to take the moral debate into every level of a company's activities, to ensure that the employee who has the vital piece of information or insight can make things happen or bring the matter to the attention of those who can make a difference.

The fourth way in which an ethical business can be helped is to set out simple, clear principles. Here, we could usefully adopt Allfirst's six guidelines, quoted earlier in this chapter, as Ethicsfirst. Of course, even the simplest questions may involve complex interpretation and require the most profound answers. For example, the first question, 'Am I being fair and honest?', raises questions of justice and also the issue touched upon elsewhere in this chapter of different meanings being attributed to the word 'honest'.

Even if the principles were easy, however, the fifth and most important element is to create and enforce practical means of implementing and monitoring the principles. If Allied Irish Bank's subsidiary had created effective procedures to check that their six principles were being applied, then the rogue trader could not have escaped detection for so long. The Nick Leeson saga had already put the worldwide banking sector on notice of the need for such control mechanisms. Discussions of business ethics have often begun from a position of hostility to profit, equating it with greed, and objecting to competition as entailing the intentional harming of the interests of others. From this cynical perspective, proper controls on a rogue trader would protect profits and promote the interests of the corporation itself. Economics and ethics, on this view, both point towards implementing checks in the spirit of these simple, good principles.

If that were all that was at stake, however, we would not feel uneasy at this catalogue of business and government failings. The ethical centre of business life can be more difficult to find than in the rogue trader case. Indeed, the essence of the problems involving New Labour, as it could see so clearly of the previous government when it was in opposition, is on this view its hubris, its overweening confidence that it is right, conflating individual ministerial interests or party interests with the interests of the government and the country as a whole. Similarly, the classic mistake when acting as a proxy in medical dilemmas, confusing the patient's best interests with your own or the community's, is never far from corporate disasters. This is not necessarily a function of the complexity of the business itself. At one level, GEC was a complicated conglomerate whereas in its new incarnation as Marconi it was moving towards a simplification of its core business. It now had the very clear aim of focusing on telecommunications. At another level, of course, it was verging on dot.com bubble thinking. Whereas GEC had aimed for profit, Marconi had as many excuses for losses as did the Internet start-up companies.

In fact, profit is not the only goal of a corporation. Profitable, profit-seeking companies can prefer ethical standards of conduct with suppliers, let alone customers or staff, to further profit, as the Body Shop demonstrated before it too teetered on the edge of convincing itself that it was purer than pure. The complexity of business behaviour becomes more apparent when business ethics moves beyond inquests into corporate disasters. From whistle-blowing to the promotion of equal opportunities, company cultures can do much beyond profit to build up the common good in a corporate community setting. In Northern Ireland, for instance, companies were forced by fair employment legislation into developing an integrated workforce of both Catholics and Protestants rather than accepting de facto segregation. The experience of working together has probably made a significant contribution to progress in Northern Ireland, notwithstanding all the difficulties of the peace process. The impact of such change should not be discounted, even if the motivation was reluctant compliance with legislation for fear of penalties, rather than willing cooperation in changing society. Along the way, employees could experience, or at least glimpse, a revealing truth. Although the equal opportunities industry is at pains to claim that this process is not one of reverse discrimination, it is easier to understand the significance if we accept that it is an experiment in social engineering and face directly the accusation that this is just as bad as the old form of discrimination. Reverse discrimination in favour of a

171

previously disadvantaged group is not morally equivalent to the former discrimination against individual members of that group. Discrimination treats one race or gender as being of less moral worth. Reverse discrimination emphasises that all races and both genders are of equal moral worth but says that a past practice of unfavourable treatment requires action now for that equality to be manifested.

One reason why a balanced workforce is so important is the equal opportunities for economic flourishing which employment brings. Another, however, is that corporate pride is not merely a delusion of management but can be a proper virtue of working as a good employee as part of an enterprise which is striving to pursue a cluster of noble objectives, ranging from good customer service to equal opportunities in the workforce. An individual's identity may include pride in their involvement in a successful, useful and fair company, where they consider that they are making a difference in a corporation which is making a difference.

Marks & Spencer used to have that reputation. As its profitability slid, perhaps again through executive complacency, so it began to receive a bad press for its treatment of suppliers. This gives us a clue as to how to see profits. It has been said that they are a way of keeping score, rather than an end in themselves. In most sport, however, it is not quite right to distinguish scores and objectives in this way. A large part of the point is to score more than the opposing team or teams, to win, both in sport and in a corporate team. If you are ahead by a reasonable margin, then you might turn on the style and play beautiful football, say, rather than a more brutal, frenetic game when the scores are even. If you are too far ahead, there is a danger of complacency. The England rugby team has in recent years shown its talent but has tended to succumb to two temptations: complacency when far ahead in the first half, so that a major score is not achieved; or complacency in the whole game, so that it does not complete a Grand Slam but loses one game a season to less gifted opposition. Governments and corporations can let themselves down in similar ways just when they seem to have an unassailable lead. The smallest company and the largest multinational need to heed the same lesson, that good business ethics stems from constant self-analysis, and preferably informed external criticism, about the purposes of the enterprise, accompanied by constant vigilance against the dangers of conflicts of interest and of hubris. Sometimes, a company does seem to need the alarm to ring before taking steps to ensure a better future. Marks & Spencer has started to emerge from its difficulties with some credit as it has begun to re-establish its former, formidable, reputation. In areas of business, the disciplines of the market in a competitive economy seem to work reasonably well in this regard. A company's success encourages others to compete, they begin to triumph over the old market leader, that company in turn dies or reinvents itself by competing on quality, fashion, price and customer service, that affects the profits of the young pretenders, and so on. Along the way, new managements are installed by shareholder demand and the share price usually reflects this cycle.

In some other areas of economic activity, however, the market does not seem to function in this way and the government has been expected to play a more vigorous part. Some industries, such as the railways, were almost monopolies, and the government was expected to run them or otherwise do something about them. Others, such as farming, were almost bankrupt and the (national or European) government had somehow come to subsidise them. When Mrs Thatcher was Prime Minister in the 1980s, she changed our understanding of the interaction between government and the economy by being prepared to abandon the coal industry, which combined both these features as a bankrupt monopoly. It is important to understand that the subsequent years have seen the ascendancy of a different function for government in business. After decades of argument about two extremes – nationalisation and privatisation – the new reality is a regulatory economy in which the free market is refereed and moderated by government or, at one remove, by quasi-government bodies.

The deeper issue, beyond the political party in power having conflicts of interest, is a lack of confidence that government in the broadest sense has come to terms with its role in this regulatory era. Just as market 'discipline' and state 'control' became misnomers because big business seemed to lack discipline and the old leviathan nationalised industries seemed to lack control, the intermediate 'third way' language of 'regulation' is just as empty. There is a need, then, to address the basic ethics, as well as the economics, of business and of government involvement in the business world. A year in the life of Stephen Byers is illuminating in many respects but needs to be set in the context of other business and government disasters of roughly the same period. Basic ethical questions surrounded Britain's foot-and-mouth epidemic which led in the first half of 2001 to severe problems for the government and for the rural economy, not just in farming but also in the tourist industry. As so often, the intertwining of economics and politics meant that the media focus was on what the government did to prevent or to worsen or to solve a business problem. In this case, timing was of particular interest and, as the epidemic spread, the government delayed the general election which it had long planned to hold at the beginning of May 2001.

Government pay-outs subsidised many of those whose businesses had suffered from a known but unlikely risk materialising for the second time in a few decades. Sceptics might wonder about the ethics of using taxpayers' money in this way when the outbreak a generation before, in 1967–8, had put all involved on notice that they needed to make arrangements, whether by preventative measures or insurance, to forestall, or cope in the event of, a recurrence. Those involved argued that insurance was not available against foot-and-mouth. Instead of those with responsibilities greeting the insurers' judgement as giving cause for concern about the likelihood and scale of losses, this line was allowed to prevail and taxpayers' money was used as the insurers of last resort. More robust approaches would have been for insurers to have been persuaded into offering cover at a price, or for a compulsory scheme to have been established so as to provide funds, or for action to have been taken to guard against 'efficiency gains' in the food industry leading to a new outbreak. The cost in each of these three cases could have been passed on to consumers of the food and/or borne by the farming industry. Perhaps the authorities' best response is to observe that food consumers and taxpayers are an overlapping group to such an extent that there is a rough justice in the way in which the government took the 'easy' option of compensating the farming industry after the event instead of one or more of those three measures in advance. The way in which the saga was handled, however, gave every impression of the government having ignored the evidence for decades, then of panicking when the problem duly recurred and finally of adding to the problem by a mixture of indecisive and inept action.

This was 'the worst epidemic of foot-and-mouth disease the world has ever seen', according to Judith Cook's account, because of 'the slaughter, at the last count, of nearly four million animals and rising (many of them quite healthy); the virtual closure of the countryside for months; continuing fears of long-term pollution of the environment from pyres and burial pits; a cost to the Treasury of billions; the postponement of a general election and, not least, the traumatic experiences of some of those who have been so severely affected'. She notes that the last major outbreak before 2001, in 1967–8 was confined to the Midlands and the north of England, with fewer than half a million animals slaughtered. The basic, obvious conclusion of the 1968 Northumberland Report was that speed of diagnosis and response was vital. That lesson appeared not to have been learned by the government or the farming industry. Moreover, the government did not seem to grasp the changes in food retailing, farming and abattoirs since the 1967–8 outbreak. There were only some three hundred abbatoirs left in the whole of the country because, as Carol Trewin, farming editor of the *Western Morning News*, observes, 'the remorseless influence of the four major supermarkets has concentrated the meat trade into a handful of super-large abbatoirs, most dealing with only one or two customers of the big four, and perhaps a handful of B-list players from the smaller supermarket chains'. This meant that the imagery of 1967–8's small, local farms, abattoirs and markets was misplaced. Judith Cook comments that 'the majority of sheep are now bought and sold in a handful of major markets, not by farmers directly but by dealers, many of whom do not even attend the markets or see the sheep. Sheep are bought, sold and resold in deals made by mobile phones.' Animals were therefore being transported round the country and the disease was harder to stop. The numbers of animals to be slaughtered were so high that there were insufficient vets to cope. Nor had the government appreciated the logistical difficulties of disposing of the carcasses, so environmental concerns were mounting. Foreign vets and the British Army were therefore deployed to help respectively in the killing and disposal of the animals. The rural economy was threatened as footpaths were closed and tourists were told to keep away, thus imperilling hotels and other small businesses in the countryside. All the signs of incompetence were there, especially the constant refrain from the government that the crisis was 'under control', a sure sign that it was not, just as the government looked ludicrous in claiming that 'the countryside is open for business' when it was patently not.

The foot-and-mouth outbreaks of 2001, therefore, raised questions about government efficiency and about the ethics of compensating or subsidising farmers. Should agriculture be subsidised, as compared to other industries such as coal or steel? Should farming have been singled out for preferential compensation, as compared to other parts of the rural economy which lost more business than farmers did as a result of the foot-and-mouth epidemic and/or the government handling of it? One of the most strident denunciations of the subsidy mentality was from Lord Haskins, seemingly the most influential government adviser on the rural economy, whose views are shaped by his own business success in building up a firm, Northern Foods, supplying the major supermarkets. He called for an end to the 'mollycoddling' of small farmers. They in turn feared that the government would accelerate the drive to larger farms and fewer abbatoirs which could add to the difficulties experienced in 2001.

Andrew O'Hagan's reflections on travelling around rural Britain during the foot-and-mouth crisis, *The End of British Farming*, capture the opposing views:

> I set out on my own rural ride feeling sorry for the farmers. I thought they were getting a raw deal: economic forces were against them, they were victims of historical realities beyond their control, and of some horrendous bad luck. They seemed to me, as the miners had once seemed, to be trying to hold onto something worth having, a decent working life, an earning, a rich British culture, and I went into their kitchens with a sense of sorrow . . . But as the months passed I could also see the sense in the opposing argument: many of the bigger farmers had exploited the subsidy system, they had done well with bumper cheques from Brussels in the 1980s, they had destroyed the land to get the

cheques, and they had nothing to fend off ruin. When I told people I was spending time with farmers, they'd say: how can you stand it, they just complain all day, and they've always got their hand out. I didn't want to believe that, and, after talking to the farmers I've written about here, I still don't believe it. But there would be no point in opting for an easy lament on the farmers' behalf, despite all the anguish they have recently suffered: it would be like singing a sad song for the 1980s men-in-red-braces, who had a similar love of Thatcher, and who did well then, but who are now reaping the rewards of bad management. As a piece of human business, British farming is a heady mixture of the terrible and the inevitable, the hopeless and the culpable, and no less grave for all that.

The gravity and the culpability suggest that the farming industry needed serious ethical analysis. Even through a year of rural agony, however, the impression given by the London-dominated sectors of politics, media and campaigning was that the primary question of ethics in the countryside was fox-hunting. Animal rights activists and sympathisers (so often to the fore in politics), the media and student union conversation about ethics seemed unmoved in comparison by the widespread slaughter of uninfected animals so that the ethical dimension to the foot-and-mouth saga was largely unexamined. Yet our moral uneasiness, bordering on queasiness, over food/animal/rural issues is better captured by the foot-and-mouth or BSE sagas than by the set-piece debates on animal rights, fox-hunting or vegetarianism, which are so often reduced to a clash of certainties. The ethical essence of this chapter, as of the next in the different setting of global terrorism, is to judge whether the taking of risks is justified or reckless and whether we should support those who suffer when a risk materialises. The 'herd' instinct applies – when those involved in an activity seem to be following one another unthinkingly in pursuit of greed or self-interest or advantage, are outsiders entitled to judge that this is unethical because, for instance, it runs a significant risk of harm to other individuals or to the community as a whole? As with a terrorist attack, once the risk of foot-and-mouth materialises, moral difficulties abound. Preventative measures, with the benefit of hindsight, would have presented fewer moral difficulties. Before the risk materialised, however, the individual and institutional pursuit of profit or subsidy or customers or market share seemed more attractive than the expense and inconvenience of putting safety first.

Finally, lurking beneath almost every example in this chapter and in the case of the most egregious of other errors of judgement in business, government and international affairs, there may be another lodestar. Business and political leaders who end up at the centre of these disasters have often put the quest for glory ahead of profit, subsidy, customers, market share or simply truth and common decency. One obvious reason why politicians and business leaders surround themselves with spin doctors is that they wish to be portrayed as engaged in a noble endeavour. This is much the same reason why they also surround themselves with each other, politicians believing that the lustre of business success is transferred by association and business leaders believing that the political success passes kudos in the opposite direction. The search for glory was at the centre of Machiavelli's account of the successful prince. Depending on what is meant by glory, there may be no harm in it and much to praise. For instance, students and their families often seem to judge universities by their prestige rather than by their ethos, their league-table performance indicators or their suitability for particular students. Yet this is understandable given that self-esteem can be enhanced by the glory of institutions with which one is associated. The quest for glory at the expense of others, however, can be the downfall of public figures. Football managers can overextend their club's credit, and therefore their own credit in a different sense, by spending too much in the transfer market. It may be that Stephen Byers was so attached to his political adviser because, at some subconscious level, the most on-message of New Labour ministers (modelling themselves on the support Tony Blair receives from Alastair Campbell?) regard the presentation of their efforts as vital for glory. The result was the opposite of what he intended, as he ultimately lost her advice, his ministerial office and his political reputation.

This may turn out to be a foretaste of the ultimate fate of the New Labour government, but along the way the quest for glory may well have brought great benefits to citizens and communities as well as to the politicians themselves. In any event, not all government ministers are motivated by glory, as shown by Estelle Morris, and not all glory is an unethical vanity, as shown by the way in which many sporting stars, business leaders and public figures add value and values to our lives, as well as to their own. From Sir Steve Redgrave to Paula Radcliffe, sporting heroes and heroines take risks, invest years in training and conduct themselves with becoming modesty when their efforts are rewarded. They have a sense of purpose, of course, which usually relates to some natural talent for, an infectious enthusiasm for and a manifest enjoyment of their sport. Estelle Morris has that for education in schools and did not wish to pretend that she had the same affection for, or command of, other aspects of a broader brief. Stephen Byers never quite convinced the public that he had that commitment to his successive responsibilities. A minister may have the luck to survive even so but Mr Byers was denied glory through some extraordinary events and his indifferent responses thereto.

What makes me uneasy about business ethics and the ethics of public life in the new millennium is the frequent assumption that downfalls are caused by glory-seeking and/or greed verging on malevolence. In the next chapter, we will meet a much more clear-cut invocation of evil. There is nothing quite so spectacular as that, however, even in the catalogue of transatlantic corporate and government disasters of this decade. It is the banality of business and government life which is more of a threat even than the corporate chancers of Enron. For the systems should already be in place to audit, monitor and restrain those who risk corporate meltdown, from Enron to rogue traders, alerting the authorities, shareholders and consumers in good time. Constant vigilance and good judgement are required, however, and this seems beyond those who are distracted by glory or greed. Many of those who take risks or suffer accidents nowadays look round to blame someone else. Even in the flawed judgement of Stephen Byers, there was something admirable about the loyalty between a beleaguered special adviser, a beleaguered government minister and a Prime Minister who could have escaped criticism by casting them adrift. Even though I think that the government, led by the Prime Minister, has taken some dubious positions and accepted some dubious donations for its political party, I do not conclude that it or he are immoral.

More generally, the inflation of moral rhetoric in the context of business and government is to be regretted. Much of this is caused by the law and is in part the unfortunate corollary of the undoubted benefits which fair employment legislation, noted above, has brought, for instance, to Northern Ireland. The language of disagreement in the workplace has become morally loaded: grievance, harassment, victimisation, discrimination. X disagrees with Y at work. This becomes a grievance with allegations of harassment, victimisation and discrimination. Even if the allegations are rejected through a process, the process can then be challenged and the workplace relationships can be further soured. This is not to deny that there are genuine grievances or cases of harassment, victimisation or discrimination at work. It is to question the equation of every disagreement or contested judgement with unethical behaviour. The answer is in part to hold on to presumptions of innocence and a critical concern to establish the facts rather than elevate allegations into truth. This is especially important when the herd instinct leads the media en masse to condemn a minister or business leader for a perceived conflict of interest or other misdemeanour.

To sum up, leadership in the overlapping spheres of economics and politics does involve ethical decision-making, often of an uneasy nature, but it has become too easy to assume that others are motivated in these endeavours by greed, dishonesty, glory-seeking or by some other manifestation of bad faith. There are mundane tasks to be done in managing risks, in monitoring, auditing, identifying conflicts of interest and the like. This should not be an excuse for the stultification of big business or government. Risks should not just be managed but calculated risks should be taken. Where tragedy looms, it is sometimes because the proper objectives of the activity in question have become obscured to those in authority or have become jumbled in their order of priority. A railway cannot run safely, on time and at a reasonable cost if the priority oscillates between punctuality and safety with insufficient investment to achieve either. A tragedy can be an accident, in the simple sense, which we have almost banished from public discourse, that no one should be blamed. Where moral fault can be found, it is not necessarily in one person or corporate body.

Although there is no moral equivalent between those with responsibility in this chapter about business and government and in the second chapter about the children who killed James Bulger, one might have thought that if moral failure can be redeemed in criminals, the same should apply to those guilty only of losing the trust of the media, electorate or shareholders. When government ministers or business executives are condemned to internal exile, removed with varying degrees of unwillingness from their offices, it should not necessarily be the end of their public or private service.

Yet while society can forgive, or at least release, murderers and others convicted of serious criminal offences, it is not always odd to seem less forgiving of those who have merely lost public trust and office. Yes, we should allow for atonement by those who have committed no crime but whose bad judgement or bad luck has undermined their reputations. No, it does not follow that they are being more harshly treated than are the criminals because the latter are not (usually) asking to be trusted in government or in corporate positions of responsibility. Where each 'side' thinks of the 'other' as having acted unforgivably, as in the third chapter's consideration of the Northern Irish peace process, the barrier to progress can be precisely this issue of trusting in authority those who are deemed to have behaved untrustworthily. As argued in that chapter, this requires going beyond rationality to have faith and generosity of spirit in the manner shown by the vineyard owner in the parable. Since 'going beyond rationality' is considered by many of those involved to be simply acting irrationally, this is a demanding test.

There may be a connection between these different contexts of entrusting responsibility to those whom you have with good reason distrusted. For if we can be more tolerant of individuals who have been at the centre of highly publicised mistakes, perhaps we could then be more generous to whole classes who can too often be dismissed for the sins or errors of judgement of one or two of their number. The media, business fat cats, managers, politicians, the unions, the railway industry, miners, farmers, Catholics, Protestants, Republicans, Unionists, nationalists and loyalists are just some of the groups who can be treated harshly through guilt by association with those individuals in the groups who have behaved badly.

In my judgement, Stephen Byers was not much worse than many other past or present government ministers. Nor was the mess he presided over as

Minister of Transport much worse than many other parts of the government or the economy. Nonetheless, the corrosive effect on government of being deemed untrustworthy is not to be taken lightly. If the Prime Minister seemed in his first five years to escape the consequences of his similar mistakes, especially over relations with donors to the Labour Party, then by 2003 he may have begun to rue the growing cynicism. For as international terrorism was met with diplomacy and military action by a Bush–Blair axis, Tony Blair began to experience what it was like to have his judgement questioned, then not trusted and eventually challenged at home and abroad.

It is not, however, these consequences of losing credibility which should ultimately determine the actions of government ministers and business executives. Traders should not engage in rogue dealing, farmers should not court foot-and-mouth disease by bad practice and ministers should not accept unseemly donations, whether or not the risks of detection materialise. Of course, traders must speculate, farmers cannot eradicate all risks and political parties need funding from somewhere. So what is needed for ethical economic activity is eternal vigilance about its purposes and lively debate about its boundaries. Just as the domestic economy seems to have conquered inflation, there is now the prospect of curbing inflationary moral rhetoric on business ethics. The old century passed with rival certainties finding little or no common ground: business was big and brash to some, almost beyond the reach of moral discourse, while to others it was big and evil, almost beneath contempt. The new millennium soon acquired a sense of proportion. International terrorism and the march towards war over Iraq's weapons of mass destruction put the misdemeanours of government and business into perspective. We need to moderate our ethical vocabulary, accepting that ministers and executives who make mistakes are not necessarily unethical monsters. On rare occasions, they act in bad faith. More often, they make bad decisions, in which case they should be held to account but not pilloried. We need to reserve our deepest moral indignation for countering evil. We need to conserve some of our everyday moral energy for our own economic decisions since most business is small and most ethical decisions are made by us, as employees and customers. The buyers', rather than the Byers', market is a moral arena for us all.

5

Countering Terrorism:
Uneasy Evil in an Uneasy World

Was it right to respond to the attacks on the USA of 11 September 2001 by launching a 'war on terror' in which innocent people were going to be killed? The US President George Bush and the UK Prime Minister Tony Blair answered 'Yes'. Others were uneasy at the outset, or became so as the conflict seemed to be settling into a long campaign. When the Taliban were suddenly defeated, it was the turn of those who had been sceptical about the war to experience unease about their position. By the first anniversary of the attacks, the balance had shifted again. As the whereabouts of Osama bin Laden remained a mystery and as President Bush contemplated pre-emptive strikes against Iraq, there was in some circles a reversion towards questioning the ethics or tactics of US responses to 11 September.

By 2003, the Israeli–Palestinian conflict continued to raise related ethical dilemmas, while tension rose between India and Pakistan over Kashmir to the point where some feared nuclear war between neighbours. Soon after the first anniversary of the 2001 attack came the bombing of tourists in Bali and then the hostage-taking by Chechens in Moscow which led to controversial, robust action by the Russian authorities in which many lives were lost even though many more were saved. The same politicians who are expected, in the circumstances of earlier chapters, to do something about medical ethics, about child killers and about business ethics, are simultaneously struggling with war and peace from Northern Ireland to northern Afghanistan, from Israel to Iraq. The connections could be seen more clearly from the USA after 11 September 2001, as illustrated by the evaporation of support for Irish Republican terrorism when Colombian connections were highlighted.

Yet still the first instinct of many who instruct others on ethics, especially church leaders, is the uneasy one of arguing for something close to pacifism. In this third millennium, church leaders tend to argue in practice against military intervention on any particular issue, from reaction to 11 September 2001 to pre-emption against Iraq a year or two later. It would be odd, of course, if bishops were militaristic, but an instinctive quasi-pacifism in the face of evil also has its uneasy elements. Arguing for pacifism itself could be seen as a noble position, albeit perhaps a naive one in a flawed world. It is dangerous, however, for the bishops or anyone else to be caught in an ethical no man's land between the morally entrenched and buttressed positions of pacifists on the one hand and those who accept in practice that a military action can sometimes be just on the other. It is debatable as to which of these positions requires the most courage or leads to the deepest unease, but no stance in these matters is untroubling.

In his first newspaper article after succeeding Dr George Carey in November 2002, the new Archbishop of Canterbury, Dr Rowan Williams, argued that it was facile to dismiss church leaders as appeasers because of the misgivings which he and others had expressed about military action against Iraq. He distinguished the circumstances of appeasement in 1938–9 and urged caution in 2002 on political, strategic and moral grounds. As we have seen in earlier chapters, especially on Northern Ireland, commentators are prone to justify their ethical preferences by reference to their superior understanding of the practicalities, such as the claim that another course of action would be 'counter-productive'. Although the archbishop is a distinguished theologian, it is unlikely that he has some political or strategic insight not vouchsafed to those more closely involved in decision-making on Iraqi weapons. His more interesting argument against Western intervention is an ethical one, which he describes as 'the classic moral challenge to colonialism of various kinds: we are not the best arbiters of the interests of others when we have interests of our own at stake (we are keenly aware of the matter of oil)'. This unease about conflicts of interest has also featured in earlier chapters, beginning with medical ethics.

This argument by the archbishop is much more intriguing, but is still not necessarily convincing. Even if he is asking the right question about interests in the region, we could dispute whether Saddam Hussein, the archbishop or George Bush is right in any judgements of the best interests of those in the Middle East. The previous chapter questioned whether a conflict of interests necessarily means that a decision-maker should abdicate responsibility or is bound to opt for the wrong course of action. Recognising that there is, or might be, such a conflict could honourably lead instead to being careful in analysing whose interests are at stake, what they might be and how they should be balanced, in the light of being aware that one's own interest in the outcome may distort perspectives but need not necessarily determine the outcome. Moreover, although the archbishop assumes that the interests at stake are those of 'the most helpless in a regional conflagration in the Middle East – minorities, refugees, ultimately the ordinary citizens of many states' .

(in which case we might, but might not, agree that Western decision-makers are not best placed to determine those interests), this need not be decisive if we believe that the primary duty of Western governments is to protect their own citizens.

At least the archbishop has not relied on the simplistic anti-Americanism which underpins some other arguments along similar lines. He was, after all, in an adjacent building when the twin towers of the World Trade Center were hit on 11 September 2001. Yet there does seem to be a visceral anti-Americanism in many other condemnations of the US response to the attacks of 11 September, including in the criticisms voiced by other religious figures. Reference to 'colonialism' gives a hint of the more troubling assumptions behind the arguments of others against the determined reaction of US leaders. Professor Fred Halliday of the London School of Economics, the expert in international relations and the Middle East, offers a corrective to such condescension. Writing soon after 11 September 2001, he acknowledges some legitimate criticisms of the USA but proceeds to observe:

> For all its faults, the USA is, to date, the most prosperous country in human history, the one to which many people, possibly half the world, would like to emigrate and work, whose vitality in a range of fields, from music to medicine, outstrips all others. It must be doing something right. It has in regard to many issues, gender and immigration among them, a record that puts most of Western Europe to shame. Much is made, especially in recent days, of American militarism and belligerency: this is, the discourse of cowboy culture aside, a myth. No other major country has a record as cautious and restrained as the USA: it had to be dragged into World War in 1941, as it was dragged into Bosnia in 1995. The USA fought three wars in the 1990s – Kuwait 1991, Bosnia 1995, Kosovo 1999 – all in response to aggression against Muslim people. Sneering at American aggressiveness comes strangely from other countries given their record in modern times: Britain and France, who trampled over half of Asia and Africa, Russia and China, not to mention Germany, Italy and Japan.

Stripping away from the 'appeasers' any pretensions to superior knowledge about what is productive or counter-productive and removing also any latent anti-Americanism, what is often left is the claim that the UN trumps the US in some moral hierarchy of decision-making. This argument may be a refined version of the previous ones, having its roots in a period when the US and the UN were in disagreement. Yet now that the Security Council of the United Nations has delivered a unanimous ultimatum to Iraq, this line from quasi-pacifists is less frequently invoked. It is quite a challenge to the argument that military action would only be moral if sanctioned by the United Nations when the UN does take steps towards supporting such action. For then we can see whether the argument was really a covert appeal to what was thought to be an appeasing body.

My own scepticism about this as an ethical argument is slightly different. For churches, which in other contexts argue that subsidiarity requires decisions to be taken at the most local level wherever possible, there is little or no analysis as to why the traditional duty of governments to secure the safety of their citizens should be ceded to a transnational body. This is a distinct point from the previous one, that process arguments may be only a cover for a substantive position against military action when church leaders believed that the UN was less likely than was the US to authorise the use of armed force. There are good *legal* arguments for engaging the UN, of course, and it may be that church leaders are laudably committed to international law with an interpretation thereof that assigns responsibility to the UN. It may also be that they are making *practical* points about international public opinion being more likely to support action which is backed by the UN. These are reasonable, *prudent* judgements, but the impression given is that they also see a *moral* element in waiting for the UN and one which is not there for other questions of morality, such as famine relief or waiving of banking debts. On those matters, church leaders expect their own charities to rush to the aid of the suffering, without waiting for a UN resolution, and they expect their own governments to forgo debts without waiting for a consensus. The church leaders are keen to point out that lives will be lost through famine or the burden of Third World debt so it cannot only be the life-and-death element which determines a different response. My rebuttable presumption is that church leaders' insistence on the UN's moral authority could wane if the UN were to disagree with them. To counter that harsh assumption, we would need some religious leaders to explain exactly why there is more *moral* authority in a global body than in governments exercising their traditional ethical and political duty to secure the safety of their citizens and, ideally, of others.

More generally, why is there such a strong urge on the part of church leaders to 'appease'? Pacifist or quasi-pacifist stances by church figures seem to rest on a selective reading of the New Testament, with the Sermon on the Mount and the injunction to turn the other cheek prominent among the explicit or implicit arguments for 'appeasement' or doing nothing in the face of international terrorism. Yet an earlier generation of Christian philosophers who argued in the 1960s *against* the possession of nuclear weapons could see that a few extracts from the New Testament were not sufficient as a basis for Christian attitudes to war and peace. Although their counsel against nuclear deterrence was rejected by church and political leaders alike and their judgement was, in my opinion, flawed and shown to be so by the enduring peace and eventual end of the Cold War, there was, nonetheless, a rigour in their approach which today's church leaders seem to have lost. As one of their number, Elizabeth Anscombe, observed, some seem to think that to follow Christianity is 'to act according to the Sermon on the Mount – to turn the other cheek and to offer no resistance to evil. In this account some of the evangelical counsels are chosen as containing the whole of Christian ethics: that is, they are made into precepts. (Only some of them; it is not likely that someone who deduces the *duty* of pacifism from the Sermon on the Mount and the rebuke to Peter, will agree to take "Give to him that asks of you" equally as a universally binding precept.)' Yet to condemn the use of force by authorities or to condemn soldiering as a profession is, according to Anscombe, to 'disregard what else is in the New Testament . . . A centurion was the first Gentile to be baptized; there is no suggestion in the New Testament that soldiering was regarded as incompatible with Christianity. The martyrology contains many names of soldiers whose occasion for martyrdom was not any objection to soldiering, but a refusal to perform idolatrous acts.' So Anscombe and others argued against nuclear weapons from a non–pacifist stance which had some intellectual, religious and ethical credibility, even if it was judged by deci-sion-makers to suffer from political naivety.

What happens now, however, is that church figures lobby against military action on the basis of their misunderstanding of their own tradition of faith and reason and their misjudgement of the realities of international terrorism. Professor George Weigel, perhaps best known as the author of *Witness to Hope: the Biography of John Paul II*, has traced the way in which the noble and influential just war tradition of the Christian Church has been corrupted into a 'presumption against violence' and how church leaders' calls for understanding the 'root causes of terrorism' amount to an expecta-tion that the victims of terrorist attacks should blame themselves (or at least their governments or 'their' corporations) for perceived injustices in the world which are alleged to have contributed to the attacks. Weigel notes how the Catholic bishops in the USA moved from regarding the just war tradition as a 'presumption in favor of peace and against war' in 1983 to talking of a 'strong presumption against the use of force' in 1993, then a 'presumption against violence' in 2001 accompanied by fears for a 'spiral of violence' which is increasingly yoked to an emphasis on those 'root causes of terrorism and/or violence' which are usually assumed to be economic inequality in the world.

Weigel gives this drift the shortest of shrift. Empirically, he notes the failure of those who use such claims to produce any evidence for a link between global economic inequality and al–Qaeda attacks. In his judgement, the 11 September 'perpetrators were well-educated, amply-funded middle-class people'. Linguistically and theologically, he shows what a difference is made, for the worse, when church leaders move in this way from 'peace' and 'war' to using 'force' and 'violence', without any discrimination between the use of force by a lawful and moral authority in defence of citizens and the use of force by those who launched the attacks of 11 September. The church leaders have gradually lost touch with their tradition's just war doctrine. For, properly understood, it leads to the conclusion not only that the US government has the right to defend its citizens, but that it has the duty to do so. Weigel puts it thus: 'The classic Catholic tradition, whose roots are found in Augustine, begins with the presumption – better, the moral judgment – that rightly-constituted public authority is under a strict moral obligation to defend the security of those for whom it has assumed responsibility, even if this puts the magistrate's own life in jeopardy.'

The theologian Robin Gill has explained the just war doctrine in the following terms:

For a law to be considered just, it must:

(1) have been undertaken by a lawful authority
(2) have been undertaken for the vindication of an undoubted right that has certainly been infringed
(3) be a last resort, all peaceful means of settlement having failed
(4) offer the possibility of the good to be achieved outweighing the evils that war would involve
(5) be waged with right intention
(6) be waged with a reasonable hope of victory for justice

As with earlier sets of questions or principles (for instance, from the Archbishop of Westminster on medical ethics or from Allfirst Bank on risk management), the clarity and simplicity of expression may belie the difficulty of judgement in answering the questions and applying them to the facts of a dilemma. There are plenty of impressive analyses of each condition. In particular, there are ingenious attempts to define 'last resort' in ways which permit pre-emptive strikes against states or terrorist networks. In the modern world of nuclear, biological and chemical 'weapons of mass destruction', it can be argued that it may be too late to wait for the last resort before tackling evil. Yet even those who enjoy Weigel's robust approach might have some unease about squeezing pre-emptive strikes against non-state terrorist networks into a doctrine which has traditionally focused on when states are entitled to wage war against other states. My answer is to question the assumption that morality is exhausted by the alternative conclusions that a war or anything else is just or unjust. Resisting evil could be regarded as an ethical option, perhaps even an ethical duty, even if the just war criteria are not satisfied. This is intended not so much to make the moral choice any easier as to downgrade the rhetoric from grandiose to accurate. Rather than asking whether President George Bush was waging a just war against al-Qaeda or Iraq, the issue is better put as to whether he was leading the necessary use of armed force to protect the world from evil.

Before considering what evil is and why evil might make a difference, the most pressing question on the day of 11 September itself was not one for the niceties of the just war doctrine. Instead, the brutal choice was whether or not it was right to authorise the shooting down of a hijacked civilian plane heading for the World Trade Center or the Pentagon or the White House. President Bush answered in the affirmative and US planes were scrambled to implement that order but were not able to carry out the instruction in time. For many armchair observers of politics, this would have been the uneasiest of ethical decisions, but elected officials seem to find it clear-cut. The UK government explained that the Prime Minister would have had to have made such a decision in this country, while the USA adjusted its arrangements after 11 September so that two generals could also issue such an order, no doubt also changing the location of its fighter planes so that they could in practice intercept in such cases.

The USA had not taken effective preventative action, perhaps because popular support would not have been so readily forthcoming for actions which would have prevented the 11 September attacks as it was for retaliation immediately afterwards. Yet there had been earlier bombings and hijackings. The World Trade Center itself had been attacked on 26 February 1993 by the less spectacular method of parking in the basement a truck laden with explosives. Six people were killed, but it seems that the towers could have collapsed had a little more explosive been placed in a slightly different place. One of those convicted of the attack asked an interviewer why the media did not place as much emphasis on those killed by the USA, citing specifically the 200,000 killed in Japan by the atomic bombs. This has opened up for some a symbolism in that the intention of the 1993 attack was said to have been to kill 200,000, calculated by assuming that there would be 50,000 workers in the twin towers, 50,000 visitors and the same numbers in the surrounding offices.

Nor was the 1993 attack on the World Trade Center an isolated event. An American military residence hall in Saudi Arabia was bombed in 1996, American embassies in Kenya and Tanzania were bombed in 1998. There was a plot to hijack eleven transpacific airliners on one day in 1995. Known as the Bojinka plot, from the file name found on the computer of the man convicted of this conspiracy, this was thought to be funded by Osama bin Laden, as were the embassy attacks in 1998. A dry run for the Bojinka plot in December 1994 led to the arrest, trial and conviction of Ramzi Yousef.

In 1997, before the embassy bombings, Osama bin Laden expressed the view that America deserved to be targeted because it was 'the biggest terrorist in the world' – citing US actions in using Saudi Arabia – and issued a fatwa calling on Muslims to join him in a war 'to kill the Americans and their allies'. Sometimes such anti-Americanism is explained by the speaker's opposition to the regimes in Muslim countries where the USA supports the government (as in the example of Saudi Arabia or the earlier example of the Shah in Iran), sometimes it is linked to US support of Israel, sometimes to its economic or cultural or military or diplomatic power.

It has become fashionable to say that 11 September has changed the world or the way we think about the world. In this chapter, the focus will be on the three aspects of countering terrorism highlighted above. In reverse order, which puts them in their proper chronological sequence, how do we understand the moral unease surrounding our failure to prevent such an atrocity, how would we have reacted if it had been possible to intercept the terrorism on the day at a cost to innocent lives but saving others, and how do we adapt 'just war' principles, or any other ethical framework, to decide the right response after the event? Each of these has uneasy elements for any Western liberal reader. Each has connections to other uneasy cases, most obviously Northern Ireland and the release of child killers, but in a sense to all our dilemmas. For instance, if the attack had been on 11 September 2000, then the dilemma on the day would probably have featured alongside Yates and Simpson in the Andes as one of the real examples, alongside the hypothetical about whether to shoot a six-year-old who was running amok shooting others in a school playground, in the Court of Appeal's judgements in the Siamese twins' case. Just as the heroism of firefighters and others on 11 September will endure in our memories, the moral dilemmas of coping with the attacks will now come to mind as we are called to make ethical judgements in other circumstances. As with the artist's sketch of the Siamese twins or the haunting video image of James Bulger being led away by one of his killers, hand in hand, our visual age has been changed for ever by the sight on television and in our newspapers of the planes crashing into the twin towers of the World Trade Center. The power and horror of the immediate and constant slow-motion video replay of the crashes was soon appreciated by the politicians and the media, so that some self-restraint was applied. After a period of accompanying any report on 11 September with the same shocking images, the media accepted that this was gratuitously distressing to the relatives of those involved and ran the risk of distorting the politics and possibly the ethics of how to respond.

On the ethics of response, three preliminary points are in order. First, it is possible to accept that pacifism is a legitimate option for an individual without agreeing that it is a legitimate option for a government, a lawful authority which has a duty to protect its citizens. Second, while process points are often invoked (the rights of parents in the case of the Siamese twins or the need for UN approval in this context), the suspicion lingers that we turn to these when we think the parental or UN position on the substantive question will match ours. Third, as with the previous chapters, media ethics and the ethics of each uneasy case are nowadays always intertwined.

The role of the media in shaping our understanding of the world can be illustrated by sporting ethics. Although omitted from these five examples of uneasy cases because sport is, by comparison, less tragic, it is an important setting for the development of all the virtues and vices considered in this book. Its importance comes less from any inherent significance than from the universal enthusiasm and therefore universal experiences which sport inspires. Schoolteachers and parents around the world can testify to the power of professional sporting examples in developing or undermining notions of fair play. Constant slow-motion replaying by the media of a video clip can nowadays bring the whole world's attention to an aspect of an incident which the referee or umpire and large sections of the crowd at the particular game did not even notice. The ubiquity of cameras in an era of saturation coverage means that even more modest games are subject to the same scrutiny. A push here, a hand there, a trip here, an overreaction to the crowd there – all the drama is captured from a variety of angles. Those of us who watched lower league soccer decades ago might have argued about what happened in an off-the-ball incident. Our view would almost certainly have been obscured, partly because in those days the crowd stood on terraces and partly because our eyes would have been trying to follow the ball. Now, armchair analysts know exactly what happened and can pass judgement in the light of slow-motion replays.

Although sporting and media ethics are sometimes assumed to be about bad behaviour, they can be a force for good, separately or in combination. For example, the London Marathon is a good metaphor for lifelong learning. It is an inclusive event of the highest quality, in which world-class athletes, on foot or in wheelchairs, compete alongside those who are just running for fun, for charity or to stretch themselves. It is not true to say that the one group holds back the other. Rather, each enhances the occasion for the other. Similarly, it is possible and inspiring in higher education to combine a commitment to widening participation and a commitment to the highest levels of research. A wonderful mix of the London Marathon itself and the creative media coverage thereof means that this analogy is immediately understood by all-comers. Capturing on film the instinctive actions of the joint winners of the first London Marathon, in trusting one another to cross the line together, has provided a lasting antidote to cynicism about sport. Media coverage which conveys the hard work involved in training for a marathon does much to prepare viewers not only for sport, but for life.

The importance of the media also applies to the challenge posed by terror and war. As the philosopher Professor Simon Blackburn observes in 'Being Good', 'A single photograph may have done more to halt the Vietnam war than all the writings of moral philosophers of the time put together', referring to Hung Cong (Nick) Ut's picture, known as 'Accidental Napalm Attack, 1972'. It is not the case, then, that the media are always to be berated for negative, unethical coverage of our world. On the contrary, the media are making ethical, responsible judgements in real time as unethical events unfold. They are not merely recording what *is* happening, however, they can affect reactions by the way in which they show what *has* happened so far and the way in which they press for comment on what *should* happen next. The media, albeit nudged by governments, quickly saw for themselves in September 2001 that there was a ghoulish sensationalism, bordering on warmongering, involved in endless slow-motion replays of the planes crashing into the twin towers of the World Trade Center. They then exercised self-restraint in the pictures and footage which accompanied their reports. More subtly, media lines of questioning can affect, for good or ill, our sense of which questions are most important in the face of such a tragedy. For example, in less traumatic crises, the media tend to press officials on the issue of resignations. In these circumstances, however, the media seemed to appreciate that responsibility for any failures of intelligence or of airport security paled by comparison with the tasks now facing those very people. Questions about resignation could be postponed for another time. The moment having passed, with the fourth hijacked plane coming down in open country probably as a result of heroic intervention by passengers, there was no point in dwelling on the question whether the President was right to have ordered that the same plane, with those heroic civilians on board, could have been shot down by a US fighter pilot. Nonetheless, the time comes eventually, after a decent interval, when it is appropriate to return to these uneasy matters.

The solemn nature of this uneasy cluster of ethical dilemmas is linked to the notion of 'evil' and the sensation that in those video clips we have seen evil manifested in slow motion. Apart from any other merits of ethical analysis, by separating these three elements of what could have been done to prevent the attacks, whether the hijacked planes should have been intercepted and how we should have reacted after the event, the danger of giving up analysis in the face of evil is avoided. Later in the chapter, however, the overused word 'evil' must be confronted. It cannot necessarily be analysed to any reader's satisfaction. For one view is that evil is the ethical nadir of disorder or irrationality, that it can suck in would-be analysts but is so powerful precisely because it is not susceptible to rational dissection. This perspective, associated with Fr Bernard Lonergan SJ and many other Christians, explains why some Catholic bishops and evangelical Protestant pastors unite in their opposition to even the seemingly lighthearted end of the occult spectrum, from Hallowe'en to Harry Potter, and would object strongly to any attempt to include witchcraft in, say, feminist theology courses. Nonetheless, the word 'evil' has been such a large element in moral reactions to the events of 11 September that its use and abuse need to be considered carefully. Again, this connects to its use in the case of the child killers and in the history of Northern Ireland. Indeed, its use has become so prevalent that it sometimes seems that we have to remind ourselves that ethical dilemmas can come from a noble disagreement in which good motives are attributed all round. From most views, for instance, the Siamese twins' case was free of any evil, but ethical unease still permeated a debate which was set very much within the realm of good intentions.

There are several uneasy aspects to the first element: could and should the USA have taken more effective steps (in the previous decade rather than just the days running up to the flights) to prevent the attacks happening on 11 September 2001?

It is likely that the USA is taking such action now to prevent similar attacks, but that has been made possible by the reactions to 11 September 2001. The liberal paradox is that the liberal consensus would not have tolerated such draconian action in the absence of the catastrophe which the action could have prevented from occurring. There are some obvious reasons why the 11 September 2001 attacks seem to have changed moral outlooks about the action which the West could take. First, they worked far more effectively than these other attempts. Second, they were covered live on television. What has been described as seeing the 'aesthetic of evil' affected the moral judgements of Western politicians and citizens in a way which radio or newspaper textual reports of earlier terrorist attacks could not achieve. Third, politicians and leaders of the armed forces who were previously restrained by criticism of unjust warmongering by liberals could now act as if the liberal agenda had contributed to the terrorist flourishing in the first place. Human rights groups could be more easily dismissed as appeasers. The liberal critique of any measure to prevent or counter terrorism is usually three-pronged. The first claim is that it would be immoral to implement X (where X might be internment or carpet bombing). The second is that X would not work. The third is that X would be counter-productive. The second and third seem to conflict (the claim of the second is negated in the assumption of the third, that X might work but would have harmful effects), yet each had a track record, until 11 September 2001, of being quite effective in the media wars which either pre-empt or presage military battles.

Those of us who have used one or more of these claims in an attempt to thwart government or military plans may have underestimated, prior to 11 September, the risks and real threats of tragedy. Some may still hold to one of the lines of argument, especially the first. Part of our unease about 11 September, however, may come from the suspicion that the atrocities could have been prevented. It is salutary to consider, therefore, why 11 September attacks did, on this view, change everything. My own conclusion is that those responsible for the 11 September attacks orchestrated a performance act of unimagined, synchronised symbolism. All the elements were there in previous terrorist incidents – suicide bombers, plane hijackings, attacks on high-profile targets – but on this occasion they were combined with simplicity (the use of knives and the turning of the fuel-laden planes into 'bombs' bypassed the need to take explosives through airport security) and literally deadly effectiveness. Two symbols of American world dominance – planes and media – were turned in on a third, fourth and possibly fifth – the World Trade Center, the Pentagon and perhaps the White House.

We are uneasy at being outwitted. Words like evil can become a surrogate for analysis or understanding. Religion in general and Islam in particular were the targets of the blame-mongers. In truth, a little more reflection on religion might have explained some of the iconic nature of the events and some of our deep unease. Western pundits and politicians, led by Tony Blair, went to the Koran to plunder quotations from holy texts. Religion is indeed partly about texts, but it is also about rites, about worship. World faiths have a rich history of spectacle, of symbolism. They have a deep belief in, and abundant experience of, the transforming, sacramental nature of performance acts. Those who wish to intimidate the faithful are often as well aware of the high moments as are the believers. In El Salvador, for instance, Archbishop Oscar Romero could have been assassinated at any time but state-sponsored terrorism chose the moment of consecration as he was celebrating Mass.

The 11 September attacks leave, in my opinion, the thesis of the clash of civilisations as implausible as it was on 10 September or in previous years. Muslim–Muslim conflicts have been a feature of world affairs in the last decade or so. At the level of states, Iraq's invasion of Kuwait and the Iran–Iraq war were both Muslim–Muslim confrontations. It is misleading to assume that the major fault line is Muslim v. the Rest of the World.

What the 11 September attacks demonstrated is something different, namely the enormity of the task facing those who are charged with the responsibility of preventing such terrorism. Unlike terrorists, democratic politicians can be constrained by their voters' squeamishness about methods. Moreover, governments regard themselves as having infinite targets to protect at all times. As the IRA more or less observed after Margaret Thatcher escaped from their Brighton bomb, states have to be lucky always to escape terrorists but terrorists have only to be lucky once. Terrorists can create unease by establishing a stark contrast between giving themselves the widest possible scope for achieving their aims and giving the authorities the narrowest possible scope for any response. Osama bin Laden, for instance, could have chosen any target, any method, any time, but his success seemed at first to dictate that the Western alliance's only criterion of success would be whether they captured him, dead or alive, while he was ensconced in a network of impenetrable caves as the Afghanistan winter approached. Even then, on the assumption that he would not be taken alive, the act of locating him would provoke further dissent within the West as to whether this was 'bringing him to justice'. In practice, America quickly established an alternative test of success, namely to bring down the Taliban regime in Afghanistan which was harbouring Osama bin Laden. When this was achieved, when the revised target was hit, the West seemed to regard that as a job well done.

There has been a notable reluctance, however, to examine the failures of intelligence, perhaps of common sense, perhaps of liberal queasiness, in the years before 11 September 2001. Instead, journalists and the authorities have meticulously reconstructed the minutiae of the days, weeks and months leading up to 11 September. It may well be the case that if the same degree of attention had been directed in real time to preventing the suicide hijackers from boarding the planes, then the tragedy could have been averted. Although this might have involved some elements of surveillance invading privacy, the main ethical dilemmas lie elsewhere. Would we have countenanced derogations from normal human rights standards years in advance if we had known what was going to happen? Would we have been prepared to anticipate and perhaps prevent such events through symbolic acts of counter-terrorism? For once we grasp that terrorist acts such as the attacks of 11 September are performances and are performative, then answers to the first question about our will to take preventative action may themselves be transformed. This is because such an understanding of the symbolism of terrorism at once rules out on pragmatic grounds certain means of *re*action while also suggesting the importance of a sense of the dramatic or the theatrical in *pre*ventative action. A classic example of a symbolic manoeuvre in the Northern Irish context was the infamous broadcasting restrictions on those who supported terrorism. The introduction of these rules was widely criticised by civil libertarians, especially in the USA, with each of the three (mutually contradictory) critiques set out above, but it may have played a part in the process whereby Sinn Fein/IRA came in from the cold. At around the same time (the late 1980s), as the media railed against these restrictions, they were embroiled in tendentious coverage of the saga which should have alerted the authorities to the 'clash of civilisations' before Samuel Huntington coined that term, namely the furore surrounding Salman Rushdie's book, *The Satanic Verses*.

These twin threats to free speech were discussed at the time in my book *The Cost of Free Speech*, so this analysis is not an attempt to be wise after the events a dozen years later. The broadcasting restrictions were not only disliked but also derided, because they seemed, as one judge put it, 'half-baked'. In a way, however, they went right to the crux of the uneasy choice facing those who supported terrorism. If you are only half committed to democracy, you can only half participate. The lesson many civil libertarians chose to deduce was that the government was being petty or incoherent. It may be, as I argued at the time, however, that those subjected to the irksome restrictions got the message even if the media pundits did not. The message was that the rights and privileges of full participation in a democracy should not be mocked by the use, or support, of violence. Hence the mark of Cain was being put on those who still condoned, or refused to condemn, the use of violence. Authority in the television age comes with appearing on camera, so the government was making it more difficult for the supporters of violence to benefit from the legitimacy which the medium bestowed. The inconvenience of dubbing their speech made broadcasters less likely to broadcast them, especially in relation to breaking news. The use of actors' voices also had a similar effect to a pulsating asterisk in the corner of the screen, acting as an irritant to viewers, reminding them that these were not fully-fledged democrats, if those are defined as eschewing violence. Moreover, the liberal Home Secretary of the day, Douglas Hurd, had in the broadcasting restrictions succeeded in doing as little as the Prime Minister, Margaret Thatcher, would allow in the wake of the IRA's bomb attacks on a coach of soldiers at Ballygawley and on the house of the leading civil servant in Northern Ireland, Kenneth (now Sir Kenneth) Bloomfield. Some action was necessary and this was a long way from the draconian end of the spectrum where internment might have been an option. It is difficult to judge the impact of these restrictions. Although all the usual arguments were deployed against them (ineffective or, if effective, counter-productive, and so on), they could be seen as a step on the journey towards peace.

Returning to the question why more was not done to prevent the attacks of 11 September, it is also the case, of course, that failures of coordination or planning were to blame. In other words, it is perhaps too easy to blame the liberal consensus for thwarting preventative action, at least until we consider whether the measures which were in place could have thwarted the attacks if properly implemented, in which case the liberal reluctance to allow more restrictions might emerge with more honour. Joseph Nye, a former chair of the USA's National Intelligence Council, wrote soon after the attacks:

The *New York Times* reported two weeks after the September 11 attacks that US intelligence and law-enforcement officials 'failed by their own admission to share information adequately or coordinate their efforts, and were caught by surprise [by the attacks]. Washington did not build a strong international coalition to focus on defeating Al Qaeda, which was seen by other nations as an American problem.' Since 1996, the FBI had had evidence of terrorists using U.S. flight schools to learn to fly jumbo jets. Two of the September 11 hijackers had been flagged by the CIA as potential terrorists, but their names were not placed on an Immigration and Naturalization Service (INS) watch list until after they had already entered the country; they also escaped placement on the larger Inter-agency Border Inspection System. Fighter planes were scrambled too late to have any effect on September 11. The North American Aerospace Defence Command (NORAD) lacked a direct telephone line to the Federal Aviation Administration. As NORAD's commanding officer later lamented, 'If somebody had called us and said, "We have a hijacking 100 miles out coming from Europe or South America, there are terrorists on board and they've taken over the airplane," that's a scenario we've practised. We did not practise – and I wish to God we had – a scenario where this takes off out of Boston, and minutes later crashes into New York City. This is a whole new ballgame.'

There are endless ways in which, with hindsight, we can see that a different mindset rather than different laws could have made a difference. To take just one more illustration, it has seemed odd to many that flight crews did not seem to have resisted the hijackers. The culture of passivity, however, was because their conditioning led them to assume that the hijackers were taking hostages rather than engaged in a suicide attack. Once mobile phone messages alerted some passengers on the later flight to what had happened with the earlier ones, they attempted to tackle the hijackers, which probably caused the crash into open ground and thus heroically prevented a fourth crash into a high-profile building.

For centuries, of course, philosophers, theologians, politicians and citizens have argued about the application of just war doctrine to the particular circumstances of their times and places. Yet deterrence has been discussed as if it were merely a function of the capacity for destruction – if we demonstrate our nuclear weaponry, then they will not dare to attack us. Perhaps not, if 'they' are a non-nuclear state or minor nuclear power, but nowadays the 'they' are more likely to be terrorists who are setting out to provoke states and especially the USA into action which in turn alienates the supporters or potential supporters of the terrorists.

The prior ethical issue, therefore, is how we *prevent* terrorist attacks, preferably without undermining the values which we are defending, including both the human rights of suspects and also the liberties of our citizens who should be able to go about their business without terror. It is a question of risk management, an unglamorous task which requires constant vigilance and which yields only exposure for failure, never glory for successful prosecution. It is also expensive and can be unpopular. It is so unfashionable a task that theologians and philosophers have tended to eschew it, preferring to focus all their attention on what to do if you are attacked first, with the sole exception mentioned above of addressing the (im)morality of relying on a nuclear deterrent. At its most sophisticated, that debate explored, during the second half of the twentieth century, the subtleties of whether it can be moral to bluff, threatening to do something which you think would be unethical but trusting that the threat will be so effective that you will never have to carry it out (or more precisely, if you are true to your ideals, that you will never have to be shown to have been bluffing).

In the new millennium, however, such extraordinary ingenuity needs to be directed at the more pressing moral issues of a world in which we know that the terrorists are not bluffing and they will not be deterred by bluffs or by actual reprisals. They need instead to be stopped. One way is by removing the supposed causes of terrorists' hatred of their targets, for instance by giving in to their demands for America to change its policy in the Middle East. If the underlying policy is ethical, however, it could be immoral to change it, either at all or under such pressure. The word 'could' signals two caveats. First, one ethical policy can sometimes be replaced by another ethical policy. There can be more than one ethical approach to the Middle East, Northern Ireland or other conflicts. Second, sometimes it can be ethical to change one's behaviour in the light of the behaviour, even the immoral behaviour, of others. Nevertheless, pusillanimous giving in to terrorist demands is not what most people have in mind when talking of 'stopping' terrorists. Apart from the gibe that this would be cowardly and the judgement that it could be unethical, it is unlikely to work. On the contrary, giving in to one set of terrorist demands, whether about policy or ransoms, is likely to encourage other terrorist groups rather than stop terrorism.

The primary ways to stop terrorist attacks such as those of 11 September 2001 are to do with prevention through intelligence, detection and tracking, whether by infiltration or surveillance. Richard Betts has noted that 'Three weeks before September 11, the director of central intelligence (DCI), George Tenet, gave an interview to *Signal* magazine that now seems tragically prescient. He agonized about the prospect of a catastrophic intelligence failure: "Then the country will want to know why we didn't make those investments; why we didn't pay the price; why we didn't develop the capability."' Betts has warned the USA, however, that surprise attacks will still happen, whatever improvements are made to the intelligence services, given 'the crafty opponents who strategize against it and the alien cultures that are not transparent to American minds'. Where prevention fails, of course, it does not follow that surprise attacks will lead to ultimate success in an ensuing war, e.g., Japan lost after the surprise attack on Pearl Harbor, Argentina lost after invading the Falklands, Iraq lost after invading Kuwait. Nonetheless, even though a surprise attack cannot always be anticipated or thwarted and even though it need not presage disaster, we need to direct more intelligence, in every sense, to a culture of prevention.

Education, in at least two contexts, would be a good starting point. First, states are less susceptible to terrorism if the cultures which foster or harbour terrorists are well educated in relation to the target state. Myths *about* America may well have played a part in the 11 September attacks. Second, education *in* America has much to do if its citizens are to understand why those other cultures hold the views they do about the USA and if the intelligence community is to operate effectively in these circumstances. As Betts has noted, 'there are very few genuinely bilingual, bicultural Americans capable of operating like natives in exotic reaches of the Middle East, Central and South Asia, or other places that shelter the bin Ladens of the world. For similar reasons there have been limitations on our capacity to translate information that does get collected. The need is not just for people who have studied Arabic, Pashto, Urdu, or Farsi, but for those who are truly fluent in those languages, and fluent in obscure dialects of them.'

Turning from the practicalities of prevention to the moralities of reactions to the 11 September attacks, what exactly are the moral dilemmas which cause unease? The immediate question, largely forgotten in the horrors which followed, was whether to shoot down the airplanes once the intentions of the hijackers were known. The longer-term question was whether to launch an attack on those who harboured those thought to be responsible. In both cases, innocent people would die as a result of presidential orders.

There is a particularly intriguing contrast between the President's instant authorisation and the vacillation of many of us who merely observe. One explanation is that, as armchair analysts, we seem to fear decision-making whereas politicians have had to be decisive to attain their positions. Another, overlapping, explanation is that armchair analysts may be squeamish, not wanting to see anyone die at our hands, at the push of our remote-control buttons, preferring to place moral weight (however mistakenly) on knowing that we would not *do* something actively to kill the innocent, even if our omission meant that other lives would have been lost. How does this relate to the hypothetical cases (about the child with a gun or indeed the plane-related issues) which the Court of Appeal considered in their Siamese twins' judgements, as well as to the greater willingness to countenance a war on terrorism in response to the attacks of 11 September? My suggestion is that our own brands of moral night vision or tunnel vision may distort our judgement. Whether through the cultural conditioning of disaster movies or otherwise, it is difficult even to think about the issue of shooting down the airplane without imagining the terror of the innocent passengers. Faced with the prospect of interception, meaning the certain death of these anguished passengers, this imagery may lead us to wishful thinking that perhaps the terrorists on board can be overpowered or that the plane will crash in a way which does not cause the death of other lives.

The dilemma was put to the President somewhat differently. He was on a school visit in Florida when his Chief of Staff told him that a plane had crashed into one of the World Trade Center towers. He was in a classroom when he was told that another had crashed, that many lives were lost and that America was under attack. He soon left the children and spoke to the Vice-President who was in the White House and then to the new director of the FBI. After these calls, he told his staff who were with him on the school trip, 'We're at war.' Before his plane took to the air with fighter plane protection, the third hijacked plane crashed into the Pentagon and the White House was evacuated. It was in these circumstances that the President was asked to authorise the interception and the shooting down of a civilian plane. Wishful thinking and squeamishness were not on the agenda in this presentation. Moreover, unlike the Siamese twins case, the release of the child killers or almost any development in Northern Ireland, there was no disagreement in the advice offered. The unease for the President would have come if the military chain of command, or other key advisers, opposed the authorisation. In fact, it was the Vice-President who proposed that the President authorise the fighter plane to intercept, if possible, the fourth plane, thought to be heading for the White House. The fighter plane had been scrambled from its Virginia base to intercept the third hijacked plane but that had crashed into the Pentagon before the fighter pilot was in a position to act. By the time authorisation was sought, therefore, it was in the light of three planes which had crashed into prominent targets. Before the fighter pilot could intercept the fourth plane, however, it crashed in open country in Pennsylvania, seemingly because passengers had heroically tackled the hijackers.

Professor Peter Hennessy has pointed towards an issue with some similarities in his book, *The Secret State*. New prime ministers have to write instructions to commanders of submarines with nuclear capability as to what they should do in the event of the UK being defeated in conflict. The consensus seems to be that prime ministers probably suggest first that the submarines should put themselves under the command of allies such as the USA or Australia. If that is impossible, then prime ministers may have authorised the use of nuclear weapons as a reprisal or at least not ruled this out in leaving the commanders with discretion to form their own judgement.

Again, the enormity of the decision seems more likely to overawe those of us who do not have to write the letters than it is to unnerve the prime ministers who do write them. This is not to say that prime ministers would find this anything but an uneasy case. Nevertheless, they understand what is expected of them in these most chilling of circumstances. Peter Hennessy reports a conversation with Lord Home, the former Prime Minister and Foreign Secretary, reflecting in his retirement about what might have happened at the height of the Cold War – 'what one might call the last contingency of retaliation – Operation Visitation as it was called. He said the Soviet leaders could not bank on a British Prime Minister not pressing the button if there were "great hordes marching right across Europe and demolishing civilisation as we know it".'

In any event, isolated readers or TV news viewers are not in the same position as world leaders surrounded by military, diplomatic and political advisers, having been schooled and rehearsed in the choices which might face them. Although 'group-think' or the herd instinct is a moral danger of which to be aware, as was pointed out in the last chapter, political leaders' decisiveness is aided by the dynamic of their entourage and the might of the military, whereas indecisiveness is likely to feed on itself as isolated television viewers ponder what they would have done.

By the end of 11 September, the President had already established the USA's answer to the question how to respond. In speaking to the US nation, he twice used the word 'evil', saying that 'Thousands of lives were suddenly ended by evil' and 'Today our nation saw evil'. He declared, 'We will make no distinction between the terrorists who committed these acts and those who harbour them.' Again, of course, the President and his advisers were making judgements in the light of more information than the armchair observer was likely to possess or could recall. For instance, after those earlier embassy attacks, President Clinton had authorised reprisals against Osama bin Laden, but they proved impossible to carry out while respecting that very distinction between those who are responsible for attacks and those who harbour them. This history was set out subsequently in the British government's statement of the evidence against Osama bin Laden.

The use of the word 'evil' poses uneasy questions not only about the particular moral dilemma but also about the moral universe, not only about the nature of humanity but also about the existence and nature of a divinity. How can a good God permit evil? More precisely, it is not just the word used to describe the events but rather the events themselves which are said by already secular commentators to present an unanswerable question. In the academy, evil events are also said to expose theology as a bogus discipline. Neither God nor theology need be abandoned, however, as a result of reflection on evil. Although believers are uneasy about the problem of evil, it does not follow that any other discipline, such as philosophy, or any other world view, such as secularism, has an easy answer. On the contrary, ethical judgement seems to presuppose choice ranging from good to bad, from ideal to evil. If God banned evil, then it would not make sense to talk of goodness or choice in pursuing the right path. For the wrong path would then have been, by definition, an impassable route. In other words, moral judgement presupposes choice of good and bad, right and wrong, what ought to be done and what ought not to be done. The fact that some choose the very worst course of action does not make a nonsense of morality or theology or divinity. Rather, it reinforces the need to seek a deeper understanding.

A simple definition of evil has eluded some of the greatest philosophers and theologians. In the context of the course of this book, from virtues such as justice and mercy to looking at bad behaviour in the previous chapter and now evil in this, a tentative understanding of evil can be garnered from Klaus Hemmerle's explanation that 'evil is more than simply what is morally bad . . . As distinguished from what is bad . . . evil means the positing of the contradiction of the good, deliberate denial of the good. . . evil has a radiating power capable of bringing into disharmony the world itself.' When put in this way, it follows that squeamish inaction is not an acceptable response to evil. Evil cannot be allowed to triumph but must be combated. It works in frightening ways which Hannah Arendt controversially tried to describe as the banality of evil in *Eichmann in Jerusalem*. Her point was, as Richard Bernstein explains in *Radical Evil*, that once evil such as that manifested in Auschwitz takes hold, it does not need demonic monsters to implement it:

> According to her account, neither blind anti-Semitism, sadistic hatred, nor even deep ideological convictions motivated him. He was motivated by the most mundane and petty considerations of advancing his career, pleasing his superiors, demonstrating that he could do his job well and efficiently. In this sense, his motives were at once banal and all too human.

This landed Arendt in trouble with those who thought, mistakenly, that she was trying to exculpate Eichmann. Rather, she was touching on an important theme of this book, the importance of honing our judgement and the dire effects when the ability to make judgements is lost through evil or otherwise. Bernstein points out that Kant's faculty of judgement, 'as she conceived it, does not require sophisticated theoretical knowledge; it is exhibited by individuals who cut across all walks of life – educated and uneducated. In her essay entitled "Thinking and Moral Considerations", she drew upon Socrates as an individual who eminently illustrated this capacity to think and to judge.' Bernstein explains that Arendt reflected on how it was that 'there were some individuals (albeit too few) from all walks of life who were able to resist evil and act in a decent manner' under the Nazis. She concluded, in her own words, that it was not knowledge but 'the ability to tell right and wrong, beautiful from ugly. And this, at the rare moments when the stakes are on the table, may indeed prevent catastrophes.' Evil threatens to engulf all-comers in a warped set of values whereby 'everybody is swept away unthinkingly by what everybody else does and believes in', whereupon we need 'Socrates' midwifery, which brings out implications of unexamined opinions and thereby destroys them – values, doctrines, theories and even convictions'.

Of course, the moral force of the word 'evil' may be undermined by overuse. It is not as if American presidents have reserved the term for 11 September 2001. In his State of the Union address of 29 January 2002, President George Bush identified an 'axis of evil' – North Korea, Iraq and Iran – perhaps echoing President Ronald Reagan's description in the 1980s of the Soviet Union as an 'evil empire'. *The Economist* observed that the phrase 'axis of evil' was intended to 'galvanise support by turning a long and tricky foreign-policy challenge into a simple, moral issue'. The New Labour government in Britain had tried in the late 1990s to turn all such challenges into simple issues by adopting an 'ethical' foreign policy. This was subjected to ridicule, especially when the ethics of the private life of the then Foreign Secretary, Robin Cook, became the subject of media attention. Of course, it is not only Western governments which like to consider their own foreign policies as ethical and their opponents' policies as 'evil'. Unsurprisingly, those attacking the West reverse these judgements, regarding the USA as 'evil' and praising resistance to the superpower as the only ethical response.

Encouragingly for the vibrancy of moral discourse, there are dissenting voices *within* cultures so that the Vietnam War, for example, led various American philosophers to turn their attention to the morality, or rather the immorality, of the conflict in the 1960s and early 1970s. Thomas Nagel, for instance, criticised the use of napalm and flame-throwers 'as an atrocity in all circumstances that I can imagine, whoever the target may be. Burns are both extremely painful and extremely disfiguring – far more than any other category of wound. That this well-known fact plays no (inhibiting) part in the determination of US weapons policy suggests that moral sensitivity among public officials has not increased markedly since the Spanish Inquisition.' Those who agree with Nagel's analysis believe that a proper understanding of morality would prohibit such actions even in a war against terrorism or evil, which is one reason for the persistence of ethical unease even when 'evil' has been diagnosed. Indeed, for those who are prepared to risk tangling with evil, deepening our understanding of its nature can make a measured response all the more vital.

The Oxford philosopher Stuart Hampshire, for example, reflects on his wartime experience in intelligence and concludes in *Innocence and Experience* that

> 'Evil' is not a term that has been prominent in contemporary philosophical ethics . . . The notion of evil is the idea of a force, or forces, which are not merely contrary to all that is most praiseworthy and admirable and desirable in human life, but a force which is actively working against all that is praiseworthy and admirable . . . The National Socialist movement in Germany is an instructive case for moral philosophy, as a historical embodiment of pure evil both in aspiration and achievement . . .
>
> The Nazi revolution was a revolution of destruction, and, more particularly, of moral destruction . . . The aim was to eliminate all notions of fairness and justice from practical politics, and, as far as possible, from person's [*sic*] minds; to create a bombed and flattened moral landscape, in which there are no boundaries and no limits . . . The deliberate aim was to substitute physical conflict and violence for fair and even-handed arbitration in settling social conflicts, or in settling oppositions between races, or states, or social groups.

If this is what evil is, then responding to it should not merely be a physical, visceral reaction but should be about building up a counter-culture of justice. Indeed, it is Hampshire's insight that we need to turn round our thinking. We tend to assume that justice is a positive and evil a negative, whereas evil is an active force and justice is how we take away its power. This is why we would be uneasy about, say, a napalm attack as a response to the events of 11 September. Jonathan Marcus of the BBC captures a proper scepticism about government overreaction and incompetence when discussing the likelihood of just or even efficient reactions to modern biological or chemical terrorism in the aftermath of the anthrax scare which followed in the autumn of 2001. He offers a link to such seemingly diverse policy failings as the government's feeble response to the foot-and-mouth epidemic and its helplessness in the face of the human tragedy of refugees:

> While the citizen wants to be defended, he or she also wants to see the maintenance of the values that make our societies worth defending. There is going to be an understandable reluctance to dilute hard-won freedoms. In the realms of biological or chemical terrorism, the authorities are dealing with areas of science and public policy in which they have a poor track record; and people are understandably sceptical about what governments can deliver. Look at the way the foot-and-mouth outbreak was handled in the UK – would, say, an anthrax outbreak necessarily be dealt with any more efficiently? Take another area: the failure of the asylum and immigration system, which seems to

deny safety to many worthy applicants while allowing entry to a small number of highly dubious characters.

In other words, while those responsible for 11 September should be brought to justice or, as President Bush put it, justice brought to them, that in itself does not redress a balance disturbed by evil hijackings. Rather, the forces of evil need to be positively countered by the building up of justice and awareness of justice in the everyday dealings which the USA and others have with the Muslim world. An unjust prosecution of the war against terrorism through, to maintain the Vietnam example, napalm would merely add to the inferno of evil. This is why the development, not least by the Prime Minister, Tony Blair, of an alliance against terrorism was so important in the weeks while the USA was positioning its forces and offering the Taliban regime the opportunity to hand over Osama bin Laden.

Stuart Hampshire captures the struggle between evil and justice in explaining why he thinks that the Nazis persecuted Jews. It was not merely random racism but the result of the Nazi brand of evil being threatened by the Jewish regard for justice:

> Justice, both in God's judgement and in the law to be observed among humans, was the central moral concept for the Jews, the very reverse of all that the Nazis wanted. The National Socialist programme was to destroy in Germany both the morality of literacy and of legality and the morality of fair negotiation. They wanted no more arguments, no more justice: just the excitement of conflict and of victory through violence.
>
> Below any level of explicit articulation, hatred of the idea of the Jews was tied to a hatred of the power of the intellect, as opposed to military power, hatred of law courts, of negotiation, of cleverness in argument, of learning and of the domination of learning: and in this way anti-Semitism is tied to hatred of justice itself, which must set a limit to the exercise of power and to domination.

Just as Stuart Hampshire was deeply influenced by his wartime service against the Nazis, so I suspect was the doyen of legal philosophers in the twentieth century, Herbert Hart. I mention him to show how we can be touched at one remove or so by some great thinker's experiences of conflict and moral dilemmas. At Oxford in the 1970s, I was tutored by the most brilliant and gentle of academics, Joseph Raz, who in the 1960s had carried out his national military service in Israel, before pursuing a doctorate with Hart as his supervisor. Raz has referred in his jurisprudence to one aspect of this experience, namely the taking of an oath in circumstances of near-compulsion. Today's students of ethics should not assume that questions of life and death, war and peace are not there to be answered in the way our tutors and we ourselves live our lives. Belfast, where I lived and worked, or the Middle East, where Joseph Raz studied, have not been easy places in which to ignore moral responsibility in recent decades, or probably in any decades. The fact that our teachers seem to carry their military experience lightly does not mean that it has had no impact on them or that it has no impact through them on us. To give another example, one of the most memorable acts of generosity and forgiveness of enemies in recent decades came in the way the then Archbishop of Canterbury, the late Robert Runcie, conducted the service of thanksgiving after the Falklands War. It was only when some observers thought he was brave to stand up for this approach in the presence of the victorious Prime Minister, Margaret Thatcher, that it became widely known that Dr Runcie had received the Military Cross in the Second World War for real bravery. This in turn gave his living out of his Christian faith in praying for all those who died in the Falklands War a special poignancy verging on moral authority.

Before the Second World War, Herbert Hart had been a chancery barrister. Both Hampshire and Hart served in intelligence during the war, before returning to Oxford as philosophy dons. I had one brief conversation with Hart in Oxford in the late 1980s about his wartime work, soon after I had been to Poland with a group of philosophers including the Oxford don, Richard Hare. It had been a chilling experience to visit Auschwitz at all and quite extraordinary to go in a group with Hare who had himself been a prisoner of war in a concentration camp in Burma. I was struck by the impact of the war on the Hart–Hare generation and would have welcomed some of them being more forthcoming about it. Hart said that the intelligence work came in fits and starts since it depended on the codes being cracked and the enemy not realising this. Once the enemy grasped what had happened, there would be a new code and a lull in intelligence work until that had been decoded. What did he do in the interim? He said that for the most part he just did his bit working manually on the armaments production line at Northolt, although at times he did have to apply his legal training in, for example, questioning prisoners of war. I do not know if there is any specific link between these wartime experiences and Hart's jurisprudence, but one possibility has subsequently occurred to me in the light of that conversation and the more recent publicity given to the code-breakers. They were led at Bletchley by Alan Turing, formerly a Cambridge don and Princeton professor, later the inventor in Manchester of the computer. Turing was prosecuted in the 1950s for his homosexual practice and ordered to undergo hormone therapy. He committed suicide. I do not know whether Hart even knew Turing but rereading Hart's *Law, Liberty & Morality*, with its opening reference to the Suicide Act, its agenda of homosexual law reform and its impassioned ending, makes me wonder if one of the greatest lawyers of the century was influenced, even subconsciously, by the disgraceful way in which his Cambridge contemporary Turing, a hero of war and peace, had been treated by the society which owed him so much.

Certainly, Stuart Hampshire found philosophy and politics to be changed utterly by the experience of encountering evil in the Second World War:

> As an intelligence officer in the war for four years I studied the espionage and counter-espionage operations of the Reichssicherheitshauptamt, Himmler's Central Command, which controlled the whole of the SS, excluding only the Waffen SS. This experience altogether changed my attitude both to politics and to philosophy, as the full scale of the SS's operations in occupied Europe and in Russia became known, and as the programme announced in *Mein Kampf* could be studied in action. I interrogated some leading Nazis in captivity at the end of the war, including Heydrich's successor as head of the Reichssicherheitshauptamt, Kaltenbrunner, with whom I talked at length when he was a prisoner with U.S. Army headquarters, and whom I brought to London for further interrogation.

The next generation of philosophers seems to understand that their immediate predecessors may have experienced evil in a way which they have been spared. In his awesome book on *Humanity*, Jonathan Glover concludes that

> Trying to learn from the twentieth-century atrocities can seem absurd. Hiroshima, the Gulag, the cruelties of Mao or of Pol Pot: their enormity transcends our imagination. Any 'lessons' drawn are bound to seem puny beside the events themselves.
>
> A few years ago a group of British philosophers was visiting Cracow. One day we were taken by bus to Auschwitz. On the way there was the buzz of philosophers' conversation: a mixture of gossip and 'People say such and such but is it really rational?' Returning, we were silent. It was hard to take in emotionally what we had seen. The fine distinctions of ethical analysis would have been grotesque on the bus back to Cracow.
>
> Inevitably, the discussion here is in the same way dwarfed by its subject. No ethical reflections, no thoughts seem adequate.
>
> All the same, we do need to learn from these events. One thought after a visit to Auschwitz is that 'never again' is the only morally serious response. The battlefields of the First World War provoke the same thought. I have not been to Hiroshima or Nagasaki, or to the sites of the Gulag, or to Cambodia, but the same thoughts must come there too.

He is referring to the same visit to Auschwitz as I have mentioned. Jonathan Glover, Richard Hare, Onora O'Neill, myself and others had been sent by the British Academy to a symposium on the ethics of life and death with a group from the Polish Academy. It was an uneasy but moving occasion to visit Auschwitz and in such company. It makes me wary of invoking the word 'evil' lightly. Without comparing tragedies or commenting on their different scales, we can reasonably summarise President Bush's response, when what he described as evil came to the World Trade Center, as, in Glover's words, 'never again'. That expresses the will but does not of itself determine the means which should, and those which should not, be deployed to give effect to the will.

This, of course, is why the attacks of 11 September represent an uneasy case. For it is when a society, or a community or a whole civilisation, feels under attack from forces it describes as 'evil' that it is most tempted to use all available means to defend itself. The herd is frightened and at its most dangerous. We must be on a heightened ethical alert, therefore, remaining ill at ease throughout any war on terrorism. This is not to do with uncertainty in the cause, or uncertainty about our ethical position. It can come from absolute certainty about what is the right response but an uneasiness nonetheless about whether we can contain those who act in our name. For when we appreciate that justice is a building up of good relations against positively evil forces, it becomes more obvious that the Mylai massacre in Vietnam can undermine the cause when it already seemed to be won. Although Thomas Nagel observes that 'no elaborate moral theory is required to account for what is wrong in cases like the Mylai massacre, since it did not serve, and was not intended to serve, any strategic purpose', its effects are still evident as one piece of the ugly jigsaw which makes up the picture of an unjust America which is used by Osama bin Laden. Nagel concedes that actions short of massacre can present what are here called uneasy cases: 'It is not easy to keep a firm grip on the idea of what is not permissible in warfare, because while some military actions are obvious atrocities, other cases are more difficult to assess, and the general principles underlying these judgements remain obscure.' He accepts that 'acute moral dilemmas' can arise where someone believes, for example, 'that by torturing a prisoner he can obtain information necessary to prevent a disaster, or that by obliterating one village with bombs he can halt a campaign of terrorism. If he believes that the gains from a certain measure will clearly outweigh its costs, yet still suspects that he ought not to adopt it, then he is in a dilemma produced by the conflict between two disparate categories of moral reason: categories that may be called *utilitarian* and *absolutist*.' He concludes that 'it is perfectly possible to feel the force of both types of reason very strongly; in that case the moral dilemma in certain situations of crisis will be acute, and it may appear that every possible course of action or inaction is unacceptable for one reason or another'.

John Rawls is clear that Churchill was justified in some of the bombing of German cities, but not of Dresden in 1945, whereas Truman was not justified in authorising the atomic bombs being dropped on Hiroshima and

Nagasaki. He thinks that there are extreme cases where what he calls the supreme emergency exemption applies:

> Were there times during World War II when Britain could properly have held that civilians' strict status was suspended, and thus could have bombed Hamburg or Berlin? Possibly, but only if it was sure that the bombing would have done some substantial good; such action cannot be justified by a doubtful marginal gain. When Britain was alone and had no other means to break Germany's superior power, the bombing of German cities was arguably justifiable. This period extended, at the least, from the fall of France in June 1940 until Russia had clearly beaten off the first German assault in the summer and fall of 1941 and showed that it would be able to fight Germany until the end. It could be argued that this period extended further until the summer and fall of 1942 or even through the Battle of Stalingrad (which ended with German surrender in February 1943). But the bombing of Dresden in February 1945 was clearly too late.
>
> Whether the supreme emergency exemption applies depends upon certain circumstances, about which judgements will still sometimes differ. Britain's bombing of Germany until the end of 1941 or 1942 could be justified because Germany could not be allowed to win the war, and this for two basic reasons. First, Nazism portended incalculable moral and political evil for civilized life everywhere. Second, the nature and history of constitutional democracy and its place in European history were at stake. Churchill really did not exaggerate when he said to the House of Commons on the day France capitulated that, 'if we fail [to stand up to Hitler], the whole world including the United States . . . will sink into a new Dark Age'. This kind of threat, in sum, justifies invoking the supreme emergency exemption, on behalf not only of constitutional democracies, but of all well-ordered societies.
>
> The peculiar evil of Nazism needs to be understood. It was characteristic of Hitler that he recognised no possibility at all of a political relationship with his enemies. They were always to be cowed by terror and brutality, and ruled by force. From the beginning, the campaign against Russia was to be a war of destruction and even at times extermination of Slavic peoples, with the original inhabitants remaining, if at all, only as serfs. When Goebbels and others protested that the war could not be won that way, Hitler refused to listen.

Rawls concludes that, 'It is clear, however, that the supreme emergency exemption never held at any time for the United States in its war with Japan.'

I have quoted great Anglo-American philosophers of the twentieth century at some length in this chapter, for a number of reasons. In the first chapter we focused on a tragic but easily understood dilemma, the archbishop's principles and the judges' hypotheticals. After some experience of considering uneasy cases for ourselves, it is helpful in this last chapter to begin to draw more on the rich tradition of ethical thought. There are lessons, for me at least, in how many of the deepest thinkers of the twentieth century were influenced by their close encounters with the evil of Nazism. It is also salutary to appreciate how quickly the lessons, and the reality of evil, came to be ignored. At the beginning of the third millennium, we have been reminded of the need to make difficult ethical decisions in a flawed world.

Of course, ethical experts of an earlier generation cannot do all the work for us and they are as unlikely to anticipate the next uneasy case as are our political or judicial leaders. Leading Anglo-American philosophers' main reference points over the past six decades, up until 11 September 2001, for the application of just war doctrine were the Second World War and Vietnam. Pride and shame, respectively, were their most common conclusions. The attacks of 11 September 2001, however, were not by a state and it was by no means obvious how any version of just war theory could be adapted to the circumstances of the Taliban harbouring in Afghanistan the leaders of the al-Qaeda terrorist network.

We may have much to learn from modern writers who would not claim to be philosophers but who do bring contemporary analysis in a range of disciplines to bear on the uneasy matter of trying to understand terrorism. Mark Juergensmeyer, for example, draws our attention to performance violence and performative acts:

> This is an idea developed by language philosophers regarding certain kinds of speech that are able to perform social functions: their very utterance has a transformative impact. Like vows recited during marriage rites, certain words not only represent reality but also shape it; they contain a certain power of their own. The same is true of some nonverbal symbolic actions, such as the gunshot that begins a race, the raising of a white flag to show defeat, or acts of terrorism.

It does not take a feminist scholar to appreciate that gender studies may have something to say about the link between terrorism and young men. Although there have been some female secular terrorists, including the suicide bomber who assassinated the Indian Prime Minister Rajiv Gandhi, and the Chechen hostage-takers in Moscow included Muslim women, the religious fanatic terrorists have usually been young men. As Juergensmeyer reminds us:

> The term guy came into use in England in the seventeenth century after Guy Fawkes was tried and executed in 1606 for his role in the Gunpowder Plot . . . the religious terrorist, Fawkes, was the original

'Guy' and his name came to be applied to all roguish men who skirted danger . . . The religious terrorists of recent years are today's guys: bands of rogue males at the margins of respectability. The gender specificity of their involvement suggests that some aspect of male sexuality – sexual roles, identity, competence or control – is a factor . . .

In these and many other ways, terrorism is posing uneasy questions not only to governments but to all of us. One recent analysis explained the dilemma in which the world's media are placed as they are inevitably caught up in uneasy ethical decision-making:

The *New York Times*, in considering whether to publish the Unabomber's 35,000-word manifesto in 1995, agonized over the role that the news media was being coerced into playing, and questioned whether the newspaper's coverage – especially its willingness to publish the bomber's writings would alleviate terrorism by helping to resolve the mystery of the bomber's identity or add to terrorism's suffering by inadvertently encouraging other activists to seek the exposure that the newspaper seemed willing to offer. The publisher of the *Times*, Arthur Sulzberger, Jr., lamented the idea of 'turning our pages over to a man who has murdered people.' But he added that he was 'convinced' that they were 'making the right choice between bad options'.

The fact that the publication of the manifesto eventually led to the identification of Theodore Kaczynski as the bomber by his brother David would seem to vindicate the decision of the *Times* publishers. It brought to an end a seventeen-year string of violence involving sixteen letter bombings that wounded twenty-three and left three others dead.

'Making the right choice between bad options' is one way of looking at uneasy ethical challenges. Not only the US President and the *New York Times* but all of us are facing such choices since the 11 September 2001 attacks showed that we are nowadays all touched by terrorism. For instance, the anthrax scare caused panic in the USA in the immediate aftermath of 11 September in a way which would not have happened before those attacks. To give another example, Unionists swiftly pointed out that it was difficult to see how the USA could any longer justify a sympathetic approach to terrorism in Northern Ireland now that it was implacably opposed to al-Qaeda terrorism. A year later, tourists in Bali and theatregoers in Moscow were tragically killed through terrorism, but it is not only, or sometimes even, those affected in this way who have to make choices. Terrorists are trying to influence others, not necessarily those they physically attack. In 1975, writing in the US publication *Foreign Affairs*, David Fromkin explained that 'Terrorism is violence used in order to create fear but it is aimed at creating fear in order that the fear, in turn, will lead somebody else – not the terrorist – to embark on some quite different programme of action that will accomplish whatever it is that the terrorist really desires.'

This is illustrated by the Northern Irish conflict, but at first it is not so clear how al-Qaeda wants its Western targets to behave differently. It means that how we all (not just our political leaders) react to our neighbours, to strangers, to our apparent enemies, in the wake of such a terrorist atrocity is part of the ethical challenge. As this chapter has argued, there is also the question of how we as citizens make decisions in advance of particular terrorist attacks. An earlier chapter addressed the question of trying to build peace and justice in the longer run rather than assuming that terrorism is a permanent feature of society or that a military solution will eradicate it. In the shorter term, however, taking action to counter evil is an awesome responsibility. It is more demanding than the more pleasant task of making the best choice between good options. Even if the ethical exercise leaves us with an uneasy conscience, it is part of the tragic yet awesome human condition to have to strive to make the right moral choice between bad options.

Even in the bleakest of times, when terrorism and war dominate the news, there is a value in reflecting on these moral choices, especially when aided by the thoughts of leading philosophers. Out of evil can come ethical guidance for the next generation and beyond. When John Rawls died in November 2002, *The Times*' obituary showed that 'the most influential political philosopher in the second half of the twentieth century' was influenced both by war and by his study of moral philosophy:

Rawl's lifelong interest in justice developed out of his concern, while a student and soldier during the war, with the basically religious questions of why there is evil in the world and whether human existence is nonetheless redeemable. This led him to enquire whether a just society is realistically possible on earth. His life's work was directed towards discovering what justice requires of us and showing that it is within human capacities to realise a just society and a just international order . . .

On graduating in 1943, Rawls joined the US Army as a private, and after initial training he was sent to fight in the war in the Pacific, in New Guinea, the Philippines, and eventually in Japan.

After his military service he began his graduate studies in philosophy at Princeton in 1946, writing his dissertation on moral knowledge and judgements on the moral worth of character. After teaching for two years, he went to Oxford on a Fulbright Scholarship for the academic year 1952–53, and was affiliated to Christ Church. This year at Oxford was one of the most formative of his long career. He was especially influenced by lectures of H. L. A. Hart on the philosophy of law, as well as by seminars held by Isaiah Berlin and Stuart Hampshire.

Conclusion

An ethical or good life is not only, not even primarily, about instantaneous decisions on what not to do in the most troubling of tragic cases. Still less is it about knowing immediately what to say on the issues of the day. Cardinal Newman noted 150 years ago the mistaken view that 'It is almost thought a disgrace not to have a view at a moment's notice on any question from the Personal Advent to the Cholera or Mesmerism.' Crafting as good a life as you can muster is, in contrast, much more to do with building up the common good through the little thoughts, words, deeds and graces of daily activity, as a unique human being living in a community, in relationships with others.

Almost all the thinkers on whose wisdom this book has rightly drawn have much more of value to say in their work about this positive side of the human condition. A good example would be the new Archbishop of Canterbury, Dr Rowan Williams, who is both a spiritual leader and a theologian of the first rank. Even he, however, seems to me to fall prey to the assumption which Newman castigated. We might expect an archbishop to have a view on the Personal Advent but commissioning editors of newspapers would also turn to Dr Williams for opinions at a moment's notice on the Cholera or Mesmerism. On known form they would not be disappointed. I would be, however, because my reading of his work, as indicated in the last chapter, is that he is at his weakest when offering thoughts on what governments should do in the light of terrorist threats. Indeed, Newman also found it difficult to resist offering his own views on the issues of the day, regularly declining to take the advice implicit in his observation about instant punditry. Many readers will know that Newman's lectures in Dublin on the idea of a university in 1852 are still of interest today. Fewer will know that, in 1853, he lectured in Liverpool on the Turkish question and that anyone who relishes 150th anniversaries will have decades more of Newman's opinions to revisit.

Nineteenth-century history, as I studied it at school, seemed big on questions of nationality, from the Turkish question to the Irish question. It is a commonplace observation that every time we come near to answering one or other of these, the question changes. My aim in this book has been to explore how we can begin to understand some of the big questions, even if we cannot agree on the answers. I have not tried to hide my own answers, but they are only works-in-progress. There are imponderables which defy any easy answer. Although I would not, for example, have shied away from authorising military action in the circumstances of recent times, no one could do so with an easy heart, especially given the possibility that the only people on the planet unaware of the impact of the 11 September attacks on the USA may have been some of the very people in Afghanistan who lost their lives as the USA struck at the Taliban for harbouring the al-Qaeda network of terrorists.

I do not, however, draw the conclusions from these sagas that we can somehow be at ethical ease with ourselves by standing idly by, under a doctrine of the (im)morality of (un)righteous omission. For that would be a mistaken complacency in which people take pride in not authorising operations, never wishing to release anyone on parole, never contemplating progress in peace talks for fear of talking to terrorists, never intervening as a government lest accusations fly of conflict of interest, watching more terrorist outrages for want of risky but targeted action to thwart their plans. On the contrary, we need more positive action to build up the common good, based on the foundation of a good understanding of the human condition. Politicians and others in positions of authority are to be supported in showing the courage to take risks for peace and justice, often by showing mercy beyond that which their voters can muster but sometimes by showing more determination to fight than their critics can stomach. Sometimes the price of leadership is living with our moral unease.

In contrast to the more important task of building up the common good, where theologians and philosophers have so much to teach us, lawyers have some experience of grappling with tragic choices. In this book, I have tried to turn that rhythm of legal life, difficult cases presenting themselves with judges having to decide one way or another under time constraints, into a framework for considering a range of ethical dilemmas. As readers try to draw together their thoughts on these five case studies in contemporary ethics, it may help to see how my own approach has changed in response to different circumstances during a quarter of a century of exploring these matters.

With the benefit of hindsight, I can now discern three phases which may be of more than autobiographical interest. The first embraced my student days and then the beginning of my academic career as I moved from Oxford to Yale and back to Oxford in the late 1970s and early 1980s. This period was one in which tutors questioned students rigorously about real and hypothetical dilemmas. The second phase ran from the early 1980s through to the first half of the 1990s, when I regarded it as part of my job as a lecturer in law at King's College London and then as Professor of Jurisprudence at Queen's University, Belfast, to profess my subject of the philosophy of law by commenting on developments as they happened, from the Warnock Report on embryo experiments and in vitro fertilisation through to the Northern Irish conflict and then the peace process. The third phase started in the mid-1990s since when my role as a chief executive has precluded me from commenting in the public domain so regularly or swiftly on the latest cases. From time to time, however, I have still been asked for behind-the-scenes advice on these ethical dilemmas and my own work requires me to make ethical judgements. Indeed, as for many readers, decision-making at work has been a salutary discipline, revealing how uneasy it can be to take responsibility in such matters.

The relevance of tracing successive phases of involvement in these ethical dilemmas is that what may seem to be only slight differences in vantage points can change one's view radically. Instant reaction to hypotheticals is different from instant public comment on actual cases, which is again different from now reflecting at leisure on some of the most uneasy of cases. In instant media comment and student interviews or tutorials, there is an expectation that one should be able to plump for a line and then defend it rigorously and vigorously. In wider life, however, there is usually time to be able to reflect on first reactions without being committed to a position. Members of the 'general public' are often nobly prepared to change their minds as they absorb new arguments or begin to see the dilemma from another vantage point, whereas those who have committed themselves to a public position often seem more caught up in defending their first instinct with ever more ingenious but unconvincing arguments.

Part of my argument is that the first of the three perspectives which I have identified has had a substantial (some would say disproportionate) impact on public decision-makers. Understanding the methodology of the academic law encounter goes a long way towards explaining politics' elusive Third Way as a mode of thought, a way of looking at uneasy politics, uneasy economics and indeed uneasy ethics, which has much in common with undergraduate law tutorials. This is no accident, as observed in Chapter Three on Northern Ireland, because so many of the politicians associated with Third Way thinking have themselves been involved in academic law, from Tony Blair (former Oxford law student) to Bill Clinton (former Yale law student), from David Trimble to Mary McAleese (both of whom were students and teachers of law at Queen's University, Belfast, before going on to become First Minister of Northern Ireland and President of Ireland respectively). Thinking about uneasy politics like a law student or law lecturer may well be at least part of the secret of understanding Third Way approaches to government on either side of the Irish Sea and on either side of the Atlantic.

It is only part of the answer because decision-makers have to make judgements which change people's lives, and another message of this book is that judgement is a neglected skill and art. Few people admit that they lack judgement or have made poor judgements. Even those who do concede that they have made an error of judgement tend to do so only in relation to another's character, implying that the fault is really the other's weakness and deception. A bad memory is readily admitted, but we need to work harder at improving the quality of our ethical judgement. Exploring ethical judgements in uneasy cases has a role to play in this.

So the dilemmas in this book should have made readers appreciate that ethical decision-making is uneasy and that it poses deep questions about what it is to be human. As the late Sir Isaiah Berlin observed:

> The task of philosophy, often a difficult and painful one, is to extricate and bring to light the hidden categories and models in terms of which human beings think (that is, their use of words, images and other symbols), to reveal what is obscure or contradictory in them, to discern the conflicts between them that prevent the construction of more adequate ways of organising and describing and explaining experience (for all description as well as explanation involves some model in terms of which the describing and explaining is done) . . . The goal of philosophy is always the same, to assist men to understand themselves.

The title 'Uneasy Ethics' indicates that reading this book does not yield a set of easy answers. Rather, the aim has been to analyse five contemporary sagas in sufficient detail that readers are more informed and more aware of arguments supporting positions which are not theirs. The attempt to understand the best possible argument against one's position is common to scholastic philosophers, to lawyers and to good negotiators in public and private lives. It guards against the tendency either to reject automatically or to accept uncritically the collective wisdom. It is always valuable to question, and it is sometimes good to marvel at, received wisdom. Discernment or ethical judgement is a skill which needs to be honed.

In successive chapters, mostly involving matters of life and death, this exploration of uneasy ethics has focused on a single good or bad concept from most readers' lexicon of (im)morality: first the laudable notions of *equality*, then *mercy* followed by *justice* before turning to the lamentable behaviour variously described as *bad faith* or *disgraceful* before finally addressing that which is *evil*. In terms of methodology, the first chapter contrasted principles with *hypotheticals*, the second looked at the detailed *facts* of a tragedy, the third explored the *rhetoric* of uneasy progress, the fourth sought to bring *order* and small-scale relevance to the chaotic world of multi-million-pound corporate and government disasters, while the fifth turned to philosophical *texts* of the twentieth century, seeing if they can be adapted to yield insight for this century into ethical ways forward when faced by the evil of terrorism which can turn modern technology against its creators.

Latent throughout the book has been the struggle between a more complex pairing of vice and virtue, the battle between a sense of hope-lessness and a true understanding of hope. It is my belief that what the socially excluded are actually excluded from, at its deepest level, is hope. In this context, hope is the firm belief, sometimes in the face of the evidence, as on 11 September 2001, that the world can be a better place and that we can make it so. In the words of the great twentieth-century ecumenist, Cardinal Suenens, 'To hope is not to dream but to turn dreams into reality.' That is why the patient, painstaking work of building up the common good is so vital.

The history of the twentieth century shows that the most appalling injustices and tragedies do not destroy the humanity of individuals, including such eyewitnesses as the many philosophers who experienced the Second World War. Similarly, in response to a devastating start to the new millennium, we can reflect, however uneasily, on these ethical dilemmas and learn from them. What we learn is to hone our judgement, to be self-critical, to seek to understand the range of perspectives, to refrain from premature mind-closing and to be courageous enough to take uneasy decisions once we have had the opportunity to reflect on an issue in the round.

As we try to take the measure of each uneasy case, we are also testing the cluster of virtues or values which form our moral compass. If they do not seem to be pointing us in the right direction, one option is to follow wheresoever they lead, however uneasy the territory. But alternatively, we might reconsider whether those values are the most reliable guide. This process of striving for a Rawlsian equilibrium is itself uneasy. The search is not, in my opinion, for a single concept such as utility or even the more inspiring ideal of justice. Even if it were, vigorous disagreement would remain because of our different conceptions of what that abstract concept might mean in a particular case and because of our different interpretations of the facts to which the concept needs to be applied.

Nor am I sure that the best way of describing the journey for ethical enlightenment is to focus on the destination, on finding instead of a single treasure a holy grail or a cluster or basket with a particular mixture of virtues. The quest is in many ways to understand ourselves, to appreciate our own vantage points, and to understand the differing perspectives of others. In other words, it is more a question of the style in which we undertake our search and the company we keep along the way. One way of reflecting on this book, if readers are looking for a starting point for the next phase of their own ethical journeys, is as offering some stepping stones. The primary lessons to draw from the ethics of these uneasy cases are the need to work towards a triple jump of values. The three virtues which should be put together in a flowing sequence of hop, skip and jump are justice, mercy and hope. As we have seen, mercy is more demanding of us. In a stepped approach, therefore, it might be appropriate to start with the other two fundamental values which were beautifully yoked together by the African-American poet, Alice Walker, when she wrote about offering to the human race flowers 'whose virtues are twin, Justice and Hope, let us begin'. Another way of considering the chapters is as potential companions on an ethical adventure. Like Dorothy in *The Wizard of Oz*, we may set out in the naive belief that someone else has the answers. Along the way, we will have to stand up to those of a wicked disposition who would take us in the wrong direction. The joyful skipping along the yellow-brick road comes in large part from the support and example offered by others, often inspiring us through their humility rather than with their views, at a moment's notice, on the issues of the day. Dorothy learned that what counts in coming to understand the need to work out our own stance is travelling together with those who are also in search of courage or a heart or wisdom.

Notes

Introduction

From the many works by my tutors, Joseph Raz, *The Morality of Freedom* (Oxford University Press, 1986), Joseph Raz, *Engaging Reason* (Oxford University Press, 1999), and Guido Calabresi and Philip Bobbitt, *Tragic Choices* (W.W. Norton, 1978) are especially relevant. From those by my colleagues, John Elford, *The Ethics of Uncertainty* (Oneworld, 2000), offers a challenging, alternative view. I first used the phrase 'uneasy cases' in my essay of that title for Brice Dickson and Paul Carmichael (eds), *The House of Lords* (Hart, 1999), in writing about the Bland case.

Of the modern introductory texts, which give a theoretical underpinning to the study of ethics, Simon Blackburn's *Think* (Oxford University Press, 1999) and *Being Good* (Oxford University Press, 2001) stand out, while Mary Warnock, *An Intelligent Person's Guide to Ethics* (Duckworth, 1998) does most to address contemporary issues, as might be expected from the doyenne of committees of inquiry, although I still admire two texts from my student days, Jonathan Glover, *Causing Death and Saving Lives* (Penguin, 1977), and J.L. Mackie, *Ethics: Inventing Right and Wrong* (Penguin, 1977).

My belief is that alongside excellent short books, which only briefly apply principles to examples, there is also a role for an alternative introductory text, which revolves around extended treatment of some contemporary uneasy cases. For a thoughtful analysis of society in the period immediately before that covered in this book, see Jonathan Sacks, *The Politics of Hope* (Jonathan Cape, 1997). See also Ronald Rolheiser, *Seeking Spirituality* (Hodder and Stoughton, 1998).

1. Siamese Twins: Separate but Equal?

The judgements can be found at www.courtservice.gov.uk, and the Archbishop of Westminster's amicus brief at www.rcdow.org.uk. *The Tablet* offers reliable, informed but critical coverage of the church in the modern world (but then I would say that as a member of the board); see www.thetablet.co.uk.

For a general background to serious thought about medial law and ethics, see the work by my former colleague, Sir Ian Kennedy, especially his influential essays collected in *Treat Me Right* (Oxford University Press, 1988), and the report of the Bristol inquiry, which he chaired, at www.bristol-inquiry.gov.uk.

The account of mountaineering referred to is Joe Simpson's *Touching the Void* (Vintage, 1997).

2. Child Killers: Uneasy Mercy

The text makes clear my debt to Blake Morrison, *As If* (Granta, 1997). Court judgments can now be traced on the Internet. For most domestic courts, see www.courtservice.gov.uk; for the House of Lords, see www.parliament.gov.uk; for the European Court of Human Rights, see www.echr.coe.int. Likewise, statements by the Pope can be read on the Vatican website, see www.vatican.va.

Media coverage is often undervalued and sometimes (including in this chapter and the rest of this book) criticised but it includes many insights on each of the chapters in this book. All the broadsheets, at home and abroad, have impressive websites. Probably the best, short contribution to the debate on the death of Myra Hindley came from Vanora Bennett, *The Times*, 16 November 2002, p.9, 'Sixties snapshot remains an image of wickedness'.

3. Northern Ireland: Uneasy Peace

The Opsahl report was edited by Andy Pollak, *A Citizens' Inquiry: The Opsahl Report on Northern Ireland* (Lilliput Press, 1993). My own submission to the Opsahl commission was reprinted by Index on Censorship, *Lost for Words* (Index on Censorship). John Hewitt's 'The Coasters', from *An Ulster Reckoning* (1971), can be found in Frank Ormsby (ed.), *The Collected Poems of John Hewitt* (Blackstaff, 1991).

Outstanding historical perspectives are offered by Marianne Elliott, *The Catholics of Ulster* (Penguin, 2000), Roy Foster, *Modern Ireland 1600–1972* (Penguin, 1988); Jonathan Bardon, *A History of Ulster* (Blackstaff, 1992); and A.T.Q. Stewart, *The Narrow Ground* (Faber, 1977). Kevin Boyle and Tom Hadden, *Northern Ireland: The Choice* (Penguin, 1994) is but one of the many influential contributions made by these two outstanding academic lawyers who have shown sustained commitment to serious analysis of Northern Ireland from the 1960s onwards. Eamonn Mallie and David McKittrick, *The Fight for Peace* (Heinemann, 1996) supplements Boyle and Hadden, for example with the text of the Downing Street Declaration. Again, these two journalists have shown extraordinary tenacity and integrity in covering Northern Ireland consistently. Although I think they focus too much on politicians and (in earlier times) terrorists, thus underplaying wider community contributions, they cover their chosen interests comprehensively.

Again, websites come to the rescue of those living outside the island of Ireland, for whom media reports are sporadic. The *Irish Times* website is especially valuable. As the text indicates, I have drawn on the wisdom of Archbishop Cahal Daly, *The Price of Peace* (Blackstaff, 1991), and have sought to learn from and apply the work of John Rawls, *A Theory of Justice* (Harvard University Press, 1971) and *Political Liberalism* (Columbia University Press, 1993), the former of which has done so much to set the modern agenda of reflecting on justice. See also Paul Boateng, 'The Hope of Things to Come', in Christopher Bryant (ed.), *Reclaiming the Ground: Christianity and Socialism* (Spire, 1993).

4. Ethics in a Spin: A Byers' Market?
Andreas R. Prindl and Bimal Prodham (eds), *The ACT Guide to Ethical Conflicts in Finance* (Blackwell, 1994) includes the essay by Sir Adrian Cadbury quoted in the text.

The press coverage is once more an excellent source for following these contemporary sagas although I have been grateful for the insights provided also in a number of perhaps ephemeral but nevertheless timely books on the latest disasters, mostly with apocalyptic titles: Andrew O'Hagan, *The End of British Farming* (Profile Books, 2001); Judith Cook, *The Year of the Pyres* (Mainstream, 2001); Christian Wolmar, *Broken Rails: How Privatisation Wrecked Britain's Railways* (Aurum, 2001); Chris Brady and Andrew Lorenz, *End of the Road: BMW and Rover – A Brand Too Far* (Financial Times, Pearson Education, 2001); Siobhan Creaton and Conor O'Clery, *Panic at the Bank* (Gill & Macmillan, 2002); Charles Cohen, *Corporate Vices* (Capstone, 2002); and Peter Fusaro and Ross Miller, *What Went Wrong at Enron* (Wiley, 2002).

For Liverpool Hope University College, see www.hope.ac.uk, and the forthcoming book edited by John Elford, *A Foundation of Hope* (University of Liverpool, 2003). For Leeds Metropolitan University, see www.lmu.ac.uk. Chris Moon and Clive Bonny, *Business Ethics: Facing up to the Issues* (Profile, 2001) gives a good general introduction from *The Economist*. See also Peter J. Dougherty, *Who's Afraid of Adam Smith? How the Market Lost its Soul* (Wiley, 2002), Anthony Giddens, *The Third Way* (Polity, 1998) and Anthony Giddens, *Where Now for New Labour?* (Polity, 2002).

5. Countering Terrorism: Uneasy Evil in an Uneasy World
The BBC coverage on 11 September 2001 was first class and the book they produced is of the same high quality: Jenny Baxter and Malcolm Downing, *The Day that Shook the World: Understanding September 11th* (BBC, 2001). Other media accounts are also important. For example, in the wake of the terrorist attack on Bali, *The Economist* of 19–25 October 2002 ('A World of

Terror') had several excellent articles.

Two other books are indispensable: Fred Halliday, *Two Hours that Shook the World* (Saqi Books, 2002) and James Hoge Jnr and Gideon Rose (eds), *How Did This Happen? Terrorism and the New War* (Public Affairs, 2001). Thoughtful analyses of the underlying issues of terrorism include Mark Jurgensmeyer, *Terror in the Mind of God* (University of California, 2001) and Conor Gearty, *Terror* (Faber, 1991). A robust counter to conventional American thinking comes from Noam Chomsky, *9–11* (Open Media, 2001).

The text demonstrates my indebtedness to Stuart Hampshire, *Innocence and Experience* (Penguin, 1989) and to Jonathan Glover, *Humanity* (Jonathan Cape, 1999). Other influential works include Isaiah Berlin, *The Proper Study of Mankind* (Pimlico, 1998); Jonathan Sacks, *The Politics of Hope* (Jonathan Cape, 1997); Thomas Nagel, *Mortal Questions* (Cambridge University Press, 1979); Bernard Williams, *Moral Luck* (Cambridge University Press, 1981); John Finnis, *Natural Law and Natural Rights* (Oxford University Press, 1980); Alasdair MacIntyre, *After Virtue* (Duckworth, 1981); Onora O'Neill, *A Question of Trust* (BBC Reith Lectures, 2002); Peter Singer (ed.), *A Companion to Ethics* (Blackwell, 1991); Robin Gill (ed.), *The Cambridge Companion to Christian Ethics* (Cambridge University Press, 2001); Mary Warnock, *An Intelligent Person's Guide to Ethics* (Duckworth, 1998); Mary Warnock, *Women Philosophers* (Everyman, 1997); Quentin Skinner, *Machiavelli* (Oxford, 1981); Richard Bernstein, *Radical Evil* (Polity, 2002); John Hick, *Evil and the God of Love* (Macmillan, 1966); Samuel Freeman (ed.), *Rawls: Collected Papers* (Harvard University Press, 1999); Francis Fukuyama, *Trust* (Penguin, 1995); Samuel Huntington, *The Clash of Civilizations and the Remaking of World Order* (Simon & Schuster, 1996); Rowan Williams, *Writing in the Dust* (Hodder & Stoughton, 2002); and Jonathan Sacks, *The Dignity of Difference* (Continuum, 2002); A. D. Lindsay, *The Two Moralities* (Eyre and Spottiswoode, 1941); Peter Hennessy, *The Secret State* (Penguin, 2002); and John Rawls, *The Law of Peoples* (Harvard University Press, 1999).

The quotation from G. E. Anscombe is taken from her essay, 'War and Murder', in Walter Stein (ed.) *Nuclear Weapons and Christian Conscience* (Merlin Press, 1961).

Conclusion

Cardinal Newman, *The Idea of a University*, based on 1852 lectures, was originally published in 1853 and is now available in many editions; see, for example the text edited by Frank Turner (Yale University Press, 1966), which contains also many valuable essays. Archbishop Rowan Williams' statements can be followed on www.archbishopofcanterbury.org, and the Church of England has an excellent website with policy statements on a wide range of ethical dilemmas at www.cofe.org.uk. The quotation is from Isaiah Berlin, *The Power of Ideas*, edited by Henry Hardy (Pimlico, 2001).

Index